MAN AND THE GODS: THREE TRAGEDIES

HOMER D. SWANDER

University of California, Santa Barbara

Man and the Gods
THREE TRAGEDIES

Harcourt, Brace & World, Inc.
New York   Chicago   Burlingame

Library of Congress Catalog Card Number: 65–10358

Printed in the United States of America

ACKNOWLEDGMENTS: The editor wishes to thank the following for permission to reproduce materials in this book:

Dodd, Mead & Company: For *Saint Joan* by George Bernard Shaw. Copyright 1924, 1930, George Bernard Shaw. Copyright 1951, 1957, The Public Trustee as Executor of the Estate of George Bernard Shaw.

Coward-McCann, Inc.: For the illustration of the Elizabethan theater by C. Walter Hodges. From *Shakespeare and the Players* by C. Walter Hodges. Reprinted by permission of Coward-McCann, Inc.

Harcourt, Brace & World, Inc.: For *The Agamemnon of Aeschylus* translated by Louis MacNeice. Reprinted by permission of Harcourt, Brace & World, Inc.

Methuen & Co., Ltd.: For extracts from H. D. F. Kitto, *Greek Tragedy*, published by Methuen & Co. and Barnes & Noble. Reprinted by permission of Methuen & Co., Ltd.

Penguin Books, Ltd.: For extracts from Homer's *Odyssey* translated by E. V. Rieu. Reprinted by permission of Penguin Books, Ltd.

To My Brother

CONTENTS

Introduction
WHAT IS DRAMA?

THE word "theater" in Greek meant "seeing place," the word "drama" meant "deed," and the dramatist has always been most clearly distinguished from other writers by his desire to make us literally *see* the *deeds* of men. If we honor this desire, we admit that the words alone of a drama are not enough; they demand voices to speak them and actors to move (sometimes even to dance) before us—an actual event. They demand, too, the space, the playing area, in which such activity will appear to its best advantage, the right costumes, the proper scenery, the appropriate music, and, furthermore, an audience: the immediate, shared response (which can of course include differing opinions) of many people gathered together—in a "seeing place."

Yet now you are to read the words—not see the deeds—of Agamemnon, Faustus, and St. Joan. And necessarily so, if you are to know the plays at all; for how many of us have ever had the opportunity to see *Agamemnon* or *Doctor Faustus* produced in any theater whatever, to say nothing of a theater resembling the one for which each was originally intended?

But what we must face at the very beginning is this: while the best introduction to poetry, for example, is a book of poems, the best introduction to drama is a book of theater tickets—precisely what I (and presumably your teacher) cannot offer you. When you read *Agamemnon* you will be, after all, a reader: a brother to the man reading a novel or a narrative poem and only a shirt-tail cousin to the man sitting in a theater. There are all those other artists upon whom the playwright is counting—the actor, the director, the composer, the musician, the architect, the set-designer, the costumier, the choreographer, the dancer—and no one of us can adequately imagine what their combined efforts would in any given instance produce. We simply cannot react to the printed words alone as we would to the theatrical event that those words were designed to initiate.

Let me put this another way. When we are reading instead of watching a play we are not in fact attending to the *form of drama* at all. That form is present only when the word of the writer has become the flesh of the actor, when the characters have come to live and to speak before our eyes.

Partly because of this fact, drama is more various in its means than any other form of art; and this, like the fact itself, contributes to a definition. You will want to notice the great many means employed by Aeschylus, for example, to achieve his end in *Agamemnon:* verse (in various forms and meters), imagery, music and song, dance (both solo and group), two stage levels (the roof and the ground), appropriate though not elaborate props (chariots, carpets, altars, statues), face masks and full robes, both single actors and a chorus, both soliloquy and dialogue. Furthermore, Aeschylus through necessity or choice did without many means that a modern writer might use—artificial lighting, for example, and darkness; walls and ceiling for interior scenes; prose in everyday speech; everyday dress; the actor's face; and many of the details of the human body that we would not hide with robes (Marlon Brando in his underwear or Elizabeth Taylor adjusting her stockings).

Clearly, the differences here between the ancient playwright and the modern are instructive, but let us emphasize for now the underlying similarity: that wide variety of means always, in whatever century and on whatever stage, legitimately available. Think how relatively limited, in this sense, is the lyric poem, the ballet, or the sonata.

To include the audience—"many people gathered together"—as part of our definition may strike you as strange; for a performance of a play is, after all, a performance, even if there be but one person—or none at all—to see it. But the truth is that while the novelist or the poet writes to a reader (a solitary man), the dramatist writes to an audience, a group. Public performance is the anticipated outcome of his work, a condition of his art that he accepts; and the theatrical event born of and shaped by his words is not complete until the anticipation is satisfied. A performance in an empty theater can in fact be no more than a rehearsal; the very rhythm of a genuine performance depends in part upon the actors' sense of how the audience is reacting. While the art of the novelist or the poet (at least since the invention of the printing press) is in this sense individualistic, the art of the playwright (at least before TV trapped us in our living rooms) is communal: he aims to make us laugh or weep or think together (which is not necessarily the same as thinking alike).

So if we content ourselves with reading—with something called "dramatic literature," a kind of novel drastically limited to dialogue—we are defying, or at least ignoring, the dramatic form. This is true even though we ought to heed a warning issued by the critic Richard Gilman:

... great plays are literature, or have become it (which is proof of their greatness), although most theater professionals and some critics keep on insisting
that a play has no life except a physical one: they would be on safer ground if
they confined their argument to the question of degrees of life and understood that only inferior plays cannot exist at all between covers since, being
nothing but notations for action, they have to get their life entirely from players and managers [*Commonweal*, April 20, 1962, p. 87].

But even those plays that have become literature by proving that they
can exist between covers deserve to be read as plays. There is a kind
of reading that cooperates with the dramatic form by preparing us for
the theater; and it leads, perhaps paradoxically, to greater pleasure in
the text. Reading a good play becomes, in a sense alien to novels or
poems, a creative act: part of our attempt to understand the words before us is quite literally an assault on the impossible, an attempt to
imagine (and thus to react to) a perfect production. Vigorous reading of this kind, far from taking us away from the words, takes us into
them in a way peculiar to drama; for we must find in the text itself a
justification for our imagined production.

I do not mean that in this book we shall try to study the techniques
of production. We have before us not stages and stage properties but
the texts of plays, and we would be wise to attend to what is available.
We *are* readers, and we shall be attending to *words*. But we shall try
to remember that the most immediate function of the words is to
stimulate the rest of the work—the theatrical event. In so doing we
shall hope to discover how much there is in the words themselves.

We hold in our minds both the events of the story and the exigen-
cies of the stage. Look at this on the simplest level. A novel, the action
of which occurs in front of a palace in prehistoric Argos, takes us, in
our imaginations, to the grounds of a palace in prehistoric Argos, simply that. A play with the same setting takes us two places: to the
grounds of the palace, to be sure, but also to a specific theatrical rep-
resentation of those grounds. This is more complicated, and it means
that, in at least this sense, reading plays is more complicated than
reading novels. Thus, for example, both the picture on page 14 and
the stage directions that I have added to the text of *Agamemnon* are
there to help you see the action taking place where *as a play* it does:
in that large circular dancing area and in the acting space between
the circle and the building called the *skenê*. It is only by means of
this theatrical scene that Aeschylus intends us to see the action taking place where *as myth or legend or story* it did: before the great
stone palace of Agamemnon.

In Shakespeare's *A Midsummer Night's Dream*, Quince (the carpenter turned playwright) faces up to this difference between a story and a play, clearly (if comically) recognizing the conflict between certain requirements of the story he wishes to dramatize and the limitations of the stage he must necessarily use:

QUINCE: But there is two hard things: that is, to bring the moonlight into a chamber, for you know Pyramus and Thisby meet by moonlight.
SNOUT: Doth the moon shine that night we play our play?
BOTTOM: A calendar, a calendar! Look in the almanac. Find out moonshine, find out moonshine.
QUINCE: Yes, it doth shine that night.
BOTTOM: Why, then may you leave a casement of the great-chamber window, where we play, open, and the moon may shine in at the casement.
QUINCE: Aye, or else one must come in with a bush of thorns and a lantern, and say he comes to disfigure, or to present, the person of moonshine.

These splendid solutions are both, strictly speaking, theatrical; but Quince's play as it is later produced shows that he is aware of still another solution, one that is, strictly speaking, rhetorical. Words can themselves "present . . . moonshine":

> PYRAMUS: Sweet Moon, I thank thee for thy sunny beams,
> I thank thee, Moon, for shining now so bright.
> For, by thy gracious, golden, glittering gleams,
> I trust to take of truest Thisby sight.

In all of this, even in the ridiculous poetry, Shakespeare was commenting upon the problem he faced in his own play: how to "present" the moonlight of a midsummer's night in a play that would be produced either inside at Court or under an afternoon sky. Any handy edition of the play will reveal his solution.

Someone has said that a stage is simply a space waiting to be filled —a space, we must now add, the special size and shape of which will partly determine what fills it, a space the nature of which, as Quince learned, constitutes some part of the playwright's opportunity and challenge. I emphasize the fifth-century theater for which *Agamemnon* was written because, if we are to read any play as a play and not as a novel, we must see the vital relationship between the playwright and the specific theatrical space that lies waiting for him, that in fact lies there only to challenge him to make the most of its particular size and shape, of its own peculiar possibilities and limitations. You will begin to see what I mean if, as you read, you will try to imagine that great moment of Agamemnon's entrance—the two horse-drawn chariots, the accompanying procession of soldiers, the statues and altars of the gods, Clytemnestra and her women with the tapestries that must be laid from the chariot to the palace door, and the twelve-man chorus that must have room to move—if you will imagine all of this crowded onto the stage of your college or community theater. The effect, and therefore the meaning, could hardly be the same as that achieved by Aeschylus in the Theater of Dionysus; such a production would be something like the *Iliad* translated into rhymed couplets: however brilliantly done (see Alexander Pope's *Iliad*), the epic is no longer epic.

But the analogy finally fails; for a play, even in a theater proper to it, encounters hazards, just as it enjoys means, unknown to any strictly literary form. A completed poem rests reasonably secure upon the page; a play submits to all the dangers of production. Stupid or irresponsible directors, shallow or untrained actors, unimaginative or vulgar set-designers—one must watch helplessly again and again as such criminals violate our favorite plays. At such moments Hamlet speaks for us: "O, it offends me to the soul to see a robustious periwig-pated fellow tear a passion to tatters, to very rags, to split the ears of the groundlings. . . . I could have such a fellow whipp'd. . . ." But the whipping, however deserved and instructive, would leave the central fact untouched. Drama, in the unique variety of its means, comes closer to the conditions of human life than any other art, engaging our mind and our senses with more of the variety of life and thus accepting, necessarily, more of the risks, more of the imperfections: the leading lady may have a crippling headache or a nasal cold; and even if she were at her best, how could she hope to equal our ideal of, say, Helen of Troy?

Mr. Stark Young, America's finest critic of the drama, has said:

We see now and again in the theatre great décor, great acting, great drama, but only two or three times in our lives do we see a quality expressed down to the last element in the theatre art, a perfect unity in idea, plot, and every other medium of theatrical expression, the music, the setting, make-ups, costumes, voice, gesture and group movement. Such completeness, such unity in essence and form, is the living principle in every work of art, the supreme soul and test of it, first and last [*Immortal Shadows* (Scribner, 1948), p. 64].

We are simply forced to admit that drama, by definition, is less likely than other forms of art to achieve this completeness. It is thus no wonder that some people are impatient with it, prefer to stick to the texts and to stay out of the theater, or prefer other arts entirely. But Mr. Young, speaking in another way of such problems, describes what holds most of us:

That final theatre creation that [the director] seeks is not so much like literature in its quality as it is like music, dancing, vivid passages in the world of
nature about us; it is elusive, penetrating, it cannot wait, it cannot depend on
some later memory or revisiting. He has the problem, and perhaps the thrill,
of knowing that in his art, just as in human life we are alive and then gone,
what he creates lives while it is before the audience, with all that living may
imply—its passionate exchange, its leaping ardor and its give and take of
beauty and quick impulse—and afterward has no existence at all [*The
Theatre* (Hill & Wang, 1958), p. 95].

The three plays in this book have all had—and will again have—
such moments of theatrical life. I have brought them together here
because they are by common consent great plays, plays that lend
themselves deeply and wholly to the intelligence and passion of the
most talented actors and directors. And they are also plays with a literary as well as a theatrical existence: men have always wanted to read
as well as to see them, and have always felt that the reading enriched
the seeing.

I have chosen them, too, because they are united by a common interest in the relationship between man and God, particularly in that
violent relationship created by heroes who are—or are thought to be
—challenging God. For Agamemnon and Faustus, as we shall see, the
case is clear: the human condition is not enough; they assert themselves, however nobly, in presumptuous—and tragic—aspirations. Aspiring to be more than men, they reject human limitations; and their
reward is inevitably death (the defining limitation) instead of the
godlike power or honor that they seek. We cannot say the same of
St. Joan, though her actions lead as inevitably to her death. In all
three plays, however the details may differ, the tragedy takes place on
that extreme frontier of human possibility where nobility and presumption live in precarious union.

For two of the plays—*Agamemnon* and *Doctor Faustus*— I have
written comments and questions. For *Saint Joan* I have included ex-
cerpts from Shaw's own introduction and have assumed that the student will enjoy using what he has learned from his study of the first
two plays as a basis for making his own comments and raising his own
questions.

Agamemnon

Translated by Louis MacNeice

AESCHYLUS

Poet, actor, musician, chorus leader and teacher, ballet master, soldier at the Battle of Marathon, Aeschylus (525–456 B.C.) began his work as a dramatist at Athens in 499 B.C. Of the ninety plays he is said to have written, seven are extant. The *Agamemnon*, together with the *Choephoroe* and the *Eumenides*, composes the *Oresteia* trilogy, his last and greatest work, which was first performed (and won the prize) at the Athenian dramatic festival in 458 B.C.

THE HOUSE OF ATREUS

AESCHYLUS wrote for auditors who already knew the story of the House of Atreus, and he counts on that knowledge. Here, then, is the story—as far as possible in the versions his audience would have known best, those that Homer gives in The Odyssey.

THE cycle of human crime and divine punishment begins with Tantalus, King of Lydia, son of Zeus, so honored by the gods that he alone of all mortals was invited to their banquets. He returned their favor with a scornful challenge: having invited them to his palace, he killed his only son, Pelops, cooked the boy's flesh, and served it to them in ironic exchange for their gifts. He thought he could deceive the gods, make cannibals of them, and thus prove his own superiority. His punishment, intended as a warning to all men, has given us the verb "to tantalize." Tantalus stands eternally thirsty and hungry in a pool in Hades, first bending to drink the water that always drains away, then stretching upward for the overhanging fruit that always moves just out of reach.

Niobe, daughter of Tantalus, was the first to disregard the warning. Married to Amphion, ruler of Thebes, she had seven daughters and seven sons. Their lives were prosperous and happy until Niobe, touched with the arrogance of her father, openly challenged the gods by declaring that the people of Thebes should worship her instead of the goddess Leto, mother of Apollo and Artemis: "Leto has only two children. I have seven times as many. I am stronger and greater than she, too great for men or gods to harm me." But Apollo (the archer god) and Artemis (goddess of the hunt) shot down all her children; and Niobe, watching them die, seemed so like a weeping stone that the gods changed her into a stone forever wet with tears.

In Atreus and Thyestes, the sons of Pelops—who was restored to life—the evil persisted. Thyestes seduced his brother's wife; and Atreus, King of Mycenae, first exiled the seducer and then, pretending to forgive, recalled and feasted him. But the meat at the banquet was the flesh of the two secretly murdered children of Thyestes, and the father (unlike the gods at that earlier banquet) ate. When he learned what he had eaten, he had strength only to curse his brother's House and leave. Later, out of his desire for revenge, he had a child by his own daughter; and this child was the Aegisthus who cuckolded and murdered Agamemnon, the elder son of Atreus.

Atreus had two sons, Agamemnon and Menelaus, who married two sisters, Clytemnestra and Helen. Paris, son of the Trojan King Priam, kidnaped—or eloped with—Helen, and so occasioned the Trojan War. The Greek army, however, was unable to leave for Troy from the port of Aulis, held there for months by the contrary winds. According to the prophet Calchas, the winds were purposely raised by Artemis, who would yield only to the sacrifice of Agamemnon's daughter Iphigeneia. Sending for the young girl, deceiving her and her mother Clytemnestra by saying that she was to come to marry the hero Achilles, Agamemnon, her father and king, ordered her death in order to free his fleet.

The war lasted ten years, and during that time Clytemnestra took Aegisthus as her lover and sent her small son Orestes to be raised in another country. In Troy, Agamemnon took captive women to his bed. When Troy fell, the Greeks sacked the temples, challenging thus the anger of the gods; and Agamemnon claimed Cassandra—the Trojan princess and priestess who had rejected the advances of Apollo —as his concubine. In his arrogance he believed that he could take with impunity the woman whose virginity even a god had respected.

Hundreds of years before Aeschylus wrote *Agamemnon*, Homer told some of the story in *The Odyssey*, putting it into the mouths of three characters: Nestor, an old Greek general, speaking to Telemachus, the son of Odysseus; Menelaus, relating the Sea Prophet's version; and Agamemnon himself speaking after death to Odysseus when the latter visits Hades.

NESTOR'S VERSION

"My child," Gerenian Nestor answered, "I shall be glad to tell you the whole tale. You can imagine for yourself what would have happened had Agamemnon's brother, red-haired Menelaus, come back from Troy and caught Aegisthus in the house alive. No barrow would have honoured his remains! Flung on the plain outside the city walls, he'd have made meat for the dogs and birds of prey, and there's no woman in Achaea who would have shed a tear for him. His was indeed no petty crime. While we that were beleaguering Troy

toiled at heroic tasks, he spent his leisured days, right in the heart of
Argos where the horses graze, besieging Agamemnon's wife with his
seductive talk. At first Queen Clytaemnestra turned a deaf ear to his
dishonourable schemes. She was a sensible woman, and besides, she
had a man with her, a minstrel by profession, to whom Agamemnon
when he left for Troy had given strict orders to watch over his queen.
But when the fatal day appointed for her conquest came, Aegisthus
took this minstrel to a desert isle, left him there as carrion for the birds
of prey and carried Clytaemnestra off to his own house, fond lover,
willing dame. This doughty deed accomplished, he heaped holy altars
of the gods with sacrificial meat and plastered the temple walls with
splendid gifts of gold brocade, thank-offerings for success beyond his
wildest dreams.

"[Meanwhile Menelaus was sailing for Troy, and Zeus] took it into
his head to give them a rough time, and sent them a howling gale with
giant waves as massive and as high as mountains. . . . Menelaus with
the remaining five vessels of his blue-prowed fleet was driven on by
wind and wave to Egypt. And so it came about that he was cruising in
those distant parts . . . while Aegisthus schemed this wickedness at
home."

THE SEA PROPHET'S VERSION
(*related by Menelaus*)

"Agamemnon set foot on the soil of his fathers with a happy heart,
and as he touched it kissed his native earth. The warm tears rolled
down his cheeks, he was so glad to see his land again. But his arrival
was observed by a spy in a watch-tower, whom Aegisthus had had the
cunning to post there with the promise of two talents of gold for his
services. This man was on the lookout for a year in case the King
should land unannounced, slip by, and himself launch an attack. He
went straight to the palace and informed the usurper. Then Aegisthus
set his brains to work and laid a clever trap. He selected twenty of the
best soldiers from the town, left them in ambush, and after ordering
a banquet to be prepared in another part of the building, set out in a
horse-chariot to bring home the King, with his heart full of ugly
thoughts. Agamemnon, never guessing that he was going to his doom,
came up with him from the coast and Aegisthus feasted and killed

him as a man might fell an ox at its manger. Not a single one of the King's following was left, nor of Aegisthus' company either. They were killed in the palace to a man."

AGAMEMNON'S VERSION

"Poseidon did not wreck my ships; nor did I fall to any hostile tribe on land. It was Aegisthus who plotted my destruction and with my accursed wife put me to death. He invited me to the palace, he feasted me, and he killed me as a man fells an ox in its manger. That was my most miserable end. And all around me my companions were cut down in ruthless succession, like white-tusked swine slaughtered in the mansion of some great and wealthy lord, for a wedding, a club-banquet, or a sumptuous public feast. You, Odysseus, have witnessed the deaths of many men in single combat or the thick of battle, but none with such horror as you would have felt had you seen us lying there by the wine-bowl and the laden tables in the hall, while the whole floor swam with our blood. Yet the most pitiable thing of all was the cry I heard from Cassandra, daughter of Priam, whom that foul traitress Clytaemnestra murdered at my side. As I lay on the ground, I raised my hands in a dying effort to grip her sword. But the harlot turned her face aside, and had not even the grace, though I was on my way to Hades, to shut my eyes with her hands or to close my mouth. And so I say that for brutality and infamy there is no one to equal a woman who can contemplate such deeds. Who else could conceive so hideous a crime as her deliberate butchery of her husband and her lord? Indeed, I had looked forward to a rare welcome from my children and my servants when I reached my home. But now, in the depth of her villainy, she has branded not herself alone but the whole of her sex and every honest woman for all time to come."

"Alas!" [Odysseus] exclaimed. "All-seeing Zeus has indeed proved himself a relentless foe to the House of Atreus, and from the beginning he has worked his will through women's crooked ways. It was for Helen's sake that so many of us met our deaths, and it was Clytaemnestra who hatched the plot against her absent lord."[1]

---

[1] I have used E. V. Rieu's translation of *The Odyssey* (Penguin Classics). Another good translation is by W. H. D. Rouse (Mentor Classics).

Homer on more than one occasion praises Orestes: "What a good thing it is, when a man dies, for a son to survive him, as Orestes survived to pay the murderer out and kill that snake in the grass, Aegisthus"—and Clytemnestra, too, of course, though Homer's purpose requires no mention of her. Killing his mother, however, drives Orestes mad. There are many different versions (none of them Homeric) of how he was at last cured, but Aeschylus apparently created his own; so that part of the story, a large part of the last play in the trilogy, would probably have been new even to the first Athenian audience.

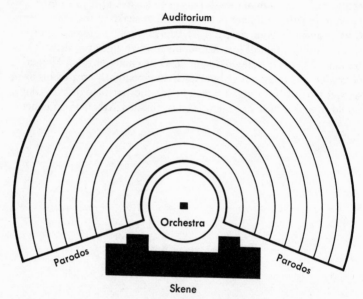

Auditorium

Orchestra

Parodos

Parodos

Skene

PLAN OF A GREEK THEATER

Greek theaters were large, seating up to 17,000 people in tiered rows rising in a semicircle from the orchestra or dancing floor up the side of a hill. Over the years, the *skenê*, which probably started as a small room for the actors, developed into an elaborate two-story building. From its function as a background (ordinarily as a temple or palace; there was little movable scenery) comes our word "scene." As the drama developed, the relationship between the chorus and the actors became increasingly remote and, eventually, a raised stage appeared; no one knows just when. For splendid pictures and authoritative information, see Margarete Bieber, *The History of the Greek and Roman Theater*, rev. ed. (Princeton University Press, 1961).

Agamemnon

PERSONS REPRESENTED

WATCHMAN

CHORUS OF OLD MEN
OF THE CITY

CLYTEMNESTRA

HERALD

AGAMEMNON

CASSANDRA

AEGISTHUS

[*Argos, a city in Greece.*[1] AGAMEMNON's *palace represented by a one-story, flat-roofed building extending across the rear of the entire playing area; a large double door at exact center. On each side of the door, close to the palace, statues of the gods—Zeus, Apollo, Artemis, Hermes, and others—each with its own altar. Between the palace and the audience a large circular playing area (the Orchestra: a name from the Greek word meaning "to dance")—seventy or eighty feet in diameter—largely reserved for the dance movements of the* CHORUS. *Throughout the play smoke rises from the altar of Dionysus at the center of this area, a visual reminder that the play occurs on sacred ground. No raised stage. Spacious side exits to right and left in front of the palace. The audience (though at a daylight performance in an outdoor theater) must imagine that it is night, shortly before dawn—the night in which the Greeks at last conquer Troy. A lone* WATCHMAN *appears on the roof of the palace. He wears a full-length gown (as will all the characters) and a full face mask so contrived as to suggest exhaustion, worry, even fear. He speaks directly to the audience.*]

WATCHMAN. The gods it is I ask to release me from this watch
A year's length now, spending my nights like a dog,
Watching on my elbow on the roof of the sons of Atreus
So that I have come to know the assembly of the nightly stars
Those which bring storm and those which bring summer to men,
The shining Masters riveted in the sky—
I know the decline and rising of those stars.
And now I am waiting for the sign of the beacon,

[1] NOTE: There are no scene or stage directions in the Greek text. The editor has substituted his own for those of the translator.

The flame of fire that will carry the report from Troy,
News of her taking. Which task has been assigned me   10
By a woman of sanguine heart but a man's mind.
Yet when I take my restless rest in the soaking dew,
My night not visited with dreams—
For fear stands by me in the place of sleep
That I cannot firmly close my eyes in sleep—
Whenever I think to sing or hum to myself
As an antidote to sleep, then every time I groan
And fall to weeping for the fortunes of this house
Where not as before are things well ordered now.
But now may a good chance fall, escape from pain,   20
The good news visible in the midnight fire.

[A *long silence while he stares into the distance. Suddenly the
beacon shines.*]

Ha! I salute you, torch of the night whose light
Is like the day, an earnest of many dances
In the city of Argos, celebration of Peace.
I call to Agamemnon's wife; quickly to rise
Out of her bed and in the house to raise
Clamour of joy in answer to this torch
For the city of Troy is taken—
Such is the evident message of the beckoning flame.
And I myself will dance my solo first   30
For I shall count my master's fortune mine
Now that this beacon has thrown me a lucky throw.

[He *dances: dignified movements suggesting relief, triumph, joy.
Suitable music. He does not dance long: thought takes over.*]

And may it be when he comes, the master of this house,
That I grasp his hand in my hand.
As to the rest, I am silent. A great ox, as they say,
Stands on my tongue. The house itself, if it took voice,
Could tell the case most clearly. But I will only speak
To those who know. For the others I remember nothing.

[He *descends into the palace as we begin to hear cries of joy
from within; the climactic cry is that of the queen,* CLYTEMNES-
TRA, *handsomely gowned, enters through the double door center with her women attendants, who light fires and sprinkle
incense on all of the altars. The full face masks of the attendants register simple joy, but* CLYTEMNESTRA'S *is designed to
anticipate—and to function as a constant reminder of—her
tragic fate. The attendants exeunt stage left, to altars elsewhere*

in the city. CLYTEMNESTRA *remains silently praying before the altar of Zeus.*]

PARODOS

[*The* CHORUS OF ELDERS—*twelve very old but important men in the kingdom—march in from stage right (through the parodos: a Greek word meaning "side way" that has given its name to the introductory choral chant). They are dressed identically in full-length gowns and probably wear identical face masks. They chant their opening lines as they move slowly toward and around the altar at the center of the Orchestra. They have not heard the news and do not at first see* CLYTEMNESTRA.]

CHORUS. The tenth year it is since Priam's high
   Adversary, Menelaus the king   40
   And Agamemnon, the double-throned and sceptred
   Yoke of the sons of Atreus
   Ruling in fee from God,
   From this land gathered an Argive army
   On a mission of war a thousand ships,
   Their hearts howling in boundless bloodlust
   In eagles' fashion who in lonely
   Grief for nestlings above their homes hang
   Turning in cycles
   Beating the air with the oars of their wings,   50
     Now to no purpose
     Their love and task of attention.

   But above there is One,
   Maybe Pan, maybe Zeus or Apollo,
   Who hears the harsh cries of the birds
   Guests in his kingdom,
   Wherefore, though late, in requital
   He sends the Avenger.
   Thus Zeus our master
   Guardian of guest and of host   60
   Sent against Paris the sons of Atreus
   For a woman of many men
   Many the dog-tired wrestlings
   Limbs and knees in the dust pressed—
     For both the Greeks and Trojans
     An overture of breaking spears.

   Things are where they are, will finish

In the manner fated and neither
Fire beneath nor oil above can soothe
The stubborn anger of the unburnt offering.   70
As for us, our bodies are bankrupt,
The expedition left us behind
And we wait supporting on sticks
Our strength—the strength of a child;
For the marrow that leaps in a boy's body
Is no better than that of the old
For the War God is not in his body;
While the man who is very old
And his leaf withering away
Goes on the three-foot way   80
No better than a boy, and wanders
A dream in the middle of the day.

[*They see* CLYTEMNESTRA *and the fresh fires on the altars before
the palace.*]

But you, daughter of Tyndareus,
Queen Clytemnestra,
What is the news, what is the truth, what have you learnt,
On the strength of whose word have you thus
Sent orders for sacrifice round?
All the gods, the gods of the town,
Of the worlds of Below and Above,
By the door, in the square,   90
Have their altars ablaze with your gifts,
From here, from there, all sides, all corners,
Sky-high leap the flame-jets fed
By gentle and undeceiving
Persuasion of sacred unguent,
Oil from the royal stores.
Of these things tell
That which you can, that which you may,
Be healer of this our trouble
Which at times torments with evil   100
Though at times by propitiations
A shining hope repels
The insatiable thought upon grief
Which is eating away our hearts.

[*She remains silent, continuing to pray and in no way acknowl-
edging the presence of the old men. Rebuffed, they turn away to
sing in unison the first choral ode (called a stasimon), moving in
austere dance steps around the central altar. For the strophe*

(which means a "turning"), they move in one direction, for the
antistrophe in another; for the epode, they halt before the statues
of the gods to whom they speak.]

FIRST STASIMON

STROPHE 1

Of the omen which powerfully speeded
That voyage of strong men, by God's grace even I
Can tell, my age can still
Be galvanized to breathe the strength of song,
To tell how the kings of all the youth of Greece
Two-throned but one in mind   110
Were launched with pike and punitive hand
Against the Trojan shore by angry birds.
Kings of the birds to our kings came,
One with a white rump, the other black,
Appearing near the palace on the spear-arm side
Where all could see them,
Tearing a pregnant hare with the unborn young
Foiled of their courses.
    Cry, cry upon Death; but may the good prevail.

ANTISTROPHE 1

But the diligent prophet of the army seeing the sons   120
Of Atreus twin in temper knew
That the hare-killing birds were the two
Generals, explained it thus—
'In time this expedition sacks the town
Of Troy before whose towers
By Fate's force the public
Wealth will be wasted.
Only let not some spite from the gods benight the bulky battalions,
The bridle of Troy, nor strike them untimely;
For the goddess feels pity, is angry   130
With the winged dogs of her father
Who killed the cowering hare with her unborn young;
Artemis hates the eagles' feast.'
    Cry, cry upon Death; but may the good prevail.

EPODE

'But though you are so kind, goddess,
To the little cubs of lions

And to all the sucking young of roving beasts
In whom your heart delights,
Fulfil us the signs of these things,
The signs which are good but open to blame,   140
And I call on Apollo the Healer
That his sister raise not against the Greeks
Unremitting gales to baulk their ships,
Hurrying on another kind of sacrifice, with no feasting,
Barbarous building of hates and disloyalties
Grown on the family. For anger grimly returns
Cunningly haunting the house, avenging the death of a child,
    never forgetting its due.'
So cried the prophet—evil and good together,
Fate that the birds foretold to the king's house.
In tune with this   150
    Cry, cry upon Death; but may the good prevail.

STROPHE 2

Zeus, whoever He is, if this
Be a name acceptable,
By this name I will call him.
There is no one comparable
When I reckon all of the case
Excepting Zeus, if ever I am to jettison
The barren care which clogs my heart.

ANTISTROPHE 2

Not He who formerly was great
With brawling pride and mad for broils   160
Will even be said to have been.
And He who was next has met
His match and is seen no more,
But Zeus is the name to cry in your triumph-song
And win the prize for wisdom.

STROPHE 3

Who setting us on the road
Made this a valid law—
    'That men must learn by suffering.'
Drop by drop in sleep upon the heart
Falls the laborious memory of pain,   170
Against one's will comes wisdom;
The grace of the gods is forced on us
    Throned inviolably.

So at that time the elder
Chief of the Greek ships
Would not blame any prophet
Nor face the flail of fortune;
For unable to sail, the people
Of Greece were heavy with famine,
Waiting in Aulis where the tides   180
   Flow back, opposite Chalcis.

But the winds that blew from the Strymon,
Bringing delay, hunger, evil harbourage,
Crazing men, rotting ships and cables,
By drawing out the time
Were shredding into nothing the flower of Argos,
When the prophet screamed a new
Cure for that bitter tempest
And heavier still for the chiefs,
Pleading the anger of Artemis so that the sons of Atreus   190
Beat the ground with their sceptres and shed tears.

Then the elder king found voice and answered:
'Heavy is my fate, not obeying,
And heavy it is if I kill my child, the delight of my house,
And with a virgin's blood upon the altar
Make foul her father's hands.
Either alternative is evil.
How can I betray the fleet
And fail the allied army?
It is right they should passionately cry for the winds to be lulled
By the blood of a girl. So be it. May it be well.'   201

But when he had put on the halter of Necessity
Breathing in his heart a veering wind of evil
Unsanctioned, unholy, from that moment forward
He changed his counsel, would stop at nothing.
For the heart of man is hardened by infatuation,
A faulty adviser, the first link of sorrow.
Whatever the cause, he brought himself to slay
His daughter, an offering to promote the voyage
To a war for a runaway wife.   210

ANTISTROPHE 5

Her prayers and her cries of father,
Her life of a maiden,
Counted for nothing with those militarists;
But her father, having duly prayed, told the attendants
To lift her, like a goat, above the altar
With her robes falling about her,
To lift her boldly, her spirit fainting,
And hold back with a gag upon her lovely mouth
By the dumb force of a bridle
The cry which would curse the house.   220

STROPHE 6

Then dropping on the ground her saffron dress,
Glancing at each of her appointed
Sacrificers a shaft of pity,
Plain as in a picture she wished
To speak to them by name, for often
At her father's table where men feasted
She had sung in celebration for her father
With a pure voice, affectionately, virginally,
The hymn for happiness at the third libation.

ANTISTROPHE 6

The sequel to this I saw not and tell not   230
But the crafts of Calchas gained their object.
To learn by suffering is the equation of Justice; the Future
Is known when it comes, let it go till then.
To know in advance is sorrow in advance.
The facts will appear with the shining of the dawn.
But may good, at the least, follow after
As the queen here wishes, who stands
Nearest the throne, the only
   Defence of the land of Argos.

FIRST EPISODE

[*The* CHORUS *turns again to* CLYTEMNESTRA, *and the* LEADER *speaks.*
CLYTEMNESTRA *is now ready to reply.*]

LEADER OF THE CHORUS. I have come, Clytemnestra, reverencing your
          authority.   240
   For it is right to honour our master's wife
   When the man's own throne is empty.

But you, if you have heard good news for certain, or if
You sacrifice on the strength of flattering hopes,
I would gladly hear. Though I cannot cavil at silence.
CLYTEMNESTRA. Bearing good news, as the proverb says, may Dawn
Spring from her mother Night.
You will hear something now that was beyond your hopes.
The men of Argos have taken Priam's city.   249
LEADER OF THE CHORUS. What! I cannot believe it. It escapes me.
CLYTEMNESTRA. Troy in the hands of the Greeks. Do I speak plain?
LEADER OF THE CHORUS. Joy creeps over me, calling out my tears.
CLYTEMNESTRA. Yes. Your eyes proclaim your loyalty.
LEADER OF THE CHORUS. But what are your grounds? Have you a proof
    of it?
CLYTEMNESTRA. There is proof indeed—unless God has cheated us.
LEADER OF THE CHORUS. Perhaps you believe the inveigling shapes of
    dreams?
CLYTEMNESTRA. I would not be credited with a dozing brain!
LEADER OF THE CHORUS. Or are you puffed up by Rumour, the wing-
    less flyer?
CLYTEMNESTRA. You mock my common sense as if I were a child. 259
LEADER OF THE CHORUS. But at what time was the city given to sack?
CLYTEMNESTRA. In this very night that gave birth to this day.
LEADER OF THE CHORUS. What messenger could come so fast?
CLYTEMNESTRA. Hephaestus, launching a fine flame from Ida,
    Beacon forwarding beacon, despatch-riders of fire,
    Ida relayed to Hermes' cliff in Lemnos
    And the great glow from the island was taken over third
    By the height of Athos that belongs to Zeus,
    And towering then to straddle over the sea
    The might of the running torch joyfully tossed
    The gold gleam forward like another sun,   270
    Herald of light to the heights of Mount Macistus,
    And he without delay, nor carelessly by sleep
    Encumbered, did not shirk his intermediary role,
    His farflung ray reached the Euripus' tides
    And told Messapion's watchers, who in turn
    Sent on the message further
    Setting a stack of dried-up heather on fire.
    And the strapping flame, not yet enfeebled, leapt
    Over the plain of Asopus like a blazing moon
    And woke on the crags of Cithaeron   280
    Another relay in the chain of fire.
    The light that was sent from far was not declined
    By the look-out men, who raised a fiercer yet,
    A light which jumped the water of Gorgopis

And to Mount Aegiplanctus duly come
Urged the reveille of the punctual fire.
So then they kindle it squanderingly and launch
A beard of flame big enough to pass
The headland that looks down upon the Saronic gulf,
Blazing and bounding till it reached at length   290
The Arachnaean steep, our neighbouring heights;
And leaps in the latter end on the roof of the sons of Atreus
Issue and image of the fire on Ida.
Such was the assignment of my torch-racers,
The task of each fulfilled by his successor,
And victor is he who ran both first and last.
Such is the proof I offer you, the sign
My husband sent me out of Troy.

LEADER OF THE CHORUS. To the gods, queen, I shall give thanks pres-
     ently.
But I would like to hear this story further,   300
To wonder at it in detail from your lips.

CLYTEMNESTRA. The Greeks hold Troy upon this day.
The cries in the town I fancy do not mingle.
Pour oil and vinegar into the same jar,
You would say they stand apart unlovingly;
Of those who are captured and those who have conquered
Distinct are the sounds of their diverse fortunes,
For *these* having flung themselves about the bodies
Of husbands and brothers, or sons upon the bodies
Of aged fathers from a throat no longer   310
Free, lament the fate of their most loved.
But *those* a night's marauding after battle
Sets hungry to what breakfast the town offers
Not billeted duly in any barracks order
But as each man has drawn his lot of luck.
So in the captive homes of Troy already
They take their lodging, free of the frosts
And dews of the open. Like happy men
They will sleep all night without sentry.
But if they respect duly the city's gods,   320
Those of the captured land and the sanctuaries of the gods,
They need not, having conquered, fear reconquest.
But let no lust fall first upon the troops
To plunder what is not right, subdued by gain,
For they must still, in order to come home safe,
Get round the second lap of the doubled course.
So if they return without offence to the gods
The grievance of the slain may learn at last

A friendly talk—unless some fresh wrong falls.
Such are the thoughts you hear from me, a woman. 330
But may the good prevail for all to see.
We have much good. I only ask to enjoy it.
LEADER OF THE CHORUS. Woman, you speak with sense like a prudent
    man.
I, who have heard your valid proofs, prepare
To give the glory to God.
Fair recompense is brought us for our troubles.

[CLYTEMNESTRA *goes into the palace. The following ode is for
the full* CHORUS, *which sings and dances in the Orchestra.*]

SECOND STASIMON

O Zeus our king and Night our friend
Donor of glories,
Night who cast on the towers of Troy
A close-clinging net so that neither the grown 340
Nor any of the children can pass
The enslaving and huge
Trap of all-taking destruction.
Great Zeus, guardian of host and guest,
I honour who has done his work and taken
A leisured aim at Paris so that neither
Too short nor yet over the stars
    He might shoot to no purpose.

STROPHE 1
From Zeus is the blow they can tell of,
This at least can be established, 350
They have fared according to his ruling. For some
Deny that the gods deign to consider those among men
Who trample on the grace of inviolate things;
It is the impious man says this,
For Ruin is revealed the child
Of not to be attempted actions
When men are puffed up unduly
And their houses are stuffed with riches.
Measure is the best. Let danger be distant,
This should suffice a man 360
With a proper part of wisdom.
    For a man has no protection
    Against the drunkenness of riches

Once he has spurned from his sight
The high altar of Justice.

ANTISTROPHE 1

Sombre Persuasion compels him,
Intolerable child of calculating Doom;
All cure is vain, there is no glozing it over
But the mischief shines forth with a deadly light
And like bad coinage   370
By rubbings and frictions
He stands discoloured and black
Under the test—like a boy
Who chases a winged bird.
He has branded his city for ever.
His prayers are heard by no god.
Who makes such things his practice
The gods destroy him.
  This way came Paris
  To the house of the sons of Atreus   380
  And outraged the table of friendship
  Stealing the wife of his host.

STROPHE 2

Leaving to her countrymen clanging of
Shields and of spears and
Launching of warships
And bringing instead of a dowry destruction to Troy
Lightly she was gone through the gates daring
Things undared. Many the groans
Of the palace spokesmen on this theme—
'O the house, the house, and its princes,
O the bed and the imprint of her limbs;   390
One can see him crouching in silence
Dishonoured and unreviling.'
Through desire for her who is overseas, a ghost
Will seem to rule the household.
  And now her husband hates
  The grace of shapely statues;
  In the emptiness of their eyes
  All their appeal is departed.

ANTISTROPHE 2

But appearing in dreams persuasive   400
Images come bringing a joy that is vain,
Vain for when in fancy he looks to touch her—
Slipping through his hands the vision
Rapidly is gone

Following on wings the walks of sleep.
Such are his griefs in his house on his hearth,
Such as these and worse than these,
But everywhere through the land of Greece which men have left
Are mourning women with enduring hearts
To be seen in all houses; many   410
Are the thoughts which stab their hearts;
    For those they sent to war
    They know, but in place of men
    That which comes home to them
    Is merely an urn and ashes.

STROPHE 3

But the money-changer War, changer of bodies,
Holding his balance in the battle
Home from Troy refined by fire
Sends back to friends the dust
That is heavy with tears, stowing   420
A man's worth of ashes
In an easily handled jar.
And they wail speaking well of the men how that one
Was expert in battle, and one fell well in the carnage—
But for another man's wife.
Muffled and muttered words;
And resentful grief creeps up against the sons
Of Atreus and their cause.
    But others there by the wall
    Entombed in Trojan ground   430
    Lie, handsome of limb,
    Holding and hidden in enemy soil.

ANTISTROPHE 3

Heavy is the murmur of an angry people
Performing the purpose of a public curse;
There is something cowled in the night
That I anxiously wait to hear.
For the gods are not blind to the
Murderers of many and the black
Furies in time
When a man prospers in sin   440
By erosion of life reduce him to darkness,
Who, once among the lost, can no more
Be helped. Over-great glory
Is a sore burden. The high peak
Is blasted by the eyes of Zeus.
    I prefer an unenvied fortune,

Not to be a sacker of cities
Nor to find myself living at another's
Ruling, myself a captive.

SECOND EPISODE

[*Excited women's voices offstage right and left; cries of joy. The
following speeches are by various members of the* CHORUS *speaking separately.*]

AN OLD MAN. From the good news' beacon a swift   450
Rumour is gone through the town.
Who knows if it be true
Or some deceit of the gods?
ANOTHER OLD MAN. Who is so childish or broken in wit
To kindle his heart at a new-fangled message of flame
And then be downcast
At a change of report?
ANOTHER OLD MAN. It fits the temper of a woman
To give her assent to a story before it is proved.   459
ANOTHER OLD MAN. The over-credulous passion of women expands
In swift conflagration but swiftly declining is gone
The news that a woman announced.

[*Exeunt. Playing area empty as offstage noise dies down. A moment of silence. Several days have passed. The* CHORUS *returns,
and the* LEADER *speaks.*]

Soon we shall know about the illuminant torches,
The beacons and the fiery relays,
Whether they were true or whether like dreams
That pleasant light came here and hoaxed our wits.
Look: I see, coming from the beach, a herald
Shadowed with olive shoots; the dust upon him,
Mud's thirsty sister and colleague, is my witness
That he will not give dumb news nor news by lighting   470
A flame of fire with the smoke of mountain timber;
In words he will either corroborate our joy—
But the opposite version I reject with horror.
To the good appeared so far may good be added.
ANOTHER SPEAKER. Whoever makes other prayers for this our city,
May he reap himself the fruits of his wicked heart.

[*Enter* HERALD *through parodos stage right.*]

HERALD. Earth of my fathers, O the earth of Argos,

In the light of the tenth year I reach you thus
After many shattered hopes achieving one,
For never did I dare to think that here in Argive land   480
I should win a grave in the dearest soil of home;
But now hail, land, and hail, light of the sun,
And Zeus high above the country and the Pythian king—
May he no longer shoot his arrows at us
(Implacable long enough beside Scamander)
But now be saviour to us and be healer,
King Apollo. And all the Assembly's gods
I call upon, and him my patron, Hermes,
The dear herald whom all heralds adore,
And the Heroes who sped our voyage, again with favour   490
Take back the army that has escaped the spear.
O cherished dwelling, palace of royalty,
O august thrones and gods facing the sun,
If ever before, now with your bright eyes
Gladly receive your king after much time,
Who comes bringing light to you in the night time,
And to all these as well—King Agamemnon.
Give him a good welcome as he deserves,
Who with the axe of judgment-awarding God
Has smashed Troy and levelled the Trojan land;   500
The altars are destroyed, the seats of the gods,
And the seed of all the land is perished from it.
Having cast this halter round the neck of Troy
The King, the elder son of Atreus, a blessed man,
Comes, the most worthy to have honour of all
Men that are now. Paris nor his guilty city
Can boast that the crime was greater than the atonement.
Convicted in a suit for rape and robbery
He has lost his stolen goods and with consummate ruin
Mowed down the whole country and his father's house.   510
The sons of Priam have paid their account with interest.

LEADER OF THE CHORUS. Hail and be glad, herald of the Greek army.

HERALD. Yes. Glad indeed! So glad that at the god's demand
I should no longer hesitate to die.

LEADER OF THE CHORUS. Were you so harrowed by desire for home?

HERALD. Yes. The tears come to my eyes for joy.

LEADER OF THE CHORUS. Sweet then is the fever which afflicts you.

HERALD. What do you mean? Let me learn your drift.

LEADER OF THE CHORUS. Longing for those whose love came back in
echo.

HERALD. Meaning the land was homesick for the army?   520

LEADER OF THE CHORUS. Yes. I would often groan from a darkened
    heart.
HERALD. This sullen hatred—how did it fasten on you?
LEADER OF THE CHORUS. I cannot say. Silence is my stock prescrip-
    tion.
HERALD. What? In your masters' absence were there some you
    feared?
LEADER OF THE CHORUS. Yes. In your phrase, death would now be a
    gratification.
HERALD. Yes, for success is ours. These things have taken time.
    Some of them we could say have fallen well,
    While some we blame. Yet who except the gods
    Is free from pain the whole duration of life?
    If I were to tell of our labours, our hard lodging,   530
    The sleeping on crowded decks, the scanty blankets,
    Tossing and groaning, rations that never reached us—
    And the land too gave matter for more disgust,
    For our beds lay under the enemy's walls.
    Continuous drizzle from the sky, dews from the marshes,
    Rotting our clothes, filling our hair with lice.
    And if one were to tell of the bird-destroying winter
    Intolerable from the snows of Ida
    Or of the heat when the sea slackens at noon
    Waveless and dozing in a depressed calm—   540
    But why make these complaints? The weariness is over;
    Over indeed for some who never again
    Need even trouble to rise.
    Why make a computation of the lost?
    Why need the living sorrow for the spites of fortune?
    I wish to say a long goodbye to disasters.
    For us, the remnant of the troops of Argos,
    The advantage remains, the pain can not outweigh it;
    So we can make our boast to this sun's light,
    Flying on words above the land and sea: 550
    'Having taken Troy the Argive expedition
    Has nailed up throughout Greece in every temple
    These spoils, these ancient trophies.'
    Those who hear such things must praise the city
    And the generals. And the grace of God be honoured
    Which brought these things about. You have the whole story.
LEADER OF THE CHORUS. I confess myself convinced by your report.
    Old men are always young enough to learn.
    This news belongs by right first to the house
    And Clytemnestra—though I am enriched also.   560

[CLYTEMNESTRA *appears at the palace door in time to hear these last words.*]

CLYTEMNESTRA. Long before this I shouted at joy's command
  At the coming of the first night-messenger of fire
  Announcing the taking and capsizing of Troy.
  And people reproached me saying, 'Do mere beacons
  Persuade you to think that Troy is already down?
  Indeed a woman's heart is easily exalted.'
  Such comments made me seem to be wandering but yet
  I began my sacrifices and in the women's fashion
  Throughout the town they raised triumphant cries
  And in the gods' enclosures   570
  Lulling the fragrant, incense-eating flame.
  And now what need is there for you to tell me more?
  From the King himself I shall learn the whole story.
  But how the best to welcome my honoured lord
  I shall take pains when he comes back—For what
  Is a kinder light for a woman to see than this,
  To open the gates to her man come back from war
  When God has saved him? Tell this to my husband,

  To come with all speed, the city's darling;
  May he returning find a wife as loyal   580
  As when he left her, watchdog of the house,
  Good to *him* but fierce to the ill-intentioned,
  And in all other things as ever, having destroyed
  No seal or pledge at all in the length of time.
  I know no pleasure with another man, no scandal,
  More than I know how to dye metal red.
  Such is my boast, bearing a load of truth,
  A boast that need not disgrace a noble wife.

[*Exit* CLYTEMNESTRA *to palace.*]

LEADER OF THE CHORUS. Thus has she spoken; if you take her meaning,
  Only a specious tale to shrewd interpreters.   590
  But do you, herald, tell me; I ask after Menelaus
  Whether he will, returning safe preserved,
  Come back with you, our land's loved master.
HERALD. I am not able to speak the lovely falsehood.
  To profit you, my friends, for any stretch of time.
LEADER OF THE CHORUS. But if only the true tidings could be also good!
  It is hard to hide a division of good and true.

HERALD. The prince is vanished out of the Greek fleet,
  Himself and ship. I speak no lie.
LEADER OF THE CHORUS. Did he put forth first in the sight of all from
      Troy,   600
  Or a storm that troubled all sweep him apart?
HERALD. You have hit the target like a master archer,
  Told succinctly a long tale of sorrow.
LEADER OF THE CHORUS. Did the rumours current among the remain-
      ing ships
  Represent him as alive or dead?
HERALD. No one knows so as to tell for sure
  Except the sun who nurses the breeds of earth.
LEADER OF THE CHORUS. Tell me how the storm came on the host of
      ships
  Through the divine anger, and how it ended.
HERALD. Day of good news should not be fouled by tongue   610
  That tells ill news. To each god his season.
  When, despair in his face, a messenger brings to a town
  The hated news of a fallen army—
  One general wound to the city and many men
  Outcast, outcursed, from many homes
  By the double whip which War is fond of,
  Doom with a bloody spear in either hand,
  One carrying such a pack of grief could well
  Recite this hymn of the Furies at your asking.
  But when our cause is saved and a messenger of good   620
  Comes to a city glad with festivity,
  How am I to mix good news with bad, recounting
  The storm that meant God's anger on the Greeks?
  For they swore together, those inveterate enemies,
  Fire and sea, and proved their alliance, destroying
  The unhappy troops of Argos.
  In night arose ill-waved evil,
  Ships on each other the blasts from Thrace
  Crashed colliding, which butting with horns in the violence
  Of big wind and rattle of rain were gone   630
  To nothing, whirled all ways by a wicked shepherd.
  But when there came up the shining light of the sun
  We saw the Aegean sea flowering with corpses
  Of Greek men and their ships' wreckage.
  But for us, our ship was not damaged,
  Whether someone snatched it away or begged it off,
  Some god, not a man, handling the tiller;
  And Saving Fortune was willing to sit upon our ship
  So that neither at anchor we took the tilt of waves

Nor ran to splinters on the crag-bound coast.⠀⠀⠀⠀⠀⠀⠀640
But then having thus escaped death on the sea,
In the white day, not trusting our fortune,
We pastured this new trouble upon our thoughts,
The fleet being battered, the sailors weary,
And now if any of *them* still draw breath,
They are thinking no doubt of us as being lost
And we are thinking of them as being lost.
May the best happen. As for Menelaus
The first guess and most likely is a disaster.
But still—if any ray of sun detects him⠀⠀⠀⠀⠀⠀650
Alive, with living eyes, by the plan of Zeus
Not yet resolved to annul the race completely,
There is some hope then that he will return home.
So much you have heard. Know that it is the truth.

[*Exit* HERALD *stage right. Full* CHORUS *again for the ode.*]

THIRD STASIMON

STROPHE 1

Who was it named her thus
In all ways appositely
Unless it was Someone whom we do not see,
Fore-knowing fate
And plying an accurate tongue?
Helen, bride of spears and conflict's⠀⠀⠀⠀⠀⠀660
Focus, who as was befitting
Proved a hell to ships and men,
Hell to her country, sailing
Away from delicately-sumptuous curtains,
Away on the wind of a giant Zephyr,
And shielded hunters mustered many
On the vanished track of the oars,
Oars beached on the leafy
Banks of a Trojan river
For the sake of bloody war.⠀⠀⠀⠀⠀⠀670

ANTISTROPHE 1

But on Troy was thrust a marring marriage
By the Wrath that working to an end exacts
In time a price from guests
Who dishonoured their host
And dishonoured Zeus of the Hearth,
From those noisy celebrants

Of the wedding hymn which fell
To the brothers of Paris
To sing upon that day.
But learning this, unlearning that,   680
Priam's ancestral city now
Continually mourns, reviling
Paris the fatal bridegroom.
The city has had much sorrow,
Much desolation in life,
From the pitiful loss of her people.

STROPHE 2

So in his house a man might rear
A lion's cub caught from the dam
In need of suckling,
In the prelude of its life   690
Mild, gentle with children,
For old men a playmate,
Often held in the arms
Like a new-born child,
Wheedling the hand,
Fawning at belly's bidding.

ANTISTROPHE 2

But matured by time he showed
The temper of his stock and payed
Thanks for his fostering
With disaster of slaughter of sheep   700
Making an unbidden banquet
And now the house is a shambles,
Irremediable grief to its people,
Calamitous carnage;
For the pet they had fostered was sent
By God as a priest of Ruin.

STROPHE 3

So I would say there came
To the city of Troy
A notion of windless calm,
Delicate adornment of riches,
Soft shooting of the eyes and flower   710
Of desire that stings the fancy.
But swerving aside she achieved
A bitter end to her marriage,

Ill guest and ill companion,
Hurled upon Priam's sons, convoyed
By Zeus, patron of guest and host,
Dark angel dowered with tears.

ANTISTROPHE 3

Long current among men an old saying
Runs that a man's prosperity   720
When grown to greatness
Comes to the birth, does not die childless—
His good luck breeds for his house
Distress that shall not be appeased.
I only, apart from the others,
Hold that the unrighteous action
Breeds true to its kind,
Leaves its own children behind it.
But the lot of a righteous house
Is a fair offspring always.   730

STROPHE 4

Ancient self-glory is accustomed
To bear to light in the evil sort of men
A new self-glory and madness,
Which sometime or sometime finds
The appointed hour for its birth,
And born therewith is the Spirit, intractable, unholy, irresistible,
The reckless lust that brings black Doom upon the house,
A child that is like its parents.

ANTISTROPHE 4

But Honest Dealing is clear
Shining in smoky homes,   740
Honours the god-fearing life.
Mansions gilded by filth of hands she leaves,
Turns her eyes elsewhere, visits the innocent house,
Not respecting the power
Of wealth mis-stamped with approval,
But guides all to the goal.

THIRD EPISODE

[*Enter* AGAMEMNON *through parodos stage right in a war chariot.
With great style: he is a victorious general, and every movement
shows it. But his tragic mask keeps before us the fate that awaits*

him. He is followed by CASSANDRA *in a second chariot; her mask
registers terror, wildness, suffering; her dress, the wreath about
her neck, and the staff she carries identify her as a priestess. Soldiers, slaves, spoils of war. Precisely as the* CHORUS *speaks its first
words,* CLYTEMNESTRA *and her attendants appear in the palace
door center.* AGAMEMNON, *turned toward the* CHORUS, *does not
see her.*]

CHORUS. Come then my King, stormer of Troy,
   Offspring of Atreus,
   How shall I hail you, how give you honour
   Neither overshooting nor falling short   750
     Of the measure of homage?
   There are many who honour appearance too much
   Passing the bounds that are right.
   To condole with the unfortunate man
   Each one is ready but the bite of the grief
     Never goes through to the heart.
   And they join in rejoicing, affecting to share it,
   Forcing their face to a smile.
   But he who is shrewd to shepherd his sheep
   Will fail not to notice the eyes of a man   760
   Which seem to be loyal but lie,
     Fawning with watery friendship.
   Even you, in my thought, when you marshalled the troops
   For Helen's sake, I will not hide it,
   Made a harsh and ugly picture,
   Holding badly the tiller of reason,
   Paying with the death of men
     Ransom for a willing whore.
   But now, not unfriendly, not superficially,
   I offer my service, well-doers' welcome.
   In time you will learn by inquiry   770
   Who has done rightly, who transgressed
     In the work of watching the city.
AGAMEMNON. First to Argos and the country's gods
   My fitting salutations, who have aided me
   To return and in the justice which I exacted
   From Priam's city. Hearing the unspoken case
   The gods unanimously had cast their vote
   Into the bloody urn for the massacre of Troy;
   But to the opposite urn   780
   Hope came, dangled her hand, but did no more.
   Smoke marks even now the city's capture.
   Whirlwinds of doom are alive, the dying ashes

Spread on the air the fat savour of wealth.
For these things we must pay some memorable return
To Heaven, having exacted enormous vengeance
For wife-rape; for a woman
The Argive monster ground a city to powder,
Sprung from a wooden horse, shield-wielding folk,
Launching a leap at the setting of the Pleiads,   790
Jumping the ramparts, a ravening lion,
Lapped its fill of the kingly blood.
To the gods I have drawn out this overture
But as for your concerns, I bear them in my mind
And say the same, you have me in agreement.
To few of men does it belong by nature
To congratulate their friends unenviously,
For a sullen poison fastens on the heart,
Doubling the pain of a man with this disease;
He feels the weight of his own griefs and when   800
He sees another's prosperity he groans.
I speak with knowledge, being well acquainted
With the mirror of comradeship—ghost of a shadow
Were those who seemed to be so loyal to me.
Only Odysseus, who sailed against his will,
Proved, when yoked with me, a ready tracehorse;
I speak of him not knowing if he is alive.
But for what concerns the city and the gods
Appointing public debates in full assembly
We shall consult. That which is well already   810
We shall take steps to ensure it remain well.
But where there is need of medical remedies,
By applying benevolent cautery or surgery
We shall try to deflect the dangers of disease.
But now, entering the halls where stands my hearth,
First I shall make salutation to the gods
Who sent me a far journey and have brought me back.
And may my victory not leave my side.

[*He is about to step from the chariot, but* CLYTEMNESTRA'S
words—spoken to the CHORUS *as she comes forward—arrest
him.*]

CLYTEMNESTRA. Men of the city, you the aged of Argos,
    I shall feel no shame to describe to you my love   820
    Towards my husband. Shyness in all of us
    Wears thin with time. Here are the facts first hand.
    I will tell you of my own unbearable life
    I led so long as this man was at Troy.

For first that the woman separate from her man
Should sit alone at home is extreme cruelty,
Hearing so many malignant rumours—First
Comes one, and another comes after, bad news to worse,
Clamour of grief to the house. If Agamemnon
Had had so many wounds as those reported   830
Which poured home through the pipes of hearsay, then—
Then he would be gashed fuller than a net has holes!
And if only he had died . . . as often as rumour told us,
He would be like the giant in the legend,
Three-bodied. Dying once for every body,
He should have by now three blankets of earth above him—
All that above him; I care not how deep the mattress under!
Such are the malignant rumours thanks to which
They have often seized me against my will and undone
The loop of a rope from my neck.   840
And this is why our son is not standing here,
The guarantee of your pledges and mine,
As he should be, Orestes. Do not wonder;
He is being brought up by a friendly ally and host,
Strophius the Phocian, who warned me in advance
Of dubious troubles, both your risks at Troy
And the anarchy of shouting mobs that might
Overturn policy, for it is born in men
To kick the man who is down.
This is not a disingenuous excuse.   850
For me the outrushing wells of weeping are dried up,
There is no drop left in them.
My eyes are sore from sitting late at nights
Weeping for you and for the baffled beacons,
Never lit up. And, when I slept, in dreams
I have been waked by the thin whizz of a buzzing
Gnat, seeing more horrors fasten on you
Than could take place in the mere time of my dream.
Having endured all this, now, with unsorrowed heart
I would hail this man as the watchdog of the farm,   860
Forestay that saves the ship, pillar that props
The lofty roof, appearance of an only son
To a father or of land to sailors past their hope,
The loveliest day to see after the storm,
Gush of well-water for the thirsty traveller.
Such are the metaphors I think befit him,
But envy be absent. Many misfortunes already
We have endured. But now, dear head, come down
Out of that car, not placing upon the ground

Your foot, O King, the foot that trampled Troy. 870
Why are you waiting, slaves, to whom the task is assigned
To spread the pavement of his path with tapestries?
At once, at once let his way be strewn with purple
That Justice lead him toward his unexpected home.
The rest a mind, not overcome by sleep
Will arrange rightly, with God's help, as destined.

[*She grovels before him as her maids spread rich purple tapestries along the ground from the chariot to the palace door.*]

AGAMEMNON. Daughter of Leda, guardian of my house,
  You have spoken in proportion to my absence.
  You have drawn your speech out long. Duly to praise me,
  That is a duty to be performed by others. 880
  And further—do not by women's methods make me
  Effeminate nor in barbarian fashion
  Gape ground-grovelling acclamations at me
  Nor strewing my path with cloths make it invidious.
  It is the gods should be honoured in this way.
  But being mortal to tread embroidered beauty
  For me is no way without fear.
  I tell you to honour me as a man, not god.
  Footcloths are very well—Embroidered stuffs
  Are stuff for gossip. And not to think unwisely 890
  Is the greatest gift of God. Call happy only him
  Who has ended his life in sweet prosperity.
  I have spoken. This thing I could not do with confidence.
CLYTEMNESTRA. Tell me now, according to your judgment.
AGAMEMNON. I tell you you shall not override my judgment.
CLYTEMNESTRA. Supposing you had feared something . . .
  Could you have vowed to God to do this thing?
AGAMEMNON. Yes. If an expert had prescribed that vow.
CLYTEMNESTRA. And how would Priam have acted in your place?
AGAMEMNON. He would have trod the cloths, I think, for certain.
CLYTEMNESTRA. Then do not flinch before the blame of men. 901
AGAMEMNON. The voice of the multitude is very strong.
CLYTEMNESTRA. But the man none envy is not enviable.
AGAMEMNON. It is not a woman's part to love disputing.
CLYTEMNESTRA. But it is a conqueror's part to yield upon occasion.
AGAMEMNON. You think such victory worth fighting for?
CLYTEMNESTRA. Give way. Consent to let me have the mastery.
AGAMEMNON. Well, if such is your wish, let someone quickly loose
  My vassal sandals, underlings of my feet,
  And stepping on these sea-purples may no god 910

Shoot me from far with the envy of his eye.
Great shame it is to ruin my house and spoil
The wealth of costly weavings with my feet.
But of this matter enough. This stranger woman here
Take in with kindness. The man who is a gentle master
God looks on from far off complacently.
For no one of his will bears the slave's yoke.
This woman, of many riches being the chosen
Flower, gift of the soldiers, has come with me.
But since I have been prevailed on by your words   920
I will go to my palace home, treading on purples.

[*He steps down, but her speech holds him standing there on the tapestries.*]

CLYTEMNESTRA. There is the sea and who shall drain it dry? It breeds
Its wealth in silver of plenty of purple gushing
And ever-renewed, the dyeings of our garments.
The house has its store of these by God's grace, King.
This house is ignorant of poverty
And I would have vowed a pavement of many garments
Had the palace oracle enjoined that vow
Thereby to contrive a ransom for his life.
For while there is root, foliage comes to the house   930
Spreading a tent of shade against the Dog Star.
So now that you have reached your hearth and home
You prove a miracle—advent of warmth in winter;
And further this—even in the time of heat
When God is fermenting wine from the bitter grape,
Even then it is cool in the house if only
Its master walk at home, a grown man, ripe.

[*With this line* CLYTEMNESTRA *indicates that she is finished, and they both move toward the palace, she following and to the side so as to avoid the tapestries.* AGAMEMNON *walks straight in. As he does so, all the women attendants and* CLYTEMNESTRA *herself raise the traditional cry of joy: alleluia.* CLYTEMNESTRA *turns at the door and prays.*]

O Zeus the Ripener, ripen these my prayers;
Your part it is to make the ripe fruit fall.

[*Exit* CLYTEMNESTRA. *Soldiers, slaves, attendants disperse, taking* AGAMEMNON's *chariot off right and the tapestries into the palace. Throughout the choral ode* CASSANDRA *remains in the second chariot; one or two soldiers unobstrusively present.*]

FOURTH STASIMON

CHORUS. Why, why at the doors   940
  Of my fore-seeing heart
  Does this terror keep beating its wings?
  And my song play the prophet
  Unbidden, unhired—
  Which I cannot spit out
  Like the enigmas of dreams
  Nor plausible confidence
  Sit on the throne of my mind?
  It is long time since
  The cables let down from the stern   950
  Were chafed by the sand when the seafaring army started for
    Troy.

And I learn with my eyes
And witness myself their return;
But the hymn without lyre goes up,
The dirge of the Avenging Fiend,
In the depths of my self-taught heart
Which has lost its dear
Possession of the strength of hope.
But my guts and my heart
Are not idle which seethe with the waves   960
Of trouble nearing its hour.
But I pray that these thoughts
May fall out not as I think
  And not be fulfilled in the end.

Truly when health grows much
It respects not limit; for disease,
Its neighbour in the next door room,
Presses upon it.
A man's life, crowding sail,
Strikes on the blind reef: 970
But if caution in advance
Jettison part of the cargo
With the derrick of due proportion,
The whole house does not sink,
Though crammed with a weight of woe

The hull does not go under.
The abundant bounty of God
And his gifts from the year's furrows
Drive the famine back.

ANTISTROPHE 2

But when upon the ground there has fallen once   980
The black blood of a man's death,
Who shall summon it back by incantations?
Even Asclepius who had the art
To fetch the dead to life, even to him
Zeus put a provident end.
But, if of the heaven-sent fates
One did not check the other,
Cancel the other's advantage,
My heart would outrun my tongue
In pouring out these fears.   990
But now it mutters in the dark,
Embittered, no way hoping
To unravel a scheme in time
    From a burning mind.

FOURTH EPISODE

[CLYTEMNESTRA *appears at the palace door.*]

CLYTEMNESTRA. Go in too, you; I speak to you, Cassandra,
    Since God in his clemency has put you in this house
    To share our holy water, standing with many slaves
    Beside the altar that protects the house,
    Step down from the car there, do not be overproud.
    Heracles himself they say was once   1000
    Sold, and endured to eat the bread of slavery.
    But should such a chance inexorably fall,
    There is much advantage in masters who have long been rich.
    Those who have reaped a crop they never expected
    Are in all things hard on their slaves and overstep the line.
    From us you will have the treatment of tradition.

[CASSANDRA *in no way indicates that she has heard. The* LEADER
OF THE CHORUS *tries to help.*]

LEADER OF THE CHORUS. You, it is you she has addressed, and clearly.
    Caught as you are in these predestined toils
    Obey her if you can. But should you disobey . . .   1009
CLYTEMNESTRA. If she has more than the gibberish of the swallow,

An unintelligible barbaric speech,
I hope to read her mind, persuade her reason.
LEADER OF THE CHORUS. As things now stand for you, she says the
    best.
Obey her; leave that car and follow her.
CLYTEMNESTRA. I have no leisure to waste out here, outside the door.
Before the hearth in the middle of my house
The victims stand already, wait the knife.
You, if you will obey me, waste no time.
But if you cannot understand my language—

[*To* CHORUS LEADER.]

You make it plain to her with the brute and voiceless hand.   1020
LEADER OF THE CHORUS. The stranger seems to need a clear inter-
    preter.
She bears herself like a wild beast newly captured.
CLYTEMNESTRA. The fact is she is mad, she listens to evil thoughts,
Who has come here leaving a city newly captured
Without experience how to bear the bridle
So as not to waste her strength in foam and blood.
I will not spend more words to be ignored.

[*Exit* CLYTEMNESTRA.]

CHORUS. But I, for I pity her, will not be angry.
Obey, unhappy woman. Leave this car.
Yield to your fate. Put on the untried yoke.   1030

[*She steps slowly down from the chariot. Her terrible cry comes
as she sees the statue of Apollo before the palace. The cry begins an intense lyric exchange (called the Kommos—Greek for
"breast beating") between* CASSANDRA *and the full* CHORUS. *The
lines are sung.*]

KOMMOS

STROPHE 1
CASSANDRA. Apollo! Apollo!
CHORUS. Why do you cry like this upon Apollo?
    He is not the kind of god that calls for dirges.

ANTISTROPHE 1
CASSANDRA. Apollo! Apollo!
CHORUS. Once more her funereal cries invoke the god
    Who has no place at the scene of lamentation.

STROPHE 2

CASSANDRA. Apollo! Apollo!
  God of the Ways! My destroyer!
  Destroyed again—and this time utterly!
CHORUS. She seems about to predict her own misfortunes.   1040
  The gift of the god endures, even in a slave's mind.

ANTISTROPHE 2

CASSANDRA. Apollo! Apollo!
  God of the Ways! My destroyer!
  Where? To what house? Where, where have you brought me?
CHORUS. To the house of the sons of Atreus. If you do not know it,
  I will tell you so. You will not find it false.

STROPHE 3

CASSANDRA. No, no, but to a god-hated, but to an accomplice
  In much kin-killing, murdering nooses,
  Man-shambles, a floor asperged with blood.
CHORUS. The stranger seems like a hound with a keen scent,   1050
  Is picking up a trail that leads to murder.

ANTISTROPHE 3

CASSANDRA. Clues! I have clues! Look! They are these.
  These wailing, these children, butchery of children;
  Roasted flesh, a father sitting to dinner.
CHORUS. Of your prophetic fame we have heard before
  But in this matter prophets are not required.

STROPHE 4

CASSANDRA. What is she doing? What is she planning?
  What is this new great sorrow?
  Great crime . . . within here . . . planning
  Unendurable to his folk, impossible   1060
  Ever to be cured. For help
    Stands far distant.
CHORUS. This reference I cannot catch. But the children
  I recognized; that refrain is hackneyed.

ANTISTROPHE 4

CASSANDRA. Damned, damned, bringing this work to completion—
  Your husband who shared your bed
  To bathe him, to cleanse him, and then—
  How shall I tell of the end?
  Soon, very soon, it will fall.
    The end comes hand over hand   1070
  Grasping in greed.

CHORUS. Not yet do I understand. After her former riddles
  Now I am baffled by these dim pronouncements.

STROPHE 5

CASSANDRA. Ah God, the vision! God, God, the vision!
  A net, is it? Net of Hell!
  But herself is the net; shared bed; shares murder.
  O let the pack ever-hungering after the family
  Howl for the unholy ritual, howl for the victim.

STROPHE 6

CHORUS. What black Spirit is this you call upon the house—
  To raise aloft her cries? Your speech does not lighten me.   1080
  Into my heart runs back the blood
  Yellow as when for men by the spear fallen
  The blood ebbs out with the rays of the setting life
    And death strides quickly.

ANTISTROPHE 5

CASSANDRA. Quick! Be on your guard! The bull—
  Keep him clear of the cow.
  Caught with a trick, the black horn's point,
  She strikes. He falls; lies in the water.
  Murder; a trick in a bath. I tell what I see.

ANTISTROPHE 6

CHORUS. I would not claim to be expert in oracles   1090
  But these, as I deduce, portend disaster.
  Do men ever get a good answer from oracles?
  No. It is only through disaster
  That their garrulous craft brings home
  The meaning of the prophet's panic.

STROPHE 7

CASSANDRA. And for me also, for me, chance ill-destined!
  My own now I lament, pour into the cup my own.
  Where is this you have brought me in my misery?
  Unless to die as well. What else is meant?

STROPHE 8

CHORUS. You are mad, mad, carried away by the god,   1100
  Raising the dirge, the tuneless
  Tune, for yourself. Like the tawny
  Unsatisfied singer from her luckless heart
  Lamenting 'Itys, Itys', the nightingale

Lamenting a life luxuriant with grief.

ANTISTROPHE 7

CASSANDRA. Oh the lot of the songful nightingale!
   The gods enclosed her in a winged body,
   Gave her a sweet and tearless passing.
   But for me remains the two-edged cutting blade.

ANTISTROPHE 8

CHORUS. From whence these rushing and God-inflicted   1110
   Profitless pains?
   Why shape with your sinister crying
   The piercing hymn—fear-piercing?
   How can you know the evil-worded landmarks
      On the prophetic path?

STROPHE 9

CASSANDRA. Oh the wedding, the wedding of Paris—death to his peo-
      ple!
   O river Scamander, water drunk by my fathers!
   When I was young, alas, upon your beaches
   I was brought up and cared for.
   But now it is the River of Wailing and the banks of Hell   1120
      That shall hear my prophecy soon.

STROPHE 10

CHORUS. What is this clear speech, too clear?
   A child could understand it.
   I am bitten with fangs that draw blood
   By the misery of your cries,
   Cries harrowing the heart.

ANTISTROPHE 9

CASSANDRA. O trouble on trouble of a city lost, lost utterly!
   My father's sacrifices before the towers,
   Much killing of cattle and sheep,
   No cure—availed not at all   1130
   To prevent the coming of what came to Troy,
   And I, my brain on fire, shall soon enter the trap.

ANTISTROPHE 10

CHORUS. This speech accords with the former.
   What god, malicious, over-heavy, persistently pressing,
   Drives you to chant of these lamentable

Griefs with death their burden?
But I cannot see the end.

FIFTH EPISODE

CASSANDRA. The oracle now no longer from behind veils
   Will be peeping forth like a newly-wedded bride;
   But I can feel it like a fresh wind swoop   1140
   And rush in the face of the dawn and, wave-like, wash
   Against the sun a vastly greater grief
   Than this one. I shall speak no more conundrums.
   And bear me witness, pacing me, that I
   Am trailing on the scent of ancient wrongs.
   For this house here a choir never deserts,
   Chanting together ill. For they mean ill,
   And to puff up their arrogance they have drunk
   Men's blood, this band of revellers that haunts the house,
   Hard to be rid of, fiends that attend the family.   1150
   Established in its rooms they hymn their hymn
   Of that original sin, abhor in turn
   The adultery that proved a brother's ruin.
   A miss? Or do my arrows hit the mark?
   Or am I a quack prophet who knocks at doors, a babbler?
   Give me your oath, confess I have the facts,
   The ancient history of this house's crimes.
LEADER OF THE CHORUS. And how could an oath's assurance, however
      finely assured,
   Turn out a remedy? I wonder, though, that you
   Being brought up overseas, of another tongue,   1160
   Should hit on the whole tale as if you had been standing by.
CASSANDRA. Apollo the prophet set me to prophesy.
LEADER OF THE CHORUS. Was he, although a god, struck by desire?
CASSANDRA. Till now I was ashamed to tell that story.
LEADER OF THE CHORUS. Yes. Good fortune keeps us all fastidious.
CASSANDRA. He wrestled hard upon me, panting love.
LEADER OF THE CHORUS. And did you come, as they do, to child-
      getting?
CASSANDRA. No. I agreed to him. And I cheated him.
LEADER OF THE CHORUS. Were you already possessed by the mystic
      art?
CASSANDRA. Already I was telling the townsmen all their future suffer-
      ing.   1170
LEADER OF THE CHORUS. Then how did you escape the doom of
      Apollo's anger?

CASSANDRA. I did not escape. No one ever believed me.
LEADER OF THE CHORUS. Yet to us your words seem worthy of belief.
CASSANDRA. Oh misery, misery!

> Again comes on me the terrible labour of true
> Prophecy, dizzying prelude; distracts . . .
> Do you see these who sit before the house,
> Children, like the shapes of dreams?
> Children who seem to have been killed by their kinsfolk,
> Filling their hands with meat, flesh of themselves,   1180
> Guts and entrails, handfuls of lament—
> Clear what they hold—the same their father tasted.
> For this I declare someone is plotting vengeance—
> A lion? Lion but coward, that lurks in bed,
> Good watchdog truly against the lord's return—
> My lord, for I must bear the yoke of serfdom.
> Leader of the ships, overturner of Troy,
> He does not know what plots the accursed hound
> With the licking tongue and the pricked-up ear will plan
> In the manner of a lurking doom, in an evil hour.   1190
> A daring criminal! Female murders male.
> What monster could provide her with a title?
> An amphisbaena or hag of the sea who dwells
> In rocks to ruin sailors—
> A raving mother of death who breathes against her folk
> War to the finish. Listen to her shout of triumph,
> Who shirks no horrors, like men in a rout of battle.
> And yet she poses as glad at their return.
> If you distrust my words, what does it matter?
> That which will come will come. You too will soon stand here
> And admit with pity that I spoke too truly.   1201

LEADER OF THE CHORUS. Thyestes' dinner of his children's meat
    I understood and shuddered, and fear grips me
    To hear the truth, not framed in parables.
    But hearing the rest I am thrown out of my course.
CASSANDRA. It is Agamemnon's death I tell you you shall witness.
LEADER OF THE CHORUS. Stop! Provoke no evil. Quiet your mouth!
CASSANDRA. The god who gives me words is here no healer.
LEADER OF THE CHORUS. Not if this shall be so. But may some chance
    avert it.
CASSANDRA. *You* are praying. But others are busy with murder.   1210
LEADER OF THE CHORUS. What man is he promotes this terrible thing?
CASSANDRA. Indeed you have missed my drift by a wide margin!
LEADER OF THE CHORUS. But I do not understand the assassin's
    method.
CASSANDRA. And yet too well I know the speech of Greece!

LEADER OF THE CHORUS. So does Delphi but the replies are hard.
CASSANDRA. Ah what a fire it is! It comes upon me.
    Apollo, Wolf-Destroyer, pity, pity . . .
    It is the two-foot lioness who beds
    Beside a wolf, the noble lion away,
    It is she will kill me. Brewing a poisoned cup   1220
    She will mix my punishment too in the angry draught
    And boasts, sharpening the dagger for her husband,
    To pay back murder for my bringing here.
    Why then do I wear these mockeries of myself,
    The wand and the prophet's garland round my neck?

[*Tears them off, throws them to the ground, and speaks to them.*]

    My hour is coming—but you shall perish first.
    Destruction! Scattered thus you give me my revenge;
    Go and enrich some other woman with ruin.
    See: Apollo himself is stripping me
    Of my prophetic gear, who has looked on   1230
    When in this dress I have been a laughing-stock
    To friends and foes alike, and to no purpose;
    They called me crazy, like a fortune-teller,
    A poor starved beggar-woman—and I bore it.
    And now the prophet undoing his prophetess
    Has brought me to this final darkness.
    Instead of my father's altar the executioner's block
    Waits me the victim, red with my hot blood.
    But the gods will not ignore me as I die.
    One will come after to avenge my death,   1240
    A matricide, a murdered father's champion.
    Exile and tramp and outlaw he will come back
    To gable the family house of fatal crime;
    His father's outstretched corpse shall lead him home.
    Why need I then lament so pitifully?
    For now that I have seen the town of Troy
    Treated as she was treated, while her captors
    Come to their reckoning thus by the god's verdict,
    I will go in and have the courage to die.
    Look, these gates are the gates of Death. I greet them. 1250
    And I pray that I may meet a deft and mortal stroke
    So that without a struggle I may close
    My eyes and my blood ebb in easy death.
LEADER OF THE CHORUS. Oh woman very unhappy and very wise,
    Your speech was long. But if in sober truth
    You know your fate, why like an ox that the gods
    Drive, do you walk so bravely to the altar?

CASSANDRA. There is no escape, strangers. No; not by postponement.
LEADER OF THE CHORUS. But the last moment has the privilege of
 hope.
CASSANDRA. The day is here. Little should I gain by flight. 1260
LEADER OF THE CHORUS. This patience of yours comes from a brave
 soul.
CASSANDRA. A happy man is never paid that compliment.
LEADER OF THE CHORUS. But to die with credit graces a mortal man.
CASSANDRA. Oh my father! You and your noble sons!

[*She moves toward the door but suddenly, with great violence,
turns back almost overcome.*]

LEADER OF THE CHORUS. What is it? What is the fear that drives you
 back?
CASSANDRA. Faugh.
LEADER OF THE CHORUS. Why faugh? Or is this some hallucination?
CASSANDRA. These walls breathe out a death that drips with blood.
LEADER OF THE CHORUS. Not so. It is only the smell of the sacrifice.
CASSANDRA. It is like a breath out of a charnel-house. 1270
LEADER OF THE CHORUS. You think our palace burns odd incense
 then!
CASSANDRA. But I will go to lament among the dead
 My lot and Agamemnon's. Enough of life!
 Strangers,
 I am not afraid like a bird afraid of a bush
 But witness you my words after my death
 When a woman dies in return for me a woman
 And a man falls for a man with a wicked wife.
 I ask this service, being about to die.
LEADER OF THE CHORUS. Alas, I pity you for the death you have fore-
 told. 1280
CASSANDRA. One more speech I have; I do not wish to raise
 The dirge for my own self. But to the sun I pray
 In face of his last light that my avengers
 May make my murderers pay for this my death,
 Death of a woman slave, an easy victim.
LEADER OF THE CHORUS. Ah the fortunes of men! When they go well
 A shadow sketch would match them, and in ill-fortune
 The dab of a wet sponge destroys the drawing.
 It is not myself but the life of man I pity.

[CASSANDRA *forces herself to enter the palace. Full* CHORUS *begins what appears at first to be another ode.*]

CHORUS. Prosperity in all men cries 1290

For more prosperity. Even the owner
Of the finger-pointed-at palace never shuts
His door against her, saying 'Come no more'.
So to our king the blessed gods had granted
To take the town of Priam, and heaven-favoured
He reaches home. But now if for former bloodshed
   He must pay blood
And dying for the dead shall cause
   Other deaths in atonement
What man could boast he was born   1300
   Secure, who heard this story?

[*Suddenly* AGAMEMNON's *voice from inside the palace.*]

AGAMEMNON. Oh! I am struck a mortal blow—within!
LEADER OF THE CHORUS. Silence! Listen. Who calls out, wounded
   with a mortal stroke?
AGAMEMNON. Again—the second blow—I am struck again.

[*The* CHORUS *is confused, its dance formation shattered. They
debate excitedly, speaking as individuals.*]

LEADER OF THE CHORUS. You heard the king cry out. I think the deed
   is done.
   Let us see if we can concert some sound proposal.
2ND OLD MAN. Well, I will tell you my opinion—
   Raise an alarm, summon the folk to the palace.
3RD OLD MAN. I say burst in with all speed possible,
   Convict them of the deed while still the sword is wet.   1310
4TH OLD MAN. And I am partner to some such suggestion.
   I am for taking some course. No time to dawdle.
5TH OLD MAN. The case is plain. This is but the beginning.
   They are going to set up dictatorship in the state.
6TH OLD MAN. We are wasting time. The assassins tread to earth
   The decencies of delay and give their hands no sleep.
7TH OLD MAN. I do not know what plan I could hit on to propose.
   The man who acts is in the position to plan.
8TH OLD MAN. So I think, too, for I am at a loss
   To raise the dead man up again with words.   1320
9TH OLD MAN. Then to stretch out our life shall we yield thus
   To the rule of these profaners of the house?
10TH OLD MAN. It is not to be endured. To die is better.
   Death is more comfortable than tyranny.
11TH OLD MAN. And are we on the evidence of groans
   Going to give oracle that the prince is dead?
12TH OLD MAN. We must know the facts for sure and *then* be angry.
   Guesswork is not the same as certain knowledge.

LEADER OF THE CHORUS. Then all of you back me and approve this
   plan—
   To ascertain how it is with Agamemnon.   1330

[*The palace doors open abruptly, revealing the bodies of* AGA-
MEMNON *and* CASSANDRA. CLYTEMNESTRA *stands over them with
blood on her hands, mask, and dress.* AGAMEMNON'S *body is
partly wrapped—as though it had been caught—in one of the
large purple tapestries upon which he has recently walked.*]

CLYTEMNESTRA. Much having been said before to fit the moment,
   To say the opposite now will not outface me.
   How else could one serving hate upon the hated,
   Thought to be friends, hang high the nets of doom
   To preclude all leaping out?
   For me I have long been training for this match,
   I tried a fall and won—a victory overdue.
   I stand here where I struck, above my victims;
   So I contrived it—this I will not deny—
   That he could neither fly nor ward off death;   1340
   Inextricable like a net for fishes
   I cast about him a vicious wealth of raiment
   And struck him twice and with two groans he loosed
   His limbs beneath him, and upon him fallen
   I deal him the third blow to the God beneath the earth,
   To the safe keeper of the dead a votive gift,
   And with that he spits his life out where he lies
   And smartly spouting blood he sprays me with
   The sombre drizzle of bloody dew and I
   Rejoice no less than in God's gift of rain   1350
   The crops are glad when the ear of corn gives birth.
   These things being so, you, elders of Argos,
   Rejoice if rejoice you will. Mine is the glory.
   And if I could pay this corpse his due libation.
   I should be right to pour it and more than right;
   With so many horrors this man mixed and filled
   The bowl—and, coming home, has drained the draught himself.
LEADER OF THE CHORUS. Your speech astonishes us. This brazen boast
   Above the man who was your king and husband!
CLYTEMNESTRA. You challenge me as a woman without foresight
   But I with unflinching heart to you who know   1361
   Speak. And you, whether you will praise or blame,
   It makes no matter. Here lies Agamemnon,
   My husband, dead, the work of this right hand,
   An honest workman. There you have the facts.

[*The* CHORUS *has come slowly together again. In the following
ode (shared, like the Kommos, by an actor and the* CHORUS*) they
react together against* CLYTEMNESTRA.]

STROPHE 1

CHORUS. Woman, what poisoned
  Herb of the earth have you tasted
  Or potion of the flowing sea
  To undertake this killing and the people's curses?
  You threw down, you cut off—The people will cast you out,
  Black abomination to the town.   1371
CLYTEMNESTRA. Now your verdict—in my case—is exile
  And to have the people's hatred, the public curses,
  Though then in no way you opposed this man
  Who carelessly, as if it were a head of sheep
  Out of the abundance of his fleecy flocks,
  Sacrificed his own daughter, to me the dearest
  Fruit of travail, charm for the Thracian winds.
  He was the one to have banished from this land,
  Pay off the pollution. But when you hear what I   1380
  Have done, you judge severely. But I warn you—
  Threaten me on the understanding that I am ready
  For two alternatives—Win by force the right
  To rule me, but, if God brings about the contrary,
  Late in time you will have to learn self-discipline.

ANTISTROPHE 1

CHORUS. You are high in the thoughts,
  You speak extravagant things,
  After the soiling murder your crazy heart
  Fancies your forehead with a smear of blood.
  Unhonoured, unfriended, you must   1390
  Pay for a blow with a blow.
CLYTEMNESTRA. Listen then to this—the sanction of my oaths:
  By the Justice totting up my child's atonement,
  By the Avenging Doom and Fiend to whom I killed this man,
  For me hope walks not in the rooms of fear
  So long as my fire is lit upon my hearth
  By Aegisthus, loyal to me as he was before.
  The man who outraged me lies here,
  The darling of each courtesan at Troy,
  And here with him is the prisoner clairvoyante,   1400
  The fortune-teller that he took to bed,
  Who shares his bed as once his bench on shipboard,

A loyal mistress. Both have their deserts.
He lies so; and she who like a swan
Sang her last dying lament
Lies his lover, and the sight contributes
An appetiser to my own bed's pleasure.

STROPHE 2

CHORUS. Ah would some quick death come not overpainful,
    Not overlong on the sickbed,
    Establishing in us the ever-   1410
    Lasting unending sleep now that our guardian
    Has fallen, the kindest of men,
    Who suffering much for a woman
    By a woman has lost his life.
      O Helen, insane, being one
      One to have destroyed so many
      And many souls under Troy,
      Now is your work complete, blossomed not for oblivion,
      Unfading stain of blood. Here now, if in any home,
      Is Discord, here is a man's deep-rooted ruin.   1420
CLYTEMNESTRA. Do not pray for the portion of death
    Weighed down by these things, do not turn
    Your anger on Helen as destroyer of men,
    One woman destroyer of many
    Lives of Greek men,
      A hurt that cannot be healed.

ANTISTROPHE 2

CHORUS. O Evil Spirit, falling on the family,
    On the two sons of Atreus and using
    Two sisters in heart as your tools,
    A power that bites to the heart—   1430
    See on the body
    Perched like a raven he gloats
    Harshly croaking his hymn.
CLYTEMNESTRA. Ah, now you have amended your lips' opinion,
    Calling upon this family's three times gorged
    Genius—demon who breeds
    Blood-hankering lust in the belly:
    Before the old sore heals, new pus collects.

STROPHE 3

CHORUS. It is a great spirit—great—
    You tell of, harsh in anger,   1440
    A ghastly tale, alas,

Of unsatisfied disaster
Brought by Zeus, by Zeus,
Cause and worker of all.
For without Zeus what comes to pass among us?
Which of these things is outside Providence?
    O my king, my king,
    How shall I pay you in tears,
    Speak my affection in words?
    You lie in that spider's web,   1450
    In a desecrating death breathe out your life,
    Lie ignominiously
    Defeated by a crooked death
    And the two-edged cleaver's stroke.
CLYTEMNESTRA. You say this is *my* work—mine?
  Do not cozen yourself that I am Agamemnon's wife.
  Masquerading as the wife
  Of the corpse there the old sharp-witted Genius
  Of Atreus who gave the cruel banquet
  Has paid with a grown man's life   1460
  The due for children dead.

ANTISTROPHE 3

CHORUS. That you are guilty of
  This murder who will attest?
  No, but you may have been abetted
  By some ancestral Spirit of Revenge.
  Wading a millrace of the family's blood
  The black Manslayer forces a forward path
  To make the requital at last
  For the eaten children, the blood-clot cold with time.
    O my king, my king,   1470
    How shall I pay you in tears,
    Speak my affection in words?
    You lie in that spider's web,
    In a desecrating death breathe out your life,
    Lie ignominiously
    Defeated by a crooked death
    And the two-edged cleaver's stroke.
CLYTEMNESTRA. Did he not, too, contrive a crooked
  Horror for the house? My child by him,
  Shoot that I raised, much-wept-for Iphigeneia,   1480
  He treated her like this;
  So suffering like this he need not make
  Any great brag in Hell having paid with death
  Dealt by the sword for work of his own beginning.

STROPHE 4

CHORUS. I am at a loss for thought, I lack
　All nimble counsel as to where
　To turn when the house is falling.
　I fear the house-collapsing crashing
　Blizzard of blood—of which these drops are earnest.
　Now is Destiny sharpening her justice　　　　　　1490
　On other whetstones for a new infliction.
　　O earth, earth, if only you had received me
　　Before I saw this man lie here as if in bed
　　　In a bath lined with silver.
　　Who will bury him? Who will keen him?
　　Will you, having killed your own husband,
　　Dare now to lament him
　　And after great wickedness make
　　　Unamending amends to his ghost?
　　And who above this godlike hero's grave　　　　1500
　　Pouring praises and tears
　　　Will grieve with a genuine heart?
CLYTEMNESTRA. It is not your business to attend to that.
　By my hand he fell low, lies low and dead,
　And I shall bury him low down in the earth,
　And his household need not weep him
　For Iphigeneia his daughter
　Tenderly, as is right,
　Will meet her father at the rapid ferry of sorrows,
　Put her arms round him and kiss him!　　　　　1510

ANTISTROPHE 4

CHORUS. Reproach answers reproach,
　It is hard to decide,
　The catcher is caught, the killer pays for his kill.
　But the law abides while Zeus abides enthroned
　That the wrongdoer suffers. That is established.
　Who could expel from the house the seed of the Curse?
　The race is soldered in sockets of Doom and Vengeance.
CLYTEMNESTRA. In this you say what is right and the will of God.
　But for my part I am ready to make a contract
　With the Evil Genius of the House of Atreus　　　1520
　To accept what has been till now, hard though it is,
　But that for the future he shall leave this house
　And wear away some other stock with deaths
　Imposed among themselves. Of my possessions
　A small part will suffice if only I
　Can rid these walls of the mad exchange of murder.

[*Enter* AEGISTHUS *triumphantly—almost running—through parodos stage left, followed by an armed bodyguard of fifteen or twenty men.*]

AEGISTHUS. O welcome light of a justice-dealing day!
From now on I will say that the gods, avenging men,
Look down from above on the crimes of earth,
Seeing as I do in woven robes of the Furies   1530
This man lying here—a sight to warm my heart—
Paying for the crooked violence of his father.
For his father Atreus, when he ruled the country,
Because his power was challenged, hounded out
From state and home his own brother Thyestes.
My father—let me be plain—was this Thyestes,
Who later came back home a suppliant,
There, miserable, found so much asylum
As not to die on the spot, stain the ancestral floor.
But to show his hospitality godless Atreus   1540
Gave him an eager if not a loving welcome,
Pretending a day of feasting and rich meats
Served my father with his children's flesh.
The hands and feet, fingers and toes, he hid
At the bottom of the dish. My father sitting apart
Took unknowing the unrecognizable portion
And ate of a dish that has proved, as you see, expensive.
But when he knew he had eaten worse than poison
He fell back groaning, vomiting their flesh,
And invoking a hopeless doom on the sons of Pelops   1550
Kicked over the table to confirm his curse—
So may the whole race perish!
Result of this—you see this man lie here.
I stitched this murder together; it was my title.
Me the third son he left, an unweaned infant,
To share the bitterness of my father's exile.
But I grew up and Justice brought me back,
I grappled this man while still beyond his door,
Having pieced together the programme of his ruin.
So now would even death be beautiful to me   1560
Having seen Agamemnon in the nets of Justice.
LEADER OF THE CHORUS. Aegisthus. I cannot respect brutality in distress.
You claim that you deliberately killed this prince
And that you alone planned this pitiful murder.
Be sure that in your turn your head shall not escape
The people's volleyed curses mixed with stones.
AEGISTHUS. Do you speak so who sit at the lower oar

While those on the upper bench control the ship?
Old as you are, you will find it is a heavy load
To go to school when old to learn the lesson of tact.   1570
For old age, too, gaol and hunger are fine
Instructors in wisdom, second-sighted doctors.
You have eyes. Cannot you see?
Do not kick against the pricks. The blow will hurt you.

LEADER OF THE CHORUS. You woman waiting in the house for those
    who return from battle
While you seduce their wives! Was it you devised
The death of a master of armies?

AEGISTHUS. And these words, too, prepare the way for tears.
Contrast your voice with the voice of Orpheus: he
Led all things after him bewitched with joy, but you   1580
Having stung me with your silly yelps shall be
Led off yourself, to prove more mild when mastered.

LEADER OF THE CHORUS. Indeed! So you are now to be king of Argos,
You who, when you had plotted the king's death,
Did not even dare to do that thing yourself!

AEGISTHUS. No. For the trick of it was clearly woman's work.
I was suspect, an enemy of old.
But now I shall try with Agamemnon's wealth
To rule the people. Any who is disobedient
I will harness in a heavy yoke, no tracehorse work for him   1590
Like barley-fed colt, but hateful hunger lodging
Beside him in the dark will see his temper soften.

LEADER OF THE CHORUS. Why with your cowardly soul did you your-
    self
Not strike this man but left that work to a woman
Whose presence pollutes our country and its gods?
But Orestes—does he somewhere see the light
That he may come back here by favour of fortune
And kill this pair and prove the final victor?

[AEGISTHUS *summons his guards.*]

AEGISTHUS. Well, if such is your design in deeds and words, you will
    quickly learn—
Here my friends, here my guards, there is work for you at hand.

LEADER OF THE CHORUS. Come then, hands on hilts, be each and all
    of us prepared.   1601

[*The old men and the guards threaten each other.*]

AEGISTHUS. Very well! I too am ready to meet death with sword in
    hand.

LEADER OF THE CHORUS. We are glad you speak of dying. We accept
　　your words for luck.
CLYTEMNESTRA. No, my dearest, do not so. Add no more to the train
　　of wrong.
　To reap these many present wrongs is harvest enough of misery.
　Enough of misery. Start no more. Our hands are red.
　But do you, and you old men, go home and yield to fate in time,
　In time before you suffer. We have acted as we had to act.
　If only our afflictions now could prove enough, we should agree—
　We who have been so hardly mauled in the heavy claws of the evil
　　god.　　　　　　　　　　　　　　　　　　　　　　　　1610
　So stands my word, a woman's, if any man thinks fit to hear.
AEGISTHUS. But to think that these should thus pluck the blooms of
　　an idle tongue
　And should throw out words like these, giving the evil god his
　　chance,
　And should miss the path of prudence and insult their master so!
LEADER OF THE CHORUS. It is not the Argive way to fawn upon a cow-
　　ardly man.
AEGISTHUS. Perhaps. But I in later days will take further steps with
　　you.
LEADER OF THE CHORUS. Not if the god who rules the family guides
　　Orestes to his home.
AEGISTHUS. Yes. I know that men in exile feed themselves on barren
　　hopes.
LEADER OF THE CHORUS. Go on, grow fat defiling justice . . . while
　　you have your hour.
AEGISTHUS. Do not think you will not pay me a price for your stu-
　　pidity.　　　　　　　　　　　　　　　　　　　　　　　1620
LEADER OF THE CHORUS. Boast on in your self-assurance, like a cock
　　beside his hen.
CLYTEMNESTRA. Pay no heed, Aegisthus, to these futile barkings. You
　　and I,
　Masters of this house, from now shall order all things well.

[*She leads him into the palace, past the bodies of* AGAMEMNON
and CASSANDRA. *The doors close. The armed guard watches arro-
gantly as the* CHORUS *goes slowly off stage right; at last the soldiers sheathe their swords and march briskly off stage left. The
playing area is empty. Smoke continues to rise from the altars of
the gods.*]

COMMENTARY

STORY, PLOT, DESIGN

AGAMEMNON is the great son of Atreus, eagle-like marshal of Hellas, captor of Troy, long-awaited master of Argos, "a blessed man," loved by his people, more worthy of honor (as the Herald says) than any other man of his day. But he is also the head of a house who inherits the sins of his ancestors; a father who murders his daughter; a husband who takes captive women to his bed; a king who leads his people to bloody and prolonged war for a trivial cause; a general who wantonly sacks a great city; and a man who offends and challenges the gods, plunders their temples, possesses their prophetess, accepts honors due to them alone.

The play named for Amamemnon tells us all of this; yet it is almost half over before he actually appears, and he speaks hardly more than eighty lines out of over sixteen hundred, providing an oddly small hero's role for the actor and almost no opportunity at all for the development of character in a specifically dramatic sense (how many of his *deeds* do we *see*?). Furthermore, to give us so many facts about a man and yet to show almost no interest in his inner life—his thoughts, emotions, motivations, the psychology of the character—is not this, too, a strange way to write a play?

Perhaps. But, we must ask, does the strangeness serve some purpose?

The *story* is what we already knew from myth and legend and Homer about the House of Atreus. The *plot*, in the bluntest sense, is what Aeschylus did to the story; it is what remains after he has cut and elaborated and rearranged the story to serve his own purposes. Another way to put this is to say that the plot is Aeschylus' unique invention and arrangement of a series of events through which he could present to our eyes and ears that part of the story that begins when the beacon flashes: the reactions of Clytemnestra and the people of Argos, the arrival of the Herald, the arrival of Agamemnon and Cassandra, and the murders. The bare plot, then, is a drama of domestic, or at most of national, proportions only—a royal husband and his wife, with infidelity on both sides. We could call it "The Murder of Agamemnon."

The whole play, however, is at once different from its story and more than its plot—more, even, than the sum of its acted events. And it asks us to contemplate something more than domestic murder.

How does it do so? Through the Chorus mainly, that solemn, digni-fied group of old men who, unlike Agamemnon, are (but for one brief moment) constantly before our eyes from the end of the Watch-man's speech to the end of the play. If we carefully follow what they say, we find that it is their function to create the universe within which the events of the plot occur. They are historians who keep the past—of Agamemnon, the House of Atreus, Paris and Helen, even the gods—always before us. They are theologians who, as they investi-gate the nature of Zeus ("whoever he is"), will not let us forget that human actions encounter divine judges; and thus the old men are moralists, too. They are poets in their method, moving toward truth through tightly constructed odes and vividly imagined scenes (Mene-laus alone with his dreams, Iphigeneia at the sacrificial altar) instead of through short stories or treatises. And they are also, more simply perhaps, decent, knowing, and intelligent beings by means of whom Aeschylus provides decent, knowing, and intelligent reactions to the events that they—and we—are called upon to witness.

Notice their first lines, the Parodos, for example, in which all these roles appear. The old men begin straight off with history ("The tenth year it is since . . . .") and an elaborate simile, a tool of the poet: Agamemnon and Menelaus, in their troubles with Paris, are first the injured (like eagles "in lonely/Grief for nestlings") and then the Avenger from Zeus. But this is to begin, too, with a simple moral theology: God punishes sinners, sometimes using the injured as his retributive instrument, and there is no way but through punishment to appease "the stubborn anger of the unburnt offering." Then the Chorus has a few lines about themselves—their age, their physical weakness—and we see them briefly for themselves; there is just enough at this point to make us aware that these are men as well as voices.

Simply men, too, for their voices are not prophetic. The future is the one thing they do not know, about which their fears are vague. But Aeschylus arranges to have Cassandra—princess, prophetess, con-cubine—bring that with her. In her painful lyric (the Kommos), just before the murders, she verifies through her supernatural vision the power of the gods and brings to a climax all the knowledge and fears of the early choral odes, adding her own knowledge of the future. Thus Cassandra drives in upon us the horror of all that has ever hap-pened in this House and of all that is about to happen—especially, perhaps, when we see her recoil before the smell of "death that drips with blood" that was shed long ago or is about to be shed. All the sins, then—past, present, and future—of the House of Atreus live for us in her voice and gestures.

So it is largely through Cassandra and the Chorus that we come to understand the universal significance of the famous domestic murder that occurred one day in Argos. The event is part of the history of man and God, the city of Argos is part of a comprehensible cosmos, and the cosmos (which contains justice but not mercy) is savagely moral: "The catcher is caught, the killer pays for his kill." The trilogy as a whole—the *Oresteia*—confronts the problem implied here: Is a new, more merciful order possible? But in *Agamemnon* itself Aeschylus is more precisely concerned with understanding the old order.

To do so he need not give us psychologically rich studies of character. Vivid characters, yes, but that is another matter. Notice, for example, that (as we learn from the opening lines of the play) the technique of the *soliloquy*—a speech delivered when a character is alone, thinking out loud—was available to Aeschylus as one way of revealing inner thoughts, fears, joys, and conflicts. But only with the Watchman does he use it. Elsewhere he never asks us to live (as Marlowe and Shakespeare so often will) in the minds of his characters. How simple it would have been, as the play moved toward the murder, to give Clytemnestra, that outraged wife and mother, a soliloquy revealing and exploring her rage and motivations. That Aeschylus does not do so constitutes one of the many proofs that he wishes to draw our attention to the reverberations of the sin, not to the nature of the sinner. The greatest sinner, of course, is Agamemnon; and everything in the play aims directly or indirectly to reveal the extent and to explore the impact of his sins in a cosmos ordered by the strict justice of Zeus.

If you consider my last sentence carefully, you will notice that the assertion it contains is large and one that you ought to challenge. As I cannot hope to support it fully in these brief comments, I can only invite you to accept it as a reasonable hypothesis and to test it. As you do so, you will begin to notice that the most frequently useful question is: What is the *function* of this speech, of that event, or of that character? And you will also notice that a good many characters and events in the play either were not in the original *story* at all or are at least not necessary to the part about Agamemnon's death; some of these things are not even necessary, speaking very strictly, to the *plot* as Aeschylus ordered it. For example: most of the Watchman's soliloquy, the Herald's tale of what happened to Menelaus on his return from Troy, and the Chorus both in its remarks about Paris and Helen and in its moral or theological generalizations. What, if anything, of the essential story would disappear if a skillful director were to cut any one of these? To what extent would the basic plot be crippled?

We are learning, I think, that there can be more even to the bare text of a play than the story and the plot. And this suggests that some other term might be useful to us, a term that would cover all the elements of a play—story, plot, characters, thought, atmosphere, imagery, spectacle, even apparent digressions—that legitimately serve the idea the playwright is exploring. The word that comes to mind is *design*, and we shall have occasion to use it.

I suggest now that you study and evaluate the following paragraph on the *function* of the Watchman:

Structurally he is unnecessary. It was possible for Aeschylus to leave the announcement of the beacon-signal to the chorus or to Clytemnestra. . . . But though the Watchman, like the Herald, is not strictly necessary to the plot, he contributes to its enormously, and in the same way. He too is not merely a dramatic decoration. He is of course a splendid prelude; his ordinary figure gives the scale of those who are to follow; he represents the plain Argive citizen whose sufferings are more than once contrasted with the misdeeds of their rulers; he gives, perhaps more vividly than the chorus could, certainly more tersely, an impression of the weariness of the years of waiting; but above all this his value to Aeschylus was that he could so suddenly and so penetratingly sound the note of uneasy foreboding. With his obscure remark, ["The house itself, if it took voice. . . ."], he starts a rhythm of apprehension which increases through the choral odes and reaches its climax with the statements of the Herald. [The Watchman appears] not for the sake of plot or characterization, but to contribute to the atmosphere [H. D. F. Kitto, *Greek Tragedy* (Doubleday, 1954), p. 72].

Next, study the Second Stasimon closely and comment on its *function* in the play. Notice how it moves from the sin and fate of Paris to the grief of Menelaus, to the grief of the people of Argos, to their anger at the House of Atreus and, finally, to the danger awaiting a man who "prospers in sin"; how it directs our attention first to the gods and the sins of Paris, then to the gods and the sins of Agamemnon. Why does Aeschylus include Paris? Menelaus? What moral and theological generalizations is the Chorus brooding over? What *line of thought* unifies the ode? In what ways (if at all) does the ode serve to *develop* the characters? the story? the plot? the atmosphere? an idea? the design?

WHAT WE SEE

But I have said very little about Aeschylus' use of the stage. Consider for a moment some ways in which what we see determines what we think and feel.

1. Silent figures on the stage frequently communicate for the dramatist simply by their presence; this is one reason we must try to imagine what would be in front of us were we fortunate enough to be in the theater. By means of a silent figure early in the play, for example, Aeschylus compresses the whole history of the war into a single stage moment: as the Chorus speaks in the Parodos about the ten-year-old beginning of war, Clytemnestra, at the altar, silently celebrates the victorious end. Knowing what the Chorus does not, she already has the upper hand; and Aeschylus emphasizes her cool, arrogant control of the situation by having her speak not when first questioned but only when she is, in her own good time, ready. Her silence creates suspense, arouses our curiosity, makes us wonder about the exact nature of her apparently devout celebration. What, we wonder, is she in fact saying to the gods? .

Later, Aeschylus brings in Cassandra and keeps her silently on stage first while others talk at some length among themselves and then when Clytemnestra and the Chorus speak directly to her; her first utterance is a sudden cry of pain to Apollo. What are the specific effects of this prolonged silence?

2. When Cassandra goes into the palace the Chorus begins what at first appears to be another ode. The old men are, as usual, chanting and dancing in unison—when suddenly the offstage murder, through the cry of Agamemnon, ends the nascent ode and shatters what is most essential about the Chorus: its unity of thought and action. They no longer speak as one, their dance formation breaks, some start off toward the city, others go toward the palace door, others are too stunned to move. Because we are accustomed by this time to choral unity, the sudden confusion provides a disturbing, even a shocking, visual image; and this image, to the degree that the actors exploit it, makes us feel the violence of the murder and reveals the chaos that such violence causes. In the Fourth Stasimon the Chorus, as one voice, does not know what to think; here, momentarily, they do not know what to do. And their later, single-minded courage as they confront Aegisthus is all the more remarkable because it contrasts with this visible confusion.

3. What precisely do we mean when we speak of the dance forma-

tions of the Chorus? That they were an important part of what the Greek audience saw is certain, but we know little more than this bare fact. I should like you to listen, however, to Professor Kitto once more as he describes the subtlety with which Aeschylus used the dance:

. . . we should count on the possibility that Aeschylus . . . was one of the finest choreographers that Europe has seen, and that his dances were as eloquent as his poetry and his stage-drama. . . . in the *Agamemnon* we can observe at least the ground-plan of a dance which becomes an idea made visible. The last six strophes of the first ode, the whole of the second ode, and the last four stanzas of the third ode are all, with occasional interruptions, composed [in the Greek] in the same slow iambic rhythm. This implies, obviously, a certain kind of music and a certain dance-form; and when we look at the text we find that this rhythm, music and dance are used always to accompany the idea of hybris [which, loosely, means excessive pride] and its punishment, the hybris of Agamemnon, the punishment and the hybris of Paris, the hybris of Agamemnon once more; an oppressive *ostinato* in the three arts at once, leading to—what? To the stage-direction: *Enter Agamemnon, with Cassandra*, as the dance ends—on the words "Justice leads all to the end appointed" [in our text poorly translated as "Honest Dealing . . . guides all to the goal"].

In this dance, which gains in weight and meaning with every repetition, we have thought and argument made visible, in the orchestra [*ibid.*, p. 109].

Unhampered by demands for realism, Aeschylus could thus embody his themes in the rhythmic movements of his chorus and could make us, in this way too, see his meaning.

4. Here is a problem in staging that you would have to solve if you were directing the play: When, for the purposes of the Third Episode, would you bring Clytemnestra on stage? In the absence of the original stage directions by Aeschylus, modern experts have widely disagreed. For example:

a. After her speech to the Herald she retires to the back of the stage and remains there through the rest of the Herald–Chorus episode, all of the Third Stasimon, and Agamemnon's entrance—until her own welcoming speech (Richmond Lattimore in Grene and Lattimore, eds., *Greek Tragedies*, Vol. 1 [University of Chicago Press, 1960]).

b. She enters after Strophe 3 of the Third Stasimon (George Thomson, *Oresteia* [Cambridge University Press, 1938]).

c. She enters after Agamemnon and his procession, just as the Chorus says, "Come then my King" (the text in this book).

d. She enters during the Chorus's speech of welcome (Edith Hamilton, *Three Greek Plays* [Norton, 1937]).

e. She enters immediately after Agamemnon has spoken, just as she is to begin her own speech (Philip Vellacott, *The Oresteian Trilogy* [Penguin, 1959]).

The problem, though a matter of what the audience is to see, may at first seem minor; but notice that what we are doing is deciding exactly how to bring about the most important confrontation in the whole play—that long-awaited reunion of Agamemnon and his queen, the reunion for which she has so carefully prepared—and we want to do so in the way that will most completely support the meaning of their words to one another. What is your solution? In deciding, consider such questions as the following: What would be the effect of Clytemnestra's presence as the Chorus speaks about the "eyes . . . Which seem to be loyal but lie"? If she is present when Agamemnon speaks, does he ignore her consciously—a calculated snub—or does he simply not see her? What, in any case, is the effect if she is silently present through his long speech to the others?

5. In discussions of tragedy one sooner or later encounters such terms from the Greek as *Dikê*, *Moira*, and *Hubris* (or *Hybris*), usually translated, respectively, as Judgment, Fate, and Pride. But they are best understood in relation to one another, as in this statement by the famous classical scholar Gilbert Murray:

[*Dikê*] is always connected with *Moira*, that due Portion which belongs to a man: his share in the tribal land, in the harvest, in the spoils of battle, in honour, and in all the natural joys and sorrows of life. Every man, and indeed every living thing, has a *Moira*; we claim more than our *Moira*, and commit *Hubris*; then *Dikê* casts us back. We try to escape from our *Moira*, but our *Moira* always overtakes us. Other people constantly invade our *Moira* and try to rob us of things: they are committing *Hubris*, and *Dikê* will get them [*Aeschylus*, (Oxford University Press, 1940), p. 83].

Human relationships, that is, are governed by a kind of Natural Law: violate it, and punishment strikes. But more than human relationships are involved; behind the law, in a way that the *Oresteia* explores, stand the gods. Furthermore, for a great king like Agamemnon to try to exceed his *Moira* meant, finally, to try to be more than a man. In his excessive pride and self-confidence—his *Hubris*—Agamemnon ends by directly challenging the gods. This is the meaning of the carpet of tapestries, the elaborate stage-business that climaxes what we see of the homecoming (and which, incidentally, was not in the *story* and is unnecessary to the *plot*).

For Clytemnestra no ordinary domestic murder will do. She must decorate the deed, and vividly define its cosmic proportions, by forcing Agamemnon to sin—purely and precisely and superfluously—against the gods in his very act of walking toward her unseen knife. To walk on the "sea-purples"—he knows what it means: "It is the gods should be honoured in this way. . . . I tell you to honour me as a man, not god." There is no reason for him to accept the honors—no urgency, no necessity, no excuse, as he could always argue there was when he took Greece to war or sacrificed Iphigeneia or sacked Troy. And his act hurts no human; in strictly human terms, it is scarcely worth noting. To step on tapestries, after all—who cares? Only one: that god with "envy [in] his eye."

Notice the audacity, the insight, the cleverness of Clytemnestra's speech leading to her introduction of the carpet; notice, in the next speech, Agamemnon's irony about the length of her greeting, and his description of her actions and the actions of her women. Then, as director, tell the actors how to move and speak so as to support the implications of the lines and to create the highly charged, florid, impressive ceremony that the situation demands. For example: When is Clytemnestra addressing the people and when Agamemnon? How do her gestures and tone change as she turns from one to the other and back? What does Agamemnon do meanwhile? (Remember, he is wearing a mask: no facial expressions can register thought or feeling.) How do the women go about "paving" his way from chariot to palace? What is his tone of voice when he speaks (for the first time in ten years) to his wife?

The next time the audience sees the carpet it is, in Clytemnestra's words, "like a net for fishes," a "vicious wealth of raiment" that has caught and holds Agamemnon's body. Exactly as she so brilliantly planned, the cloth that he violated has become, literally, his death-trap and his purple shroud. And not until then does the specifically *theatrical* character of Aeschylus' invention of the carpet scene stand fully revealed. Try to put into your own words the idea that he has, in this particular sequence of events, made visible.

Do you find in the play any other references to a net? In what way do these purely verbal references—figures, as they are called, or *images*—cooperate with the *sight* of the carpet-shroud to develop the meaning of the play? Is there, for example, any relationship between these sights and the net in which Night (in the Second Stasimon) entangles the towers of Troy? Are both Troy and Agamemnon caught figuratively in the same net and actually in the inexorable working of the same fierce law? Does the figure help Aeschylus to explore the nature of the actual? How does the presence of the figure elsewhere—for example, in Clytemnestra's welcoming speech or in the Fourth Episode ("Caught . . . in these . . . toils") or in the Kommos—cooperate with such an exploration? "Night our friend," says the Chorus when the punished transgressor is Troy; is there some irony operating, then, when the old men weep at the sight of the Greek transgressor, Agamemnon, entangled in the same "net"?

Most playwrights would have given us a quite different, more obvious stage picture of sin: Agamemnon sacrificing Iphigeneia, perhaps, or violating Trojan temples, or forcing his love upon Cassandra. When Aeschylus chose, instead, to show us Agamemnon stepping onto a carpet it was not because there existed (as you will sometimes be told) an inviolable rule outlawing violence from the Greek stage. It was, one imagines, simply because he saw how such an action could, as we have been discovering, serve his particular purpose:

—how it would allow him to reveal that hard brilliance in Clytemnestra, the deadly coldness between her and Agamemnon, and her ability to maneuver him exactly as she desires;

—how, because the act of stepping on a carpet is in itself so insignificant, it would expose and isolate the challenge to the gods, thus defining the nature of Agamemnon's hubris;

—how, by making the audience see the carpet-turned-shroud, it would make visible (would emphasize in specifically theatrical terms) the inevitability and justice of divine retribution;

—and, finally, how these stage pictures would develop theatrically the suggestions to be carried in the verse by images of the net, helping thus to point to the harsh impartiality of the law that punishes first Paris and then the man who sins in the course of bringing Paris to justice.

The affair of the carpet is, in other words, theatrical strategy at its best: a significant idea perfectly embodied.

FOR FURTHER THOUGHT

The deed is done; the bodies are there before our eyes; this is the consummation toward which the play has moved. But it is not the end. There are some three hundred more lines—a fierce, dialectical ode between Clytemnestra and the Chorus, and a clash, nearly physical, between the Chorus and Aegisthus. Aeschylus did not write these lines primarily in order to reveal his characters reacting to murder (though they do react) or to wind up his plot (though that occurs) but initially, at least, to face two questions—Did Agamemnon deserve his death? Was Clytemnestra justified in murdering him?—for these are the questions about which she and the Chorus argue so bitterly. Follow the progress of the thought in this final ode to its culmination in Antistrophe 4. What is the truth upon which the queen and the elders are able to agree? Do they also agree about the nature of the future under the law of this truth? What is the precise nature of the "contract" Clytemnestra wishes to make with the "Evil Genius"? Is it a full contract, or does she hope now for some milder dispensation under which order will be achieved at less cost than that exacted by the law of murder for murder, an eye for an eye? (If, as I hope, you go on to read the *Choephoroe* and the *Eumenides*, you will watch Clytemnestra's failure to escape the law, and will wonder: Is the law in fact eternal, or can it possibly be altered? Can justice be tempered with mercy and not at the same time bring chaos?)

With fewer than a hundred lines remaining, Aegisthus enters. Knowing the legend, we knew of his existence; there have been vague references to him in the play; and Clytemnestra, in the preceding ode, at last named him. But by this time we may have concluded that the Aeschylean version of the story means (as is quite within its artistic rights) to make only indirect use of him; and then, when it is much too late for him to do anything except bluster a little, suddenly there he is. Why? What is his *function* in the *design* of the play?

Let me suggest some answers, leaving you to check them with the evidence of the play:

1. Aegisthus presents his own interpretation of the morality of the murder, reminding us that Agamemnon's death was more than the simple death of a man; it was also the working-out of that old curse upon the House of Atreus.

2. His bullying motivates a shift of attitude in the Chorus, bringing them out of their despair until, with the naming of Orestes, they call for the murder of both Aegisthus and Clytemnestra, for the law to operate, that is, with all its severity.

3. His threats of violence against the Chorus motivate Clytemnestra to emphasize twice more her deep desire for the peace that will, we know, never be hers.

4. His words and actions, and the final taunts of the Chorus, specifically reintroduce at the end the important theme of hubris, for Agamemnon is not the only one who can so act as to catch the jealous eye of Justice.

Notice how at every point here Aeschylus is doing three things: bringing the action of this play to an end, preparing for the action of the next play in the trilogy, and uniting the actions not simply so that they grow out of one another but so that they serve his developing investigation of the response of the gods to human sin.

Can you now add anything to my answers about Aegisthus? Would your own answers differ in any way? Cite specific words and gestures from the play that, in your judgment, support or refute my suggestions.

The Tragical History of
Doctor Faustus

CHRISTOPHER MARLOWE

An important lyric and narrative poet and a translator of Ovid and Lucan, Marlowe (1564–93) was also the first great tragic dramatist after the deaths of Sophocles and Euripides near the end of the fifth century B.C. The plays for which he is famous are *Tamburlaine the Great* (two parts), *Doctor Faustus*, *The Jew of Malta*, and *Edward the Second*. His influence upon Shakespeare, a contemporary, was considerable but has often been exaggerated. As Marlowe was apparently a secret agent for the government of Elizabeth I, his murder in a tavern quarrel may have been politically inspired.

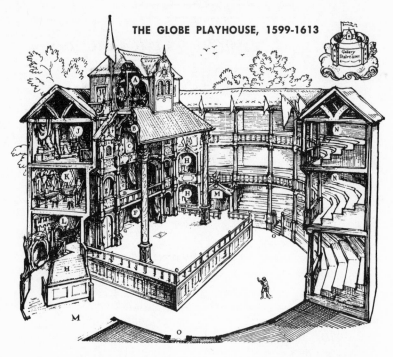

THE GLOBE PLAYHOUSE, 1599-1613

Key: A—The "Hut," with machinery for lowering the Heavenly throne to the stage; B—The "Heavens"; C—Top stage, sometimes used as a music gallery; D—Upper stage; E—Window stages; F—Inner stage, sometimes called the "Study"; G—"Traps" leading down to the "Hell" under the stage; H—"Gentlemen's Rooms" or "Lords' Rooms"; J—Storage lofts, dressing rooms, etc.; K—Dressing rooms; L—Backstage area; M—Main entrances to auditorium; N—Doorways connecting with gallery staircase; O—Entrance to galleries and staircases.

The Elizabethan theater, developing even as Marlowe wrote, became, shortly after his death, the kind of building shown above. It is open to the sky and presents an architecturally unchanging background. The curtained inner stage, useful for preparing oncoming scenes, can represent a tomb, a cave, or the Pope's privy-chamber. Action that begins here usually flows quickly out onto the platform. The upper stage and windows can be Juliet's balcony, the wall of a fortress, or the vantage point of the Good Angel. Part of the audience of about 2000 stood in the pit on three sides of the stage, and everyone in the theater was closer to the action than were most of the spectators in a Greek theater. For other pictures and information see C. Walter Hodges, *The Globe Restored* (Coward-McCann, 1954), especially pp. 170–77.

The Tragical History of Doctor Faustus

FROM THE QUARTO OF 1604

PERSONS IN THE PLAY

CHORUS
DOCTOR FAUSTUS
WAGNER, *his Servant*
GOOD ANGEL *and* EVIL ANGEL
VALDES *and* CORNELIUS, *Conjurors*
THREE SCHOLARS
MEPHISTOPHILIS, *a Devil*
THE CLOWN
BALIOL, BELCHER, LUCIFER, BELZE-
    BUB, *and other Devils*
THE SEVEN DEADLY SINS
THE POPE
CARDINAL OF LORRAIN

FRIARS
ROBIN, *the Ostler*
RAFE
A VINTNER
THE EMPEROR
A KNIGHT *and* ATTENDANTS
Spirits of ALEXANDER *and his*
    PARAMOUR
A HORSE-COURSER
THE DUKE OF VANHOLT *and his*
    DUCHESS
AN OLD MAN
The Spirit of HELEN OF TROY

SCENE: *Mainly the study of* DOCTOR FAUSTUS; *otherwise a grove, the* POPE'S *Privy-Chamber at Rome, the Courts of the* EMPEROR *and the* DUKE OF VANHOLT *and elsewhere.*[1]

[*Enter* CHORUS.]

CHORUS. Not marching now in fields of Thrasimene,
　　Where Mars did mate the Carthaginians;
　　Nor sporting in the dalliance of love,
　　In courts of kings where state is overturned;
　　Nor in the pomp of proud audacious deeds,
　　Intends our Muse to vaunt his heavenly verse:
　　Only this, gentlemen—we must perform
　　The form of Faustus' fortunes, good or bad;
　　To patient judgments we appeal our plaud,
　　And speak for Faustus in his infancy.
　　Now is he born, his parents base of stock,
　　In Germany, within a town called Rhodes;
　　Of riper years to Wittenberg he went,

1 [The text and footnotes for this play were prepared by Francis Connolly for his anthology *Man and His Measure* and are reprinted by permission. The reader should notice that Faustus often immediately translates his own Latin.—H. S.]

Whereas his kinsmen chiefly brought him up.
So soon he profits in divinity,
The fruitful plot of scholarism graced,
That shortly he was graced with doctor's name,
Excelling all whose sweet delight disputes
In heavenly matters of theology;
Till swollen with cunning, of a self-conceit,
His waxen wings did mount above his reach,
And, melting, heavens conspired his overthrow;
For, falling to a devilish exercise,
And glutted now with learning's golden gifts,
He surfeits upon cursèd necromancy.
Nothing so sweet as magic is to him,
Which he prefers before his chiefest bliss.
And this the man that in his study sits!   [*Exit.*]

SCENE I

[*Enter* FAUSTUS *in his study.*]

FAUST. Settle thy studies, Faustus, and begin
To sound the depth of that thou wilt profess;
Having commenced, be a divine in show,
Yet level at the end of every art,
And live and die in Aristotle's works.
Sweet Analytics, 'tis thou hast ravished me—   [*Reads.*]
Bene dissere est finis logices.[2]
Is to dispute well logic's chiefest end?
Affords this art no greater miracle?
Then read no more, thou hast attained the end;
A greater subject fitteth Faustus' wit:
Bid ὅν χαὶ μὴ ὅν [3] farewell; Galen come,
Seeing *Ubi desinit philosophus ibi incipit medicus,*[4]
Be a physician, Faustus, heap up gold,
And be eternized for some wondrous cure.   [*Reads.*]
Summum bonum medicinœ sanitas,[5]
The end of physic is our body's health.
Why, Faustus, hast thou not attained that end?
Is not thy common talk sound aphorisms?
Are not thy bills hung up as monuments,
Whereby whole cities have escaped the plague,

2 [To dispute well is the end of logic.]
3 [Being and nonbeing.]
4 [Where the philosopher ends there begins the physician.]
5 [Health is the highest good of medicine.]

And thousand desperate maladies been eased?
Yet art thou still but Faustus and a man.
Wouldst thou make men to live eternally,
Or, being dead, raise them to life again,
Then this profession were to be esteemed.
Physic, farewell.—Where is Justinian?   [*Reads.*]
Si una eademque res legatur duobus, alter rem, alter valorem rei,
     etc.⁶
A pretty case of paltry legacies!   [*Reads.*]
Exhœreditare filium non potest pater nisi, etc.⁷
Such is the subject of the Institute
And universal body of the law.
His study fits a mercenary drudge,
Who aims at nothing but external trash;
Too servile and illiberal for me.
When all is done divinity is best;
Jerome's Bible, Faustus, view it well.   [*Reads.*]
Stipendium peccati mors est. Ha! *Stipendium,* etc.
The reward of sin is death. That's hard.   [*Reads.*]
Si peccasse negamus, fallimur, et nulla est in nobis veritas. ⁸
If we say that we have no sin we deceive ourselves, and there's no
truth in us. Why, then, belike we must sin, and so consequently die.
Ay, we must die an everlasting death.
What doctrine call you this, *Che sera sera,*
What will be, shall be? Divinity, adieu!
These metaphysics of magicians
And necromantic books are heavenly:
Lines, circles, scenes, letters, and characters:
Ay, these are those that Faustus most desires.
O, what a world of profit and delight,
Of power, of honor, of omnipotence
Is promised to the studious artisan!
All things that move between the quiet poles
Shall be at my command: emperors and kings
Are but obey'd in their several provinces,
Nor can they raise the wind or rend the clouds;
But his dominion that exceeds in this
Stretcheth as far as doth the mind of man,
A sound magician is a mighty god:
Here, Faustus, try thy brains to gain a deity.
Wagner!

6 [If one and the same thing be willed to two people, one is given the thing and
the other the value of the thing.]
7 [A father cannot disinherit a son unless . . .]
8 [If we deny we have sinned we err, and the truth is not in us.]

[*Enter* WAGNER.]

        Commend me to my dearest friends,
The German Valdes and Cornelius;
Request them earnestly to visit me.

WAG. I will, sir.   [*Exit.*]

FAUST. Their conference will be a greater help to me
Than all my labors, plod I ne'er so fast.

[*Enter* GOOD ANGEL *and* EVIL ANGEL.]

G. ANG. O Faustus! lay that damnèd book aside,
And gaze not on it lest it tempt thy soul,
And heap God's heavy wrath upon thy head.
Read, read the Scriptures: that is blasphemy.

E. ANG. Go forward, Faustus, in that famous art,
Wherein all Nature's treasure is contained:
Be thou on earth as Jove is in the sky,
Lord and commander of these elements.   [*Exeunt* ANGELS.]

FAUST. How am I glutted with conceit of this!
Shall I make spirits fetch me what I please,
Resolve me of all ambiguities,
Perform what desperate enterprise I will?
I'll have them fly to India for gold,
Ransack the ocean for orient pearl,
And search all corners of the new-found world
For pleasant fruits and princely delicates;
I'll have them read me strange philosophy
And tell the secrets of all foreign kings;
I'll have them wall all Germany with brass,
And make swift Rhine circle fair Wittenberg,
I'll have them fill the public schools with silk,
Wherewith the students shall be bravely clad;
I'll levy soldiers with the coin they bring,
And chase the Prince of Parma from our land,
And reign sole king of all the provinces;
Yea, stranger engines for the brunt of war
Than was the fiery keel at Antwerp's bridge,
I'll make my servile spirits to invent.

[*Enter* VALDES *and* CORNELIUS.]

Come, German Valdes and Cornelius,
And make me blest with your sage conference.
Valdes, sweet Valdes, and Cornelius,
Know that your words have won me at the last
To practise magic and concealèd arts:

Yet not your words only, but mine own fantasy
That will receive no object; for my head
But ruminates on necromantic skill.
Philosophy is odious and obscure,
Both law and physic are for petty wits;
Divinity is basest of the three,
Unpleasant, harsh, contemptible, and vile:
'Tis magic, magic that hath ravished me.
Then, gentle friends, aid me in this attempt;
And I that have with concise syllogisms
Gravelled the pastors of the German church,
And made the flowering pride of Wittenberg
Swarm to my problems, as the infernal spirits
On sweet Musæus, when he came to hell,
Will be as cunning as Agrippa was,
Whose shadows made all Europe honor him.

VALD. Faustus, these books, thy wit, and our experience
Shall make all nations to canònize us.
As Indian Moors obey their Spanish lords,
So shall the spirits of every element
Be always serviceable to us three;
Like lions shall they guard us when we please;
Like Almain rutters with their horsemen's staves
Or Lapland giants, trotting by our sides;
Sometimes like women or unwedded maids,
Shadowing more beauty in their airy brows
Than have the white breasts of the queen of love
From Venice shall they drag huge argosies,
And from America the golden fleece
That yearly stuffs old Philip's treasury;
If learnèd Faustus will be resolute.

FAUST. Valdes, as resolute am I in this
As thou to live; therefore object it not.

CORN. The miracles that magic will perform
Will make thee vow to study nothing else.
He that is grounded in astrology,
Enriched with tongues, well seen in minerals,
Hath all the principles magic doth require.
Then doubt not, Faustus, but to be renowned,
And more frequented for this mystery
Than heretofore the Delphian Oracle.
The spirits tell me they can dry the sea,
And fetch the treasure of all foreign wracks,
Ay, all the wealth that our forefathers hid
Within the massy entrails of the earth;

Then tell me, Faustus, what shall we three want?

FAUST. Nothing, Cornelius! O, this cheers my soul!
Come show me some demonstrations magical,
That I may conjure in some lusty grove,
And have these joys in full possession.

VALD. Then haste thee to some solitary grove,
And bear wise Bacon's and Albanus' works,
The Hebrew Psalter and New Testament!
And whatsoever else is requisite
We will inform thee ere our conference cease.

CORN. Valdes, first let him know the words of art;
And then, all other ceremonies learned,
Faustus may try his cunning by himself.

VALD. First I'll instruct thee in the rudiments,
And then wilt thou be perfecter than I.

FAUST. Then come and dine with me, and after meat,
We'll canvass every quiddity thereof;
For ere I sleep I'll try what I can do:
This night I'll conjure tho' I die therefore.   [*Exeunt.*]

SCENE II

Before FAUSTUS' *house.*

[*Enter two* SCHOLARS.]

1 SCHOL. I wonder what's become of Faustus that was wont to make
our schools ring with *sic probo?*[9]

2 SCHOL. That shall we know, for see here comes his boy.

[*Enter* WAGNER.]

1 SCHOL. How now, sirrah! Where's thy master?

WAG. God in heaven knows!

2 SCHOL. Why, dost not thou know?

WAG. Yes, I know. But that follows not.

1 SCHOL. Go to, sirrah! leave your jesting, and tell us where he is.

WAG. That follows not necessary by force of argument, that you,
being licentiate, should stand upon't: therefore acknowledge your
error and be attentive.

2 SCHOL. Why, didst thou not say thou knewest?

WAG. Have you any witness on't?

1 SCHOL. Yes, sirrah, I heard you.

WAG. Ask my fellow if I be a thief.

2 SCHOL. Well, you will not tell us?

9 [Thus I prove.]

WAG. Yes, sir, I will tell you; yet if you were not dunces, you would
never ask me such a question; for is not he *corpus naturale?*[10] and
is not that *mobile?*[11] Then wherefore should you ask me such a
question? But that I am by nature phlegmatic, slow to wrath,
and prone to lechery (to love, I would say), it were not for you
to come within forty feet of the place of execution, although I do
not doubt to see you both hanged the next sessions. Thus having
triumphed over you, I will set my countenance like a precisian,
and begin to speak thus: Truly, my dear brethren, my master is
within at dinner, with Valdes and Cornelius, as this wine, if it
could speak, would inform your worships; and so the Lord bless
you, preserve you, and keep you, my dear brethren, my dear
brethren.   [*Exit.*]

1 SCHOL. Nay, then, I fear he has fallen into that damned art, for
which they two are infamous through the world.

2 SCHOL. Were he a stranger, and not allied to me, yet should I
grieve for him. But come, let us go and inform the rector, and see
if he by his grave counsel can reclaim him.

1 SCHOL. O, but I fear me nothing can reclaim him.

2 SCHOL. Yet let us try what we can do.   [*Exeunt.*]

SCENE III

[*Enter* FAUSTUS *to conjure in a grove.*]

FAUST. Now that the gloomy shadow of the earth
  Longing to view Orion's drizzling look,
  Leaps from the antarctic world unto the sky,
  And dims the welkin with her pitchy breath,
  Faustus, begin thine incantations,
  And try if devils will obey thy hest,
  Seeing thou hast prayed and sacrificed to them.
  Within this circle is Jehovah's name,
  Forward and backward anagrammatized,
  The breviated names of holy saints,
  Figures of every adjunct to the heavens,
  And characters of signs and erring stars,
  By which the spirits are enforced to rise:
  Then fear not, Faustus, but be resolute,
  And try the uttermost magic can perform.
  Sint mihi dei Acherontis propitii! Valeat numen triplex Jehovæ!
  Ignei, aerii, aquatani spiritus, salvete! Orientis princeps Belzebub,
  inferni ardentis monarcha, et Demogorgon, propitiamus vos, ut

10 [Natural body.]
11 [Moving.]

appareat et surgat Mephistophilis. Quid tu moraris? per Jehovam,
Gehennam, et consecratam aquam quam nunc spargo, signumque
crucis quod nunc facio, et per vota nostra, ipse nunc surgat nobis
dicatus Mephistophilis![12]

[*Enter* MEPHISTOPHILIS, *a Devil.*]

I charge thee to return and change thy shape;
Thou art too ugly to attend on me.
Go, and return an old Franciscan friar;
That holy shape becomes a devil best.   [*Exit* MEPH.]
I see there's virtue in my heavenly words;
Who would not be proficient in this art?
How pliant is this Mephistophilis,
Full of obedience and humility!
Such is the force of magic and my spells:
No, Faustus, thou art conjurer laureat,
That canst command great Mephistophilis:
Quin regis Mephistophilis fratris imagine.[13]

[*Re-enter* MEPHISTOPHILIS, *like a Franciscan friar.*]

MEPH. Now, Faustus, what would'st thou have me to do?
FAUST. I charge thee wait upon me whilst I live,
To do whatever Faustus shall command,
Be it to make the moon drop from her sphere,
Or the ocean to overwhelm the world.
MEPH. I am a servant to great Lucifer,
And may not follow thee without his leave:
No more than he commands must we perform.
FAUST. Did not he charge thee to appear to me?
MEPH. No, I came hither of mine own accord.
FAUST. Did not my conjuring speeches raise thee? Speak.
MEPH. That was the cause, but yet *per accidens,*[14]
For when we hear one rack the name of God,
Abjure the Scriptures and his Saviour Christ,
We fly in hope to get his glorious soul;
Nor will we come, unless he use such means
Whereby he is in danger to be damned:
Therefore the shortest cut for conjuring
Is stoutly to abjure the Trinity,

12 [May the gods of Acheron (Hell) be propitious! May the triple might of
Jehovah prevail! Hail spirits of fire, air, water! We pay homage to you, Belzebub,
prince of the East and king of burning Hell, and you, Demogorgon, in order
that Mephistophilis may rise and appear. Why do you delay? By Jehovah,
Gehenna, and the holy water I now sprinkle, and the sign of the cross I now do
make, and by our prayers, let the said Mephistophilis now rise before us.]
13 [Yea, rather rule thou in the image of the brother, Mephistophilis.]
14 [By accident, that is, not essentially.]

And pray devoutly to the Prince of Hell.
FAUST. So Faustus hath
  Already done; and holds this principle,
  There is no chief, but only Belzebub,
  To whom Faustus doth dedicate himself.
  This word "damnation" terrifies not him,
  For he confounds hell in Elysium;
  His ghost be with the old philosophers!
  But, leaving these vain trifles of men's souls,
  Tell me what is that Lucifer thy lord?
MEPH. Arch-regent and commander of all spirits.
FAUST. Was not that Lucifer an angel once?
MEPH. Yes, Faustus, and most dearly loved of God.
FAUST. How comes it then that he is prince of devils?
MEPH. O, by aspiring pride and insolence;
  For which God threw him from the face of heaven.
FAUST. And what are you that live with Lucifer?
MEPH. Unhappy spirits that fell with Lucifer,
  Conspired against our God with Lucifer,
  And are for ever damned with Lucifer.
FAUST. Where are you damned?
MEPH. In hell.
FAUST. How comes it then that thou art out of hell?
MEPH. Why this is hell, nor am I out of it:
  Think'st thou that I who saw the face of God,
  And tasted the eternal joys of heaven,
  Am not tormented with ten thousand hells,
  In being deprived of everlasting bliss?
  O Faustus! leave these frivolous demands,
  Which strike a terror to my fainting soul.
FAUST. What, is great Mephistophilis so passionate
  For being deprivèd of the joys of heaven?
  Learn thou of Faustus manly fortitude,
  And scorn those joys thou never shalt possess.
  Go bear these tidings to great Lucifer:
  Seeing Faustus hath incurred eternal death.
  By desperate thoughts against Jove's deity,
  Say he surrenders up to him his soul,
  So he will spare him four and twenty years,
  Letting him live in all voluptuousness;
  Having thee ever to attend on me;
  To give me whatsoever I shall ask,
  To tell me whatsoever I demand,
  To slay mine enemies, and aid my friends,
  And always be obedient to my will.

Go and return to mighty Lucifer,
And meet me in my study at midnight,
And then resolve me of thy master's mind.
MEPH. I will, Faustus. [*Exit.*]
FAUST. Had I as many souls as there be stars,
I'd give them all for Mephistophilis.
By him I'll be great Emperor of the world,
And make a bridge thorough the moving air,
To pass the ocean with a band of men:
I'll join the hills that bind the Afric shore,
And make that country continent to Spain,
And both contributory to my crown.
The Emperor shall not live but by my leave,
Nor any potentate of Germany.
Now that I have obtained what I desire,
I'll live in speculation of this art
Till Mephistophilis return again. [*Exit.*]

SCENE IV

Before FAUSTUS' *house.*

[*Enter* WAGNER *and* CLOWN.]

WAG. Sirrah, boy, come hither.
CLOWN. How, boy! Swowns, boy! I hope you have seen many boys
with such pickadevaunts as I have; boy, quotha.
WAG. Tell me, sirrah, hast thou any comings in?
CLOWN. Ay, and goings out too. You may see else.
WAG. Alas, poor slave! see how poverty jesteth in his nakedness! The
villain is bare and out of service, and so hungry that I know he
would give his soul to the Devil for a shoulder of mutton though
it were blood-raw.
CLOWN. How? My soul to the Devil for a shoulder of mutton, though
'twere blood-raw! Not so, good friend. By'r lady, I had need have
it well roasted and good sauce to it, if I pay so dear.
WAG. Well, wilt thou serve me, and I'll make thee go like *Qui mihi
discipulus?*[15]
CLOWN. How, in verse?
WAG. No, sirrah; in beaten silk and stavesacre.
CLOWN. How, now, Knave's acre! Ay, I thought that was all the land
his father left him. Do you hear? I would be sorry to rob you of
your living.
WAG. Sirrah, I say in stavesacre.
CLOWN. Oho! Oho! Stavesacre! Why then belike if I were your man
I should be full of vermin.
  15 [(One) who is my disciple.]

WAG. So thou shalt, whether thou beest with me or no. But, sirrah, leave your jesting, and bind yourself presently unto me for seven years, or I'll turn all the lice about thee into familiars, and they shall tear thee in pieces.

CLOWN. Do you hear, sir? You may save that labor: they are too familiar with me already: swowns! they are as bold with my flesh as if they had paid for their meat and drink.

WAG. Well, do you hear, sirrah? Hold, take these guilders.

[*Gives money.*]

CLOWN. Gridirons! what be they?

WAG. Why, French crowns.

CLOWN. Mass, but in the name of French crowns, a man were as good have as many English counters. And what should I do with these?

WAG. Why, now, sirrah, thou art at an hour's warning, whensoever and wheresoever the Devil shall fetch thee.

CLOWN. No, no. Here, take your gridirons again.

WAG. Truly I'll none of them.

CLOWN. Truly but you shall.

WAG. Bear witness I gave them him.

CLOWN. Bear witness I give them you again.

WAG. Well, I will cause two devils presently to fetch thee away—Baliol and Belcher!

CLOWN. Let your Baliol and your Belcher come here, and I'll knock them, they were never so knocked since they were devils! Say I should kill one of them, what would folks say? "Do you see yonder tall fellow in the round slop—he has killed the devil." So I should be called Kill-devil all the parish over.

[*Enter two* DEVILS: *the* CLOWN *runs up and down crying.*]

WAG. Baliol and Belcher! Spirits, away!   [*Exeunt* DEVILS.]

CLOWN. What, are they gone? A vengeance on them, they have vile long nails! There was a he-devil, and a she-devil. I'll tell you how you shall know them; all he-devils has horns, and all she-devils has clifts and cloven feet.

WAG. Well, sirrah, follow me.

CLOWN. But, do you hear—if I should serve you, would you teach me to raise up Banios and Belcheos?

WAG. I will teach thee to turn thyself to anything; to a dog, or a cat, or a mouse, or a rat, or anything.

CLOWN. How! a Christian fellow to a dog or a cat, a mouse or a rat! No, no, sir. If you turn me into anything, let it be in the likeness of a little pretty frisking flea, that I may be here and there and everywhere. O, I'll tickle the pretty wenches' plackets; I'll be amongst them, i' faith.

WAG. Well, sirrah, come.

CLOWN. But, do you hear, Wagner?

WAG. How! Baliol and Belcher!

CLOWN. O Lord! I pray, sir, let Banio and Belcher go sleep.

WAG. Villain—call me Master Wagner, and let thy left eye be diam-
etarily fixed upon my right heel, with *quasi vestigiis nostris insis-
tere.*[16]   [*Exit.*]

CLOWN. God forgive me, he speaks Dutch fustian. Well, I'll follow
him: I'll serve him, that's flat.   [*Exit.*]

SCENE V

[*Enter* FAUSTUS *in his study.*]

FAUST. Now, Faustus, must
Thou needs be damned, and canst thou not be saved:
What boots it then to think of God or heaven?
Away with such vain fancies, and despair:
Despair in God, and trust in Belzebub;
Now go not backward: no, Faustus, be resolute:
Why waver'st thou? O, something soundeth in mine ears
"Abjure this magic, turn to God again!"
Ay, and Faustus will turn to God again.
To God?—He loves thee not—
The God thou serv'st is thine own appetite,
Wherein is fixed the love of Belzebub;
To him I'll build an altar and a church,
And offer lukewarm blood of new-born babes.

[*Enter* GOOD ANGEL *and* EVIL ANGEL.]

G. ANG. Sweet Faustus, leave that execrable art.

FAUST. Contrition, prayer, repentance! What of them?

G. ANG. O, they are means to bring thee unto heaven.

E. ANG. Rather, illusions—fruits of lunacy,
That makes men foolish that do trust them most.

G. ANG. Sweet Faustus, think of heaven and heavenly things.

E. ANG. No, Faustus, think of honor and of wealth. [*Exeunt* ANGELS.]

FAUST. Of wealth!
Why the signiory of Embden shall be mine.
When Mephistophilis shall stand by me,
What God can hurt thee? Faustus, thou art safe:
Cast no more doubts. Come, Mephistophilis,
And bring glad tidings from great Lucifer;
Is't not midnight? Come, Mephistophilis;
Veni, veni, Mephistophile!

16 [As if to tread in our footsteps.]

[*Enter* MEPHISTOPHILIS.]

Now tell me, what says Lucifer, thy lord?
MEPH. That I shall wait on Faustus whilst he lives,
 So he will buy my service with his soul.
FAUST. Already Faustus hath hazarded that for thee.
MEPH. But, Faustus, thou must bequeath it solemnly,
 And write a deed of gift with thine own blood,
 For that security craves great Lucifer.
 If thou deny it, I will back to hell.
FAUST. Stay, Mephistophilis! and tell me what good
 Will my soul do thy lord.
MEPH. Enlarge his kingdom.
FAUST. Is that the reason why he tempts us thus?
MEPH. *Solamen miseris socios habuisse doloris.*¹⁷
FAUST. Why, have you any pain that tortures others?
MEPH. As great as have the human souls of men.
 But tell me, Faustus, shall I have thy soul?
 And I will be thy slave, and wait on thee,
 And give thee more than thou hast wit to ask.
FAUST. Ay, Mephistophilis, I give it thee.
MEPH. Then, Faustus, stab thine arm courageously,
 And bind thy soul that at some certain day
 Great Lucifer may claim it as his own;
 And then be thou as great as Lucifer.
FAUST. [*Stabbing his arm.*] Lo, Mephistophilis, for love of thee,
 I cut mine arm, and with my proper blood
 Assure my soul to be great Lucifer's,
 Chief lord and regent of perpetual night!
 View here the blood that trickles from mine arm,
 And let it be propitious for my wish.
MEPH. But, Faustus, thou must
 Write it in manner of a deed of gift.
FAUST. Ay, so I will.[*Writes.*] But, Mephistophilis,
 My blood congeals, and I can write no more.
MEPH. I'll fetch thee fire to dissolve it straight. [*Exit.*]
FAUST. What might the staying of my blood portend?
 Is it unwilling I should write this bill?
 Why streams it not that I may write afresh?
 Faustus gives to thee his soul. Ah, there it stayed.
 Why should'st thou not? Is not thy soul thine own?
 Then write again, *Faustus gives to thee his soul.*

[*Re-enter* MEPHISTOPHILIS *with a chafer of coals.*]

MEPH. Here's fire. Come, Faustus, set it on.

17 [It is a comfort to have companions in misery.]

FAUST. So now the blood begins to clear again;
   Now will I make an end immediately.   [*Writes.*]
MEPH. O, what will not I do to obtain his soul.   [*Aside.*]
FAUST. *Consummatum est:*[18] this bill is ended.
   And Faustus hath bequeathed his soul to Lucifer.
   But what is this inscription on mine arm?
   Homo, fuge![19] Whither should I fly?
   If unto God, he'll throw me down to hell.
   My senses are deceived; here's nothing writ—
   I see it plain; here in this place is writ
   Homo, fuge! Yet shall not Faustus fly.
MEPH. I'll fetch him somewhat to delight his mind.   [*Exit.*]

    [*Re-enter* MEPHISTOPHILIS *with* DEVILS, *giving crowns and
    rich apparel to* FAUSTUS, *and dance, and then depart.*]

FAUST. Speak, Mephistophilis, what means this show?
MEPH. Nothing, Faustus, but to delight thy mind withal,
   And to show thee what magic can perform.
FAUST. But may I raise up spirits when I please?
MEPH. Ay, Faustus, and do greater things than these.
FAUST. Then there's enough for a thousand souls.
   Here, Mephistophilis, receive this scroll,
   A deed of gift of body and of soul:
   But yet conditionally that thou perform
   All articles prescribed between us both.
MEPH. Faustus, I swear by hell and Lucifer
   To effect all promises between us made.
FAUST. Then hear me read them: *On these conditions following.
   First, that Faustus may be a spirit in form and substance. Secondly,
   that Mephistophilis shall be his servant, and at his command.
   Thirdly, that Mephistophilis shall do for him and bring him what-
   soever. Fourthly, that he shall be in his chamber or house invisible.
   Lastly, that he shall appear to the said John Faustus, at all times, in
   what form or shape soever he please. I, John Faustus, of Wittenberg, Doctor, by these presents, to give both body and soul to Lucifer, Prince of the East, and his minister, Mephistophilis: and furthermore grant unto them, that, twenty-four years being expired,
   the articles above written inviolate, full power to fetch or carry the
   said John Faustus, body and soul, flesh, blood, or goods, into their
   habitation wheresoever. By me,*   *John Faustus.*
MEPH. Speak, Faustus, do you deliver this as your deed?
FAUST. Ay, take it, and the Devil give thee good on't!
MEPH. Now, Faustus, ask what thou wilt.
FAUST. First will I question with thee about hell.

18 [It is consummated.]   19 [Flee, man!]

Tell me where is the place that men call hell?

MEPH. Under the heavens.

FAUST. Ay, but whereabout?

MEPH. Within the bowels of these elements,
    Where we are tortured and remain for ever;
    Hell hath no limits, nor is circumscribed
    In one self place; for where we are is hell,
    And where hell is there must we ever be:
    And, to conclude, when all the world dissolves,
    And every creature shall be purified,
    All places shall be hell that is not heaven.

FAUST. Come, I think hell's a fable.

MEPH. Ay, think so still, till experience change thy mind.

FAUST. Why, think'st thou then that Faustus shall be damned?

MEPH. Ay, of necessity, for here's the scroll
    Wherein thou hast given thy soul to Lucifer.

FAUST. Ay, and body too; but what of that?
    Think'st thou that Faustus is so fond to imagine
    That, after this life, there is any pain?
    Tush; these are trifles and mere old wives' tales.

MEPH. But, Faustus, I am an instance to prove the contrary.
    For I am damnèd, and am now in hell.

FAUST. How! now in hell?
    Nay, an this be hell, I'll willingly be damnèd here;
    What? walking, disputing, etc.?
    But, leaving off this, let me have a wife,
    The fairest maid in Germany;
    For I am wanton and lascivious,
    And cannot live without a wife.

MEPH. How—a wife?
    I prithee, Faustus, talk not of a wife.

FAUST. Nay, sweet Mephistophilis, fetch me one, for I will have one.

MEPH. Well—thou wilt have one. Sit there till I come:
    I'll fetch thee a wife in the Devil's name.   [*Exit.*]

[*Re-enter* MEPHISTOPHILIS *with a* DEVIL *dressed
like a woman, with fireworks.*]

MEPH. Tell me, Faustus, how dost thou like thy wife?

FAUST. A plague on her for a hot whore!

MEPH. Tut, Faustus,
    Marriage is but a ceremonial toy;
    And if thou lovest me, think no more of it.
    I'll cull thee out the fairest courtesans,
    And bring them every morning to thy bed;
    She whom thine eye shall like, thy heart shall have,

Be she as chaste as was Penelope,
And ás wise as Saba, or as beautiful
As was bright Lucifer before his fall.
Here, take this book, peruse it thoroughly: [*Gives a book.*]
The iterating of these lines brings gold;
The framing of this circle on the ground
Brings whirlwinds, tempests, thunder and lightning;
Pronounce this thrice devoutly to thyself,
And men in armor shall appear to thee,
Ready to execute what thou desir'st.

FAUST. Thanks, Mephistophilis; yet fain would I have a book wherein I might behold all spells and incantations, that I might raise up spirits when I please.

MEPH. Here they are, in this book.   [*There turn to them.*]

FAUST. Now would I have a book where I might see all characters and planets of the heavens, that I might know their motions and dispositions.

MEPH. Here they are too.   [*Turn to them.*]

FAUST. Nay, let me have one book more—and then I have done—wherein I might see all plants, herbs, and trees that grow upon the earth.

MEPH. Here they be.

FAUST. O, thou art deceived.

MEPH. Tut, I warrant thee.   [*Turn to them. Exeunt.*]

SCENE VI

[*Enter* FAUSTUS *in his study, and* MEPHISTOPHILIS.]

FAUST. When I behold the heavens, then I repent,
    And curse thee, wicked Mephistophilis,
    Because thou hast deprived me of those joys.

MEPH. Why, Faustus,
    Think'st thou heaven is such a glorious thing?
    I tell thee 'tis not half so fair as thou,
    Or any man that breathes on earth.

FAUST. How prov'st thou that?

MEPH. 'Twas made for man, therefore is man more excellent.

FAUST. If it were made for man, 'twas made for me; I will renounce this magic and repent.

[*Enter* GOOD ANGEL *and* EVIL ANGEL.]

G. ANG. Faustus, repent; yet God will pity thee.

E. ANG. Thou art a spirit; God cannot pity thee.

FAUST. Who buzzeth in mine ears I am a spirit?

Be I a devil, yet God may pity me;
Ay, God will pity me if I repent.
E. ANG. Ay, but Faustus never shall repent.   [*Exeunt* ANGELS.]
FAUST. My heart's so hardened I cannot repent.
Scarce can I name salvation, faith, or heaven,
But fearful echoes thunder in mine ears
"Faustus, thou art damned!" Then swords and knives,
Poison, gun, halters, and envenomed steel
Are laid before me to dispatch myself,
And long ere this I should have slain myself,
Had not sweet pleasure conquered deep despair.
Have not I made blind Homer sing to me
Of Alexander's love and Œnon's death?
And hath not he that built the walls of Thebes
With ravishing sound of his melodious harp,
Made music with my Mephistophilis?
Why should I die then, or basely despair?
I am resolved: Faustus shall ne'er repent—
Come, Mephistophilis, let us dispute again,
And argue of divine astrology.
Tell me, are there many heavens above the moon?
Are all celestial bodies but one globe,
As is the substance of this centric earth?
MEPH. As are the elements, such are the spheres
Mutually folded in each other's orb,
And, Faustus,
All jointly move upon one axle-tree
Whose terminine is termed the world's wide pole;
Nor are the names of Saturn, Mars, or Jupiter
Feigned, but are erring stars.
FAUST. But tell me, have they all one motion, both *situ et tempore?*[20]
MEPH. All jointly move from east to west in twenty-four hours upon
the poles of the world; but differ in their motion upon the poles of
the zodiac.
FAUST. Tush!
These slender trifles Wagner can decide;
Hath Mephistophilis no greater skill?
Who knows not the double motion of the planets?
The first is finished in a natural day;
The second thus: as Saturn in thirty years;
Jupiter in twelve; Mars in four; the Sun, Venus, and Mercury in a
year; the moon in twenty-eight days. Tush, these are freshmen's
suppositions. But tell me, hath every sphere a dominion or *intelli-*
gentia?[21]

20 [In place and time?]
21 [Intelligence or spirit.]

MEPH. Ay.

FAUST. How many heavens, or spheres, are there?

MEPH. Nine: the seven planets, the firmament, and the empyreal heaven.

FAUST. Well, resolve me in this question: Why have we not conjunctions, oppositions, aspects, eclipses, all at one time, but in some years we have more, in some less?

MEPH. *Per inœqualem motum respectu totius.*[22]

FAUST. Well, I am answered. Tell me who made the world.

MEPH. I will not.

FAUST. Sweet Mephistophilis, tell me.

MEPH. Move me not, for I will not tell thee.

FAUST. Villain, have I not bound thee to tell me anything?

MEPH. Ay, that is not against our kingdom; but this is. Think thou on hell, Faustus, for thou art damned.

FAUST. Think, Faustus, upon God that made the world.

MEPH. Remember this.   [*Exit.*]

FAUST. Ay, go, accursèd spirit, to ugly hell.
 'Tis thou hast damned distressèd Faustus' soul.
 Is't not too late?

[*Re-enter* GOOD ANGEL *and* EVIL ANGEL.]

E. ANG. Too late.

G. ANG. Never too late, if Faustus can repent.

E. ANG. If thou repent, devils shall tear thee in pieces.

G. ANG. Repent, and they shall never raze thy skin. [*Exeunt* ANGELS.]

FAUST. Ah, Christ my Saviour,
 Seek to save distressèd Faustus' soul!

[*Enter* LUCIFER, BELZEBUB, *and* MEPHISTOPHILIS.]

LUC. Christ cannot save thy soul, for he is just;
 There's none but I have interest in the same.

FAUST. O, who art thou that look'st so terrible?

LUC. I am Lucifer,
 And this is my companion-prince in hell.

FAUST. O Faustus! they are come to fetch away thy soul!

LUC. We come to tell thee thou dost injure us;
 Thou talk'st of Christ contrary to thy promise;
 Thou should'st not think of God: think of the Devil.

BELZ. And of his dam, too.

FAUST. Nor will I henceforth: pardon me in this,
 And Faustus vows never to look to heaven,
 Never to name God, or to pray to him,
 To burn his Scriptures, slay his ministers,

22 [Through unequal motion in respect to the whole.]

And make my spirits pull his churches down.

LUC. Do so and we will highly gratify thee. Faustus, we are come from hell to show thee some pastime: sit down, and thou shalt see all the Seven Deadly Sins appear in their proper shapes.

FAUST. That sight will be as pleasing unto me,
As Paradise was to Adam the first day
Of his creation.

LUC. Talk not of Paradise nor creation, but mark this show: talk of the Devil, and nothing else: come away!

[*Enter the* SEVEN DEADLY SINS.]

Now, Faustus, examine them of their several names and dispositions.

FAUST. What art thou—the first?

PRIDE. I am Pride. I disdain to have any parents. I am like to Ovid's flea: I can creep into every corner of a wench; sometimes, like a periwig, I sit upon her brow; or like a fan of feathers, I kiss her lips; indeed I do—what do I not? But, fie, what a scent is here! I'll not speak another word, except the ground were perfumed, and covered with cloth of arras.

FAUST. What art thou—the second?

COVET. I am Covetousness, begotten of an old churl in an old leathern bag; and, might I have my wish, I would desire that this house and all the people in it were turned to gold, that I might lock you up in my good chest. O, my sweet gold!

FAUST. What art thou—the third?

WRATH. I am Wrath. I had neither father nor mother; I leapt out of a lion's mouth when I was scarce half an hour old; and ever since I have run up and down the world with this case of rapiers, wounding myself when I had nobody to fight withal. I was born in hell; and look to it, for some of you shall be my father.

FAUST. What art thou—the fourth?

ENVY. I am Envy, begotten of a chimney-sweeper and an oyster-wife. I cannot read, and therefore wish all books were burnt. I am lean with seeing others eat. O, that there would come a famine through all the world, that all might die, and I live alone! then thou should'st see how fat I would be. But must thou sit and I stand? Come down with a vengeance!

FAUST. Away, envious rascal! What art thou—the fifth?

GLUT. Who, I, sir? I am Gluttony. My parents are all dead, and the devil a penny they have left me, but a bare pension, and that is thirty meals a day and ten bevers—a small trifle to suffice nature. O, I come of a royal parentage! My grandfather was a Gammon of Bacon, my grandmother was a Hogshead of Claret wine; my godfathers were these, Peter Pickle-herring, and Martin Martlemasbeef; O, but my godmother, she was a jolly gentlewoman, and well beloved in every good town and city; her name was Mistress Margery March-beer. Now, Faustus, thou hast heard all my progeny, wilt thou bid me to supper?

FAUST. No, I'll see thee hanged: thou wilt eat up all my victuals.

GLUT. Then the Devil choke thee!

FAUST. Choke thyself, glutton! What are thou—the sixth?

SLOTH. I am Sloth. I was begotten on a sunny bank, where I have lain ever since; and you have done me great injury to bring me from thence: let me be carried thither again by Gluttony and Lechery. I'll not speak another word for a king's ransom.

FAUST. What are you, Mistress Minx, the seventh and last?

LECHERY. Who, I, sir? I am the one that loves an inch of raw mutton better than an ell of fried stock-fish; and the first letter of my name begins with L.

LUC. Away to hell, to hell!   [*Exeunt the* SINS.]

Now, Faustus, how dost thou like this?

FAUST. O, this feeds my soul!

LUC. Tut, Faustus, in hell is all manner of delight.

FAUST. O, might I see hell, and return again,
How happy were I then!

LUC. Thou shalt; I will send for thee at midnight.
In meantime take this book; peruse it thoroughly,
And thou shalt turn thyself into what shape thou wilt.

FAUST. Great thanks, mighty Lucifer!
This will I keep as chary as my life.

LUC. Farewell, Faustus, and think on the Devil.

FAUST. Farewell, great Lucifer! Come, Mephistophilis.

[*Exeunt omnes.*]

[*Enter* CHORUS.]

CHORUS. Learned Faustus,
To know the secrets of astronomy,
Graven in the book of Jove's high firmament,
Did mount himself to scale Olympus' top,
Being seated in a chariot burning bright,
Drawn by the strength of yoky dragons' necks.
He now is gone to prove cosmography,
And, as I guess, will first arrive at Rome,
To see the Pope and manner of his court,
And take some part of holy Peter's feast,
That to this day is highly solemnized.   [*Exit.*]

The Privy-Chamber of the POPE.

[*Enter* FAUSTUS *and* MEPHISTOPHILIS.]

FAUST. Having now, my good Mephistophilis,
Passed with delight the stately town of Trier,
Environed round with airy mountain tops,
With walls of flint, and deep entrenchèd lakes,
Not to be won by any conquering prince;
From Paris next, coasting the realm of France,
We saw the river Maine fall into Rhine,
Whose banks are set with groves of fruitful vines;
Then up to Naples, rich Campania,
Whose buildings fair and gorgeous to the eye,
The streets straight forth, and paved with finest brick,
Quarter the town in four equivalents:
There saw we learned Maro's golden tomb,
The way he cut, an English mile in length,
Thorough a rock of stone in one night's space;
From thence to Venice, Padua, and the rest,
In one of which a sumptuous temple stands,
That threats the stars with her aspiring top.
Thus hitherto has Faustus spent his time:
But tell me, now, what resting-place is this?
Hast thou, as erst I did command,
Conducted me within the walls of Rome?
MEPH. Faustus, I have; and because we will not be unprovided, I have
taken up his Holiness' privy-chamber for our use.
FAUST. I hope his Holiness will bid us welcome.
MEPH. Tut, 'tis no matter, man, we'll be bold with his good cheer.
And now, my Faustus, that thou may'st perceive
What Rome containeth to delight thee with,
Know that this city stands upon seven hills
That underprop the groundwork of the same:
Just through the midst runs flowing Tiber's stream,
With winding banks that cut it in two parts:
Over the which four stately bridges lean,
That make safe passage to each part of Rome:
Upon the bridge called Ponte Angelo
Erected is a castle passing strong,
Within whose walls such store of ordnance are,
And double cannons framed of carvèd brass,
As match the days within one complete year;

Besides the gates, and high pyramides,
Which Julius Cæsar brought from Africa.
FAUST. Now, by the kingdoms of infernal rule,
Of Styx, of Acheron, and the fiery lake
Of ever-burning Phlegethon, I swear
That I do long to see the monuments
And situation of bright-splendent Rome:
Come, therefore, let's away.
MEPH. Nay, Faustus, stay; I know you'd fain see the Pope,
And take some part of holy Peter's feast,
Where thou shalt see a troop of bald-pate friars,
Whose *summum bonum*[23] is in belly-cheer.
FAUST. Well, I'm content to compass then some sport,
And by their folly make us merriment.
Then charm me, Mephistophilis, that I
May be invisible, to do what I please
Unseen of any whilst I stay in Rome.
[MEPHISTOPHILIS *charms him.*]
MEPH. So, Faustus, now
Do what thou wilt, thou shalt not be discerned.

[*Sound a sennet. Enter the* POPE *and the* CARDINAL OF LORRAIN
to the banquet, with FRIARS *attending.*]

POPE. My lord of Lorrain, wilt please you draw near?
FAUST. Fall to, and the devil choke you an you spare!
POPE. How now! Who's that which spake?—Friars, look about.
FRIAR. Here's nobody, if it like your Holiness.
POPE. My lord, here is a dainty dish was sent me from the Bishop of
Milan.
FAUST. I thank you, sir. [*Snatches it.*]
POPE. How now! Who's that which snatched the meat from me? Will
no man look? My lord, this dish was sent me from the Cardinal of
Florence.
FAUST. You say true; I'll ha't. [*Snatches the dish.*]
POPE. What, again! My lord, I'll drink to your grace.
FAUST. I'll pledge your grace. [*Snatches the cup.*]
C. OF LOR. My lord, it may be some ghost newly crept out of purga-
tory, come to beg a pardon of your Holiness.
POPE. It may be so. Friars, prepare a dirge to lay the fury of this ghost.
Once again, my lord, fall to. [*The* POPE *crosseth himself.*]
FAUST. What, are you crossing of yourself?
Well, use that trick no more I would advise you. [*Cross again.*]
Well, there's the second time. Aware the third,

23 [Highest good.]

I give you fair warning.
> [*Cross again, and* FAUSTUS *hits him a box of the ear; they all run away.*]

Come on, Mephistophilis, what shall we do?

MEPH. Nay, I know not. We shall be cursed with bell, book, and candle.

FAUST. How! bell, book, and candle—candle, book, and bell,
Forward and backward to curse Faustus to hell!
Anon you shall hear a hog grunt, a calf bleat, and an ass bray,
Because it is Saint Peter's holiday.

> [*Re-enter all the* FRIARS *to sing the dirge.*]

FRIAR. Come, brethren, let's about our business with good devotion.
> [*Sing this.*]
Cursed be he that stole away his Holiness' meat from the table!
Maledicat Dominus![24]
Cursed be he that struck his Holiness a blow on the face! *Maledicat Dominus!*
Cursed be he that took Friar Sandelo a blow on the pate! *Maledicat Dominus!*
Cursed be he that disturbeth our holy dirge! *Maledicat Dominus!*
Cursed be he that took away his Holiness' wine! *Maledicat Dominus! Et omnes sancti!*[25] *Amen!*

> [MEPHISTOPHILIS *and* FAUSTUS *beat the* FRIARS, *and fling fireworks among them; and so exeunt.*]

> [*Enter* CHORUS.]

CHORUS. When Faustus had with pleasure ta'en the view
Of rarest things, and royal courts of kings,
He stayed his course, and so returnèd home;
Where such as bear his absence but with grief,
I mean his friends, and near'st companions,
Did gratulate his safety with kind words,
And in their conference of what befell,
Touching his journey through the world and air,
They put forth questions of astrology,
Which Faustus answered with such learnèd skill,
As they admired and wondered at his wit.
Now is his fame spread forth in every land;
Amongst the rest the Emperor is one,
Carolus the Fifth, at whose palace now
Faustus is feasted 'mongst his noblemen.
What there he did in trial of his art,
I leave untold—your eyes shall see performed.   [*Exit.*]

24 [May God curse.]   25 [And all the saints!]

SCENE VIII

An Inn-yard.

[*Enter* ROBIN *the Ostler, with a book in his hand.*]

ROBIN. Oh, this is admirable! here I ha' stolen one of Doctor Faustus'
conjuring books, and i' faith I mean to search some circles for my
own use. Now will I make all the maidens in our parish dance at
my pleasure, stark-naked before me; and so by that means I shall
see more than e'er I felt or saw yet.

[*Enter* RAFE, *calling* ROBIN.]

RAFE. Robin, prithee, come away; there's a gentleman tarries to have
his horse, and he would have his things rubbed and made clean; he
keeps such a chafing with my mistress about it; and she has sent me
to look thee out; prithee, come away.

ROBIN. Keep out, keep out, or else you are blown up; you are dismem-
bered, Rafe: keep out, for I am about a roaring piece of work.

RAFE. Come, what dost thou with that same book? Thou can'st not
read.

ROBIN. Yes, my master and mistress shall find that I can read, he for
his forehead, she for her private study; she's born to bear with me,
or else my art fails.

RAFE. Why, Robin, what book is that?

ROBIN. What book! Why, the most intolerable book for conjuring
that e'er was invented by any brimstone devil.

RAFE. Can'st thou conjure with it?

ROBIN. I can do all these things easily with it; first, I can make thee
drunk with ippocras at any tabern in Europe for nothing; that's
one of my conjuring works.

RAFE. Our Master Parson says that's nothing.

ROBIN. True, Rafe; and more, Rafe, if thou hast any mind to Nan
Spit, our kitchen-maid, then turn her and wind her to thy own use
as often as thou wilt, and at midnight.

RAFE. O brave Robin, shall I have Nan Spit, and to mine own use?
On that condition I'll feed thy devil with horsebread as long as he
lives, of free cost.

ROBIN. No more, sweet Rafe: let's go and make clean our boots, which
lie foul upon our hands, and then to our conjuring in the devil's
name. [*Exeunt.*]

SCENE IX

The same.

[*Enter* ROBIN *and* RAFE *with a silver goblet.*]

ROBIN. Come, Rafe, did not I tell thee we were for ever made by this
Doctor Faustus' book? *ecce signum,*[26] here's a simple purchase for
horse-keepers; our horses shall eat no hay as long as this lasts.
RAFE. But, Robin, here comes the Vintner.
ROBIN. Hush! I'll gull him supernaturally.

[*Enter* VINTNER.]

Drawer, I hope all is paid: God be with you; come, Rafe.
VINT. Soft, sir; a word with you. I must yet have a goblet paid from
you, ere you go.
ROBIN. I, a goblet, Rafe; I, a goblet! I scorn you, and you are but a, etc.
I, a goblet! search me.
VINT. I mean so, sir, with your favor. [*Searches him.*]
ROBIN. How say you now?
VINT. I must say somewhat to your fellow. You, sir!
RAFE. Me, sir! me, sir! search your fill. [VINTNER *searches him.*] Now,
sir, you may be ashamed to burden honest men with a matter of
truth.
VINT. Well, t'one of you hath this goblet about you.
ROBIN. You lie, drawer, 'tis afore me. [*Aside.*]—Sirrah you, I'll teach
you to impeach honest men—stand by—I'll scour you for a goblet!
—stand aside you had best, I charge you in the name of Belzebub.
—Look to the goblet, Rafe. [*Aside to* RAFE.]
VINT. What mean you, sirrah?
ROBIN. I'll tell you what I mean. [*Reads from a book.*] Sanctobulorum
Periphrasticon[27]—nay, I'll tickle you, Vintner. Look to the goblet,
Rafe. [*Aside to* RAFE.]
[*Reads.*] Polypragmos Belseborams framanto pacostiphos tostu,
Mephistophilis, etc.

[*Enter* MEPHISTOPHILIS, *sets squibs at their backs, and then
exits. They run about.*]

VINT. O nomine Domini![28] what meanest thou, Robin? thou hast no
goblet.
RAFE. Peccatum peccatorum.[29] Here's thy goblet, good Vintner.
[*Gives the goblet to* VINTNER, *who exits.*]

26 [Behold the sign.]
27 [Nonsense, as is the next pseudo-Latin phrase.]
28 [Oh in God's name!]
29 [Sin of sins.]

ROBIN. *Misericordia pro nobis!*[30] What shall I do? Good Devil, forgive me now, and I'll never rob thy library more.

[*Re-enter* MEPHISTOPHILIS.]

MEPH. Monarch of hell, under whose black survey
Great potentates do kneel with awful fear,
Upon whose altars thousand souls do lie,
How am I vexed with these villains' charms!
From Constantinople am I hither come
Only for pleasure of these damnèd slaves.

ROBIN. How, from Constantinople! You have had a great journey: will you take sixpence in your purse to pay for your supper, and begone?

MEPH. Well, villains, for your presumption I transform thee into an ape, and thee into a dog and so begone.　　　　　　　[*Exit.*]

ROBIN. How, into an ape; that's brave! I'll have fine sport with the boys. I'll get nuts and apples enow.

RAFE. And I must be a dog.

ROBIN. I' faith thy head will never be out of the pottage pot.

[*Exeunt.*]

SCENE X

The court.

[*Enter* EMPEROR, FAUSTUS, *and a* KNIGHT, *with* ATTENDANTS.]

EMP. Master Doctor Faustus, I have heard strange report of thy knowledge in the black art, how that none in my empire nor in the whole world can compare with thee for the rare effects of magic; they say thou hast a familiar spirit, by whom thou canst accomplish what thou list. This, therefore, is my request, that thou let me see some proof of thy skill, that mine eyes may be witnesses to confirm what mine ears have heard reported; and here I swear to thee by the honor of mine imperial crown, that, whatever thou doest, thou shalt be no ways prejudiced or endamaged.

KNIGHT. I' faith he looks much like a conjuror.　　　　　[*Aside.*]

FAUST. My gracious sovereign, though I must confess myself far inferior to the report men have published, and nothing answerable to the honor of your imperial majesty, yet for that love and duty binds me thereunto, I am content to do whatsoever your majesty shall command me.

EMP. Then, Doctor Faustus, mark what I shall say.
As I was sometimes solitary set

30 [Mercy upon us!]

Within my closet, sundry thoughts arose
About the honor of mine ancestors,
How they had won by prowess such exploits,
Got such riches, subdued so many kingdoms
As we that do succeed, or they that shall
Hereafter possess our throne, shall
(I fear me) ne'er attain to that degree
Of high renown and great authority;
Amongst which kings is Alexander the Great,
Chief spectacle of the world's pre-eminence,
The bright shining of whose glorious acts
Lightens the world with his reflecting beams,
As when I hear but motion made of him
It grieves my soul I never saw the man.
If therefore thou by cunning of thine art
Canst raise this man from hollow vaults below,
Where lies entombed this famous conqueror,
And bring with him his beauteous paramour,
Both in their right shapes, gesture, and attire
They used to wear during their time of life,
Thou shalt both satisfy my just desire,
And give me cause to praise thee whilst I live.

FAUST. My gracious lord, I am ready to accomplish your request so far
forth as by art, and power of my spirit, I am able to perform.

KNIGHT. I' faith that's just nothing at all.   [*Aside.*]

FAUST. But, if it like your grace, it is not in my ability to present before
your eyes the true substantial bodies of those two deceased princes,
which long since are consumed to dust.

KNIGHT. Ay, marry, Master Doctor, now there's a sign of grace in you,
when you will confess the truth.   [*Aside.*]

FAUST. But such spirits as can lively resemble Alexander and his paramour shall appear before your grace in that manner that they both
lived in, in their most flourishing estate; which I doubt not shall
sufficiently content your imperial majesty.

EMP. Go to, Master Doctor, let me see them presently.

KNIGHT. Do you hear, Master Doctor? You bring Alexander and his
paramour before the Emperor!

FAUST. How then, sir?

KNIGHT. I' faith that's as true as Diana turned me to a stag!

FAUST. No, sir, but when Actæon died, he left the horns for you.
Mephistophilis, begone.   [*Exit* MEPH.]

KNIGHT. Nay, an you go to conjuring, I'll begone.   [*Exit* KNIGHT.]

FAUST. I'll meet with you anon for interrupting me so. Here they are,
my gracious lord.

[*Re-enter* MEPHISTOPHILIS *with spirits in the shapes of* ALEXANDER *and his* PARAMOUR.]

EMP. Master Doctor, I heard this lady while she lived had a wart or mole in her neck: how shall I know whether it be so or no?

FAUST. Your highness may boldly go and see.

EMP. Sure these are no spirits, but the true substantial bodies of those two deceased princes.   [*Exeunt* SPIRITS.]

FAUST. Will't please your highness now to send for the knight that was so pleasant with me here of late?

EMP. One of you call him forth!   [*Exit* ATTENDANT.]

[*Re-enter the* KNIGHT *with a pair of horns on his head.*]

How now, sir Knight! why I had thought thou had'st been a bachelor, but now I see thou hast a wife, that not only gives thee horns, but makes thee wear them. Feel on thy head.

KNIGHT. Thou damnèd wretch and execrable dog,
Bred in the concave of some monstrous rock,
How darest thou thus abuse a gentleman?
Villain, I say, undo what thou hast done!

FAUST. O, not so fast, sir; there's no haste; but, good, are you remembered how you crossed me in my conference with the Emperor? I think I have met with you for it.

EMP. Good Master Doctor, at my entreaty release him; he hath done penance sufficient.

FAUST. My gracious lord, not so much for the injury he offered me here in your presence, as to delight you with some mirth, hath Faustus worthily requited this injurious knight; which, being all I desire, I am content to release him of his horns: and, sir Knight, hereafter speak well of scholars. Mephistophilis, transform him straight. [MEPHISTOPHILIS *removes the horns.*] Now, my good lord, having done my duty I humbly take my leave.

EMP. Farewell, Master Doctor; yet, ere you go,
Expect from me a bounteous reward.

                         [*Exeunt* EMPEROR, KNIGHT, *and* ATTENDANTS.]

SCENE XI

A Green, then FAUSTUS' *house.*

[*Enter* FAUSTUS *and* MEPHISTOPHILIS.]

FAUST. Now, Mephistophilis, the restless course
That time doth run with calm and silent foot,
Shortening my days and thread of vital life,
Calls for the payment of my latest years:

Therefore, sweet Mephistophilis, let us
Make haste to Wittenberg.
MEPH. What, will you go on horse-back or on foot?
FAUST. Nay, till I'm past this fair and pleasant green, I'll walk on foot.

[*Enter a* HORSE-COURSER.]

HORSE-C. I have been all this day seeking one Master Fustian: mass,
see where he is! God save you, Master Doctor!
FAUST. What, Horse-Courser! You are well met.
HORSE-C. Do you hear, sir? I have brought you forty dollars for your
horse.
FAUST. I cannot sell him so: if thou likest him for fifty, take him.
HORSE-C. Alas, sir, I have no more.—I pray you, speak for me.
MEPH. I pray you, let him have him: he is an honest fellow, and he
has a great charge, neither wife nor child.
FAUST. Well, come, give me your money. [HORSE-COURSER *gives*
FAUSTUS *the money.*] My boy will deliver him to you. But I must
tell you one thing before you have him; ride him not into the water
at any hand.
HORSE-C. Why, sir, will he not drink of all waters?
FAUST. O, yes, he will drink of all waters, but ride him not into the
water: ride him over hedge or ditch, or where thou wilt, but not into
the water.
HORSE-C. Well, sir.—Now am I made man for ever: I'll not leave my
horse for twice forty: if he had but the quality of hey-ding-ding,
hey-ding-ding, I'd make a brave living on him: he has a buttock as
slick as an eel. [*Aside.*] Well, God b' wi' ye, sir, your boy will deliver him me: but hark you, sir; if my horse be sick or ill at ease, if
I bring his water to you, you'll tell me what it is?
FAUST. Away, you villain; what, dost think I am a horse-doctor?

[*Exit* HORSE-COURSER.]

What art thou, Faustus, but a man condemned to die?
Thy fatal time doth draw to final end;
Despair doth drive distrust unto my thoughts:
Confound these passions with a quiet sleep:
Tush, Christ did call the thief upon the cross;
Then rest thee, Faustus, quiet in conceit.   [*Sleeps in his chair.*]

[*Re-enter* HORSE-COURSER, *all wet, crying.*]

HORSE-C. Alas, alas! Doctor Fustian quotha? Mass, Doctor Lopus was
never such a doctor. Has given me a purgation, has purged me of
forty dollars; I shall never see them more. But yet, like an ass as I
was, I would not be ruled by him, for he bade me I should ride him
into no water. Now I, thinking my horse had had some rare quality

that he would not have had me known of, I, like a venturous youth,
rid him into the deep pond at the town's end. I was no sooner in
the middle of the pond, but my horse vanished away, and I sat
upon a bottle of hay, never so near drowning in my life. But I'll seek
out my Doctor, and have my forty dollars again, or I'll make it the
dearest horse!—O, yonder is his snipper-snapper.—Do you hear?
you hey-pass, where's your master?

MEPH. Why, sir, what would you? You cannot speak with him.

HORSE-C. But I will speak with him.

MEPH. Why, he's fast asleep. Come some other time.

HORSE-C. I'll speak with him now, or I'll break his glass windows about
his ears.

MEPH. I tell thee he has not slept this eight nights.

HORSE-C. An he have not slept this eight weeks I'll speak with him.

MEPH. See where he is, fast asleep.

HORSE-C. Ay, this is he. God save you, Master Doctor, Master Doctor,
Master Doctor Fustian!—Forty dollars, forty dollars for a bottle of
hay!

MEPH. Why, thou seest he hears thee not.

HORSE-C. So-ho, ho!—so-ho ho! [*Hollas in his ear.*] No, will you not
wake? I'll make you wake ere I go. [*Pulls him by the leg, and pulls
it away.*] Alas, I am undone! What shall I do?

FAUST. O, my leg, my leg! Help, Mephistophilis! call the officers. My
leg, my leg!

MEPH. Come, villain, to the constable.

HORSE-C. O lord, sir, let me go, and I'll give you forty dollars more.

MEPH. Where be they?

HORSE-C. I have none about me. Come to my ostry and I'll give them
you.

MEPH. Begone quickly.   [HORSE-COURSER *runs away.*]

FAUST. What, is he gone? Farewell he! Faustus has his leg again, and
the horse-courser, I take it, a bottle of hay for his labor. Well, this
trick shall cost him forty dollars more.

[*Enter* WAGNER.]

How now, Wagner, what's the news with thee?

WAG. Sir, the Duke of Vanholt doth earnestly entreat your company.

FAUST. The Duke of Vanholt! an honorable gentleman, to whom I
must be no niggard of my cunning. Come, Mephistophilis, let's
away to him.   [*Exeunt.*]

Court of the DUKE.

[*Enter the* DUKE OF VANHOLT, *the* DUCHESS,
FAUSTUS, *and* MEPHISTOPHILIS.]

DUKE. Believe me, Master Doctor, this merriment hath much pleased
me.

FAUST. My gracious lord, I am glad it contents you so well.—But it
may be, madam, you take no delight in this. I have heard that great
bellied women do long for some dainties or other: what is it,
madam? tell me, and you shall have it.

DUCHESS. Thanks, good Master Doctor; and, for I see your courteous
intent to pleasure me, I will not hide from you the thing my heart
desires; and, were it now summer, as it is January and the dead time
of winter, I would desire no better meat than a dish of ripe grapes.

FAUST. Alas, madam, that's nothing! Mephistophilis, begone. [*Exit*
MEPHISTOPHILIS.] Were it a greater thing than this, so it would
content you, you should have it.

[*Re-enter* MEPHISTOPHILIS *with the grapes.*]

Here they be, madam; wilt please you taste on them?

DUKE. Believe me, Master Doctor, this makes me wonder above the
rest, that being in the dead time of winter, and in the month of
January, how you should come by these grapes.

FAUST. If it like your grace, the year is divided into two circles over the
whole world, that, when it is here winter with us, in the contrary
circle it is summer with them, as in India, Saba, and farther countries in the East; and by means of a swift spirit that I have, I had
them brought hither, as you see.—How do you like them, madam;
be they good?

DUCHESS. Believe me, Master Doctor, they be the best grapes that e'er
I tasted in my life before.

FAUST. I am glad they content you so, madam.

DUKE. Come, madam, let us in, where you must well reward this
learned man for the great kindness he hath showed to you.

DUCHESS. And so I will, my lord; and, whilst I live, rest beholding for
this courtesy.

FAUST. I humbly thank your grace.

DUKE. Come, Master Doctor, follow us and receive your reward.

[*Exeunt.*]

SCENE XIII

FAUSTUS' *study.*

[*Enter* WAGNER *solus.*]

WAG. I think my master means to die shortly,
   For he hath given to me all his goods
   And yet, methinks, if that death were [so] near,
   He would not banquet, and carouse and swill
   Amongst the students, as even now he doth,
   Who are at supper with such belly-cheer
   As Wagner ne'er beheld in all his life.
   See where they come! belike the feast is ended.

[*Enter* FAUSTUS, *with two or three* SCHOLARS
   and MEPHISTOPHILIS.]

1 SCHOL. Master Doctor Faustus, since our conference about fair ladies, which was the beautifullest in all the world, we have determined with ourselves that Helen of Greece was the admirablest
   lady that ever lived: therefore, Master Doctor, if you will do us that
   favor, as to let us see that peerless dame of Greece, whom all the
   world admires for majesty, we should think ourselves much beholding unto you.

FAUST. Gentlemen,
   For that I know your friendship is unfeignèd,
   And Faustus' custom is not to deny
   The just requests of those that wish him well,
   You shall behold that peerless dame of Greece,
   No otherways for pomp and majesty,
   Than when Sir Paris crossed the seas with her,
   And brought the spoils to rich Dardania.
   Be silent, then, for danger is in words.

[*Music sounds and* HELEN *passeth over the stage.*]

2 SCHOL. Too simple is my wit to tell her praise,
   Whom all the world admires for majesty.

3 SCHOL. No marvel though the angry Greeks pursued
   With ten years' war the rape of such a queen,
   Whose heavenly beauty passeth all compare.

1 SCHOL. Since we have seen the pride of Nature's works,
   And only paragon of excellence,

[*Enter an* OLD MAN.]

Let us depart; and for this glorious deed
Happy and blest be Faustus evermore.

FAUST. Gentlemen, farewell—the same I wish to you.

[*Exeunt* SCHOLARS *and* WAGNER.]

OLD MAN. Ah, Doctor Faustus, that I might prevail
    To guide thy steps unto the way of life,
    By which sweet path thou may'st attain the goal
    That shall conduct thee to celestial rest!
    Break heart, drop blood, and mingle it with tears,
    Tears falling from repentant heaviness
    Of thy most vile and loathsome filthiness,
    The stench whereof corrupts the inward soul
    With such flagitious crimes of heinous sins
    As no commiseration may expel,
    But mercy, Faustus, of thy Saviour sweet,
    Whose blood alone must wash away thy guilt.

FAUST. Where art thou, Faustus? wretch, what hast thou done?
    Damned art thou, Faustus, damned; despair and die!
    Hell calls for right, and with a roaring voice
    Says, "Faustus! come! thine hour is [almost] come!"
    And Faustus now will come to do thee right.

[MEPHISTOPHILIS *gives him a dagger.*]

OLD MAN. Ah stay, good Faustus, stay thy desperate steps!
    I see an angel hovers o'er thy head,
    And, with a vial full of precious grace,
    Offers to pour the same into thy soul:
    Then call for mercy, and avoid despair.

FAUST. Ah, my sweet friend, I feel
    Thy words do comfort my distressèd soul.
    Leave me a while to ponder on my sins.

OLD MAN. I go, sweet Faustus, but with heavy cheer,
    Fearing the ruin of thy hopeless soul.   [*Exit.*]

FAUST. Accursèd Faustus, where is mercy now?
    I do repent; and yet I do despair;
    Hell strives with grace for conquest in my breast:
    What shall I do to shun the snares of death?

MEPH. Thou traitor, Faustus, I arrest thy soul
    For disobedience to my sovereign lord;
    Revolt, or I'll in piecemeal tear thy flesh.

FAUST. Sweet Mephistophilis, entreat thy lord
    To pardon my unjust presumption.
    And with my blood again I will confirm
    My former vow I made to Lucifer.

MEPH. Do it then quickly, with unfeignèd heart,
    Lest greater danger do attend thy drift.   [FAUSTUS *stabs his*
                  arm and writes on a paper with his blood.]

FAUST. Torment, sweet friend, that base and crookèd age,

That durst dissuade me from thy Lucifer,
With greatest torments that our hell affords.
MEPH. His faith is great: I cannot touch his soul;
  But what I may afflict his body with
  I will attempt, which is but little worth.
FAUST. One thing, good servant, let me crave of thee,
  To glut the longing of my heart's desire—
  That I might have unto my paramour
  That heavenly Helen, which I saw of late,
  Whose sweet embracings may extinguish clean
  These thoughts that do dissuade me from my vow,
  And keep mine oath I made to Lucifer.
MEPH. Faustus, this or what else thou shalt desire
  Shall be performed in twinkling of an eye.

[*Re-enter* HELEN.]

FAUST. Was this the face that launched a thousand ships
  And burnt the topless towers of Ilium?
  Sweet Helen, make me immortal with a kiss.   [*She kisses him.*]
  Her lips suck forth my soul; see where it flies!
  Come, Helen, come, give me my soul again.   [*He kisses her.*]
  Here will I dwell, for heaven be in these lips,
  And all is dross that is not Helena.

[*Enter the* OLD MAN.]

I will be Paris, and for love of thee,
Instead of Troy, shall Wittenberg be sacked
And I will combat with weak Menelaus,
And wear thy colors on my plumèd crest:
Yea, I will wound Achilles in the heel,
And then return to Helen for a kiss.
O, thou art fairer than the evening air
Clad in the beauty of a thousand stars;
Brighter art thou than flaming Jupiter
When he appeared to hapless Semele:
More lovely than the monarch of the sky
In wanton Arethusa's azured arms:
And none but thou shalt be my paramour!   [*Exeunt.*]
OLD MAN. Accursèd Faustus, miserable man,
  That from thy soul exclud'st the grace of heaven,
  And fly'st the throne of his tribunal seat!

[*Enter* DEVILS.]

Satan begins to sift me with his pride:

As in this furnace God shall try my faith.
My faith, vile hell, shall triumph over thee.
Ambitious fiends! see how the heavens smile
At your repulse, and laugh your state to scorn!
Hence, hell! for hence I fly unto my God.   [*Exeunt.*]

SCENE XIV

The same.

[*Enter* FAUSTUS *with the* SCHOLARS.]

FAUST. Ah, gentlemen!

1 SCHOL. What ails Faustus?

FAUST. Ah, my sweet chamber-fellow, had I lived with thee, then had I lived still! but now I die eternally. Look, comes he not, comes he not?

2 SCHOL. What means Faustus?

3 SCHOL. Belike he is grown into some sickness by being over solitary.

1 SCHOL. If it be so, we'll have physicians to cure him. 'Tis but a surfeit. Never fear, man.

FAUSTUS. A surfeit of deadly sin that hath damned both body and soul.

2 SCHOL. Yet, Faustus, look up to heaven: remember God's mercies are infinite.

FAUST. But Faustus' offence can ne'er be pardoned: the serpent that tempted Eve may be saved, but not Faustus. Ah, gentlemen, hear me with patience, and tremble not at my speeches! Though my heart pants and quivers to remember that I have been a student here these thirty years, O, would I had never seen Wittenberg, never read book! And what wonders I have done, all Germany can witness, yea, all the world; for which Faustus hath lost both Germany and the world, yea heaven itself, heaven, the seat of God, the throne of the blessed, the kingdom of joy; and must remain in hell for ever, hell, ah, hell, for ever! Sweet friends! what shall become of Faustus being in hell for ever?

3 SCHOL. Yet, Faustus, call on God.

FAUST. On God, whom Faustus hath abjured! on God, whom Faustus hath blasphemed! Ah, my God, I would weep, but the Devil draws in my tears. Gush forth blood instead of tears! Yea, life and soul! O, he stays my tongue! I would lift up my hands, but see, they hold them, they hold them!

ALL. Who, Faustus?

FAUST. Lucifer and Mephistophilis. Ah, gentlemen, I gave them my soul for my cunning!

ALL. God forbid!

FAUST. God forbade it indeed; but Faustus hath done it: for vain
pleasure of twenty-four years hath Faustus lost eternal joy and
felicity. I writ them a bill with mine own blood: the date is expired; the time will come, and he will fetch me.

1 SCHOL. Why did not Faustus tell us of this before, that divines
might have prayed for thee?

FAUST. Oft have I thought to have done so: but the Devil threatened
to tear me in pieces if I named God; to fetch both body and soul if
I once gave ear to divinity: and now 'tis too late. Gentlemen,
away! lest you perish with me.

2 SCHOL. O, what shall we do to save Faustus?

FAUST. Talk not of me, but save yourselves, and depart.

3 SCHOL. God will strengthen me. I will stay with Faustus.

1 SCHOL. Tempt not God, sweet friend; but let us into the next room,
and there pray for him.

FAUST. Ay, pray for me, pray for me! and what noise soever ye hear,
come not unto me, for nothing can rescue me.

2 SCHOL. Pray thou, and we will pray that God may have mercy upon
thee.

FAUST. Gentlemen, farewell: if I live till morning I'll visit you; if
not—Faustus is gone to hell.

ALL. Faustus, farewell. [*Exeunt* SCHOLARS.]

[*The clock strikes éleven.*]

FAUST. Ah, Faustus,
Now hast thou but one bare hour to live,
And then thou must be damned perpetually!
Stand still, you ever-moving spheres of heaven,
That time may cease, and midnight never come;
Fair Nature's eye, rise, rise again and make
Perpetual day; or let this hour be but
A year, a month, a week, a natural day,
That Faustus may repent and save his soul!
O lente, lente, currite noctis equi!³¹
The stars move still, time runs, the clock will strike,
The Devil will come, and Faustus must be damned.
Oh, I'll leap up to my God! Who pulls me down?
See, see where Christ's blood streams in the firmament!
One drop would save my soul—half a drop: ah, my Christ!
Ah, rend not my heart for naming of my Christ!
Yet will I call on him: O, spare me, Lucifer!—
Where is it now? 'tis gone; and see where God
Stretcheth out his arm, and bends his ireful brows!
Mountain and hills come, come and fall on me,

31 [Run slowly, slowly, horses of the night.]

And hide me from the heavy wrath of God!
No! no!
Then will I headlong run into the earth;
Earth gape! O, no, it will not harbor me!
You stars that reigned at my nativity,
Whose influence hath allotted death and hell,
Now draw up Faustus like a foggy mist
Into the entrails of yon laboring clouds,
That when you vomit forth into the air,
My limbs may issue from their smoky mouths,
So that my soul may but ascend to heaven.
                    [*The clock strikes the half hour.*]
Ah, half the hour is past! 'twill all be past anon!
O God!
If thou wilt not have mercy on my soul,
Yet for Christ's sake whose blood hath ransomed me,
Impose some end to my incessant pain;
Let Faustus live in hell a thousand years—
A hundred thousand, and—at last—be saved!
O, no end is limited to damnèd souls!
Why wert thou not a creature wanting soul?
Or why is this immortal that thou hast?
Ah, Pythagoras' metempsychosis! were that true,
This soul should fly from me, and I be changed
Unto some brutish beast! all beasts are happy,
For, when they die,
Their souls are soon dissolved in elements;
But mine must live, still to be plagued in hell.
Curst be the parents that engendered me!
No, Faustus: curse thyself; curse Lucifer
That hath deprived thee of the joys of heaven.
                    [*The clock strikes twelve.*]
O, it strikes, it strikes! Now, body, turn to air,
Or Lucifer will bear thee quick to hell.   [*Thunder and lightning.*]
O soul, be changed into little water-drops,
And fall into the ocean—ne'er be found.

                    [*Enter* DEVILS.]

My God! my God! look not so fierce on me!
Adders and serpents, let me breathe awhile!
Ugly hell, gape not! come not, Lucifer!
I'll burn my books!—Ah Mephistophilis!   [*Exeunt with him.*]
                    [*Enter* CHORUS.]

CHORUS. Cut is the branch that might have grown full straight,

And burnèd is Apollo's laurel bough,
That sometime grew within this learnèd man.
Faustus is gone; regard his hellish fall,
Whose fiendful fortune may exhort the wise
Only to wonder at unlawful things,
Whose deepness doth entice such forward wits
To practise more than heavenly power permits.   [*Exit.*]

Terminat hora diem; terminat auctor opus.[32]

32 [The hour ends the day; the author ends the work.]

COMMENTARY

Two thousand years after Aeschylus, the opposite side of Europe, another religion, a new kind of theater, a different set of conventions for playwright and actor, a play unlike *Agamemnon* in dozens of ways —and yet: its purpose is still to make us see the significant deeds of men, its deepest concern is still with the relations of man and God, especially with those men who yield to a desire for some more-than-human honor or power or knowledge.

Unfortunately, we do not know the full "form of Faustus' fortunes" as Christopher Marlowe envisioned them. The text of the play as we have it (in two versions that differ greatly from one another) presents problems about which scholars still debate. Nearly everyone agrees, however, that some additions have been made to the play by writers other than Marlowe (possibly working with him, possibly only after his death), and that probably some of what Marlowe himself wrote has been lost. The six scenes that are most certainly his are (as numbered in this book) Scenes I, III, V, VI, XIII, and XIV. The scenes that were most probably written by other, inferior playwrights are those involving the clowns Robin and Rafe, the Horse-Courser, the Pope, the Emperor, and the Duke and Duchess of Vanholt—Scenes VII through XII.

The play thus presents us with a Marlovian beginning and end but with an uncertain middle; we cannot be certain about how, for most of the twenty-four years covered by the play, a strictly Marlovian Faustus would have used the powers for which he gave his soul. This difficulty often leads to lengthy discussions of what has been called the "problem of the middle" (see *Understanding Drama*, edited by Cleanth Brooks and Robert Heilman [Holt, 1948]), but I have thought it far more profitable to concentrate upon Marlowe's own work. You will thus discover that all the following remarks concern themselves with the six Marlovian scenes listed above.

In the Elizabethan theater a good share of the audience is very close to the action. When Mephistophilis, in all his ugliness, suddenly appears through the trap door, accompanied by smoke, thunder, and lightning, some of us would be as close and as terrified as Faustus himself, who, significantly, cannot take the devil *as he really is* and insists that he adopt a disguise. We can measure the effect upon Elizabethan audiences in part by the anecdotes that were told about those who went to see "shagge-hayr'd Devills runne roaring over the Stage": the "Theatre crackt and frighted the audience"; the "visible apparition of the Devill on the Stage at the Belsavage Playhouse" drove some of the spectators mad "with that fearefull sight"; the appearance of "one devell too many" on an Exeter stage emptied the theater and sent the actors to their prayers; and Edward Alleyn, the most famous actor who played Faustus, retired from the stage entirely when his conjuring brought forth not a fellow-actor but an "Apparition of the Devil."

Of course, those who have not seen the Devil may come to think he does not exist. Faustus, who knows that invisibility is merely one of the Devil's disguises (see point four of his pact), nevertheless errs similarly: he forgets that Christ exists. In the Christian context of the play, his hubris—what the Chorus calls his "self-control"—is to forget that Christ is, for the scholar as much as for others, the Way and the Truth.

The withholding until Scene VI of Christ's name as any part of Faustus' calculations is one of the principal foundations of the design of the play as we have it. When Faustus, to support his rejection of theology in the first scene, reads from the Bible, the biblical contexts (which the audience is expected to know) are what matter most. When you look at these contexts as quoted below, from which Faustus speaks only those words that are *not* in italics, you will notice that he has distorted everything by willfully or blindly omitting the name of Christ and all that the name means. But—and this is important—the omitted words are as much a part of the play as any that he actually speaks.

The reward of sin is death, *but the gift of God is life everlasting in Christ Jesus our Lord* (Romans 6:23).

. . . *the blood of Jesus Christ, His Son, cleanses us from all sin.* If we say that we have no sin, we deceive ourselves, and there is no truth in us. *If we acknowledge our sins, He is faithful and just to forgive us our sins and to cleanse us from all iniquity* (I John 1:7–9).

For a scholar with the text right before him, the omissions are astonishing, are they not? It is clear that the complete quotations mean quite the opposite of the deterministic conclusion—"What will be, shall be"—that Faustus derives from his two fragments. His omissions create a vacuum that he never wholly fills. For although he

finally calls to Christ and even sees His blood, he never truly acknowl-
edges his sins.

Examine closely the way Marlowe develops this level of his design.
Scene I: the above omissions appear immediately after Faustus has
said to himself, "Jerome's Bible, Faustus, *view it well.*" Scene III:
in the newly created vacuum, Mephistophilis, serving as a strange
contrast to Faustus, names Christ the *Saviour.* Scene V: Faustus,
having signed his soul away in blood, speaks (unconsciously? or in-
tending blasphemy?) the very words—*consummatum est*—that
Christ used to mark the consummation of His gift of blood to save all
souls. Scene VI: Faustus at last calls upon "Christ my *Saviour.*"
Scene XIII: the Old Man speaks of Christ as the *Saviour* and refers to
His cleansing blood. Scene XIV: Faustus sees Christ's blood streaming in the firmament, and then says (note how precisely this reminds
us of his original fatal omissions), "Ah, rend not my heart for *naming
of my Christ!*" The implications of all this are more rich than I have
space to indicate.

SOLILOQUIES AND ANGELS

The first scene opens—and there should be some moments of silence
while we take in the familiar picture—with the scholar at work:
Faustus alone in his study, deep in the books upon which he has thus
far, as the prologue tells us, so fruitfully built his life. It is this stage
image that we remember when near the end he says in despair, "O,
would I had never seen Wittenberg, never read book." The books
that immediately surround him, and that one by one he rejects in his
first speech, contain (symbolically) all *human* knowledge—that de-
rived through the light of human reason, intuition, or divine revelation. But this is for him not enough, that is the point, and he reaches
for books containing knowledge gained only through traffic with the
Devil, those necromantic books "which he prefers before his chiefest
bliss"—before, that is, the salvation of his soul.

For sixty lines he speaks to himself, a *soliloquy,* a dramatic technique that Aeschylus used only once in *Agamemnon* but that here
dominates and finally characterizes that part of the play that we can
be sure Marlowe wrote. Faustus alone, speaking to himself or calling
upon God or the Devil—so he begins and so he ends, soliloquies
comprising about one-fifth of the Marlovian scenes. The reason is
clear. *Doctor Faustus,* unlike *Agamemnon,* is about one man, about
his mind and soul, about his life in time (in the body) only as it

bears upon his life in eternity (in the spirit). Thus the soliloquy—
the stage convention that allows us to hear a man thinking—becomes
essential. Marlowe takes us inside his character not, as Shakespeare
does in *Hamlet*, because he wants to develop a profound study of
character (we really learn surprisingly little about Faustus) but because *inside* is where the real action occurs.

Another, stranger theatrical strategy—the two angels—arose with
equal directness from the demand of the subject (although Marlowe
borrowed them, to be sure, from a simpler and earlier form of drama
known as the morality play). He needed the angels so that we would
not think, from the extent and force of the soliloquies, that the represented conflict is no more than a man arguing with himself. The conflict does go on inside Faustus, but it is at all times part of the universal struggle between Good and Evil: every man's soul is, after all,
the ground on which (and for which) the Devil attacks God.

What as readers we must try to observe is how, in the theater, the
archaic device of the angels would serve Marlowe's purpose. Notice
that they first appear almost immediately after Faustus' long opening soliloquy, at a time when he has just made his decision and when
no doubts have yet disturbed him. More than that, the actor who
plays Faustus, never going beyond what the text authorizes, must in
no way indicate that he is aware of their conflict over him. Faustus
never sees them: Scene VI, line 14, is the best proof; he does not
know the source of the buzzing in his ears. On the first appearance of
the angels, we cannot even be sure that he hears them; apparently he
doesn't or, if he does, he ignores them (the reference in Faustus' use
of the word "this" seems, on Marlowe's part, deliberately ambigu-
ous). The lack of awareness or recognition in Faustus—he goes right
on reading the "damnèd book" as the angels speak to him—emphasizes that what is happening to and in him is part of a conflict in
which real forces distinct from the man himself take part. Marlowe
makes his audience see and hear that conflict before Faustus gives it a
thought.

The second time the angels appear (Scene V) they interrupt a
soliloquy in which Faustus is for the first time at war with himself.
Just before they appear he hears and quotes "something" that
"soundeth" in his ears. It could be the Good Angel, for the advice
is the same; but the audience does not hear it, and if Marlowe gave
us only this kind of voice—the distinction here is important—we
could conclude that Faustus was merely hearing things or that the
voice was simply his own worried conscience. But we already know

better, and the second appearance of the angels, at this moment, verifies our knowledge. The angels are real, and Faustus is the prize for which they battle. It is clear that he now hears them (he repeats their last words), but for him they are only sounding or buzzing voices, some anonymous adjunct to his own inner dialogue and conflict. For us they are genuine and identifiable presences: the angels that speak to men, the forces of Good and Evil that contend against one another for men's souls. The conflict is—as we see—both internal and external, both individual and universal. Toward the end of the play (Scene XIII) Marlowe suddenly confronts us with a vivid stage picture: Mephistophilis handing Faustus a dagger with which to commit suicide (the ultimate act of despair) while the Good Angel offers to pour a "vial full of precious grace" into his soul. And Faustus himself now says, "Hell strives with grace for conquest in my breast."

DRAMATIC IRONY

As Marlowe communicates much of his meaning through *irony*, an originally rhetorical strategy long common in most forms of art and especially in drama, he provides us with the opportunity to observe various manifestations of a basic technique. Let us begin with the two most relevant meanings of the word (from the *Standard College Dictionary*):

An effect achieved by making the audience aware of something a character or participant does not know.

A result, ending, etc., the reverse of what was expected.

And we must then ask what it was that Faustus *expected* from his contract with the Devil. Marlowe spells it out precisely in Faustus' first two scenes, and it comes to this:

    1. unlimited possessions ("what I please": mainly wealth, women, and rare delicacies);

    2. absolute knowledge ("resolve me of *all* ambiguities");

    3. infinite power (political, scientific, and necromantic—over, that is, men, nature, and the dead; over the Emperor, the moon, and Helen).

He wants also, in some sense, to escape the "everlasting death" that he says the Bible promises: he will "confound hell" by spending eternity with Plato and Aristotle in Elysium. Faustus is, in other words, dissatisfied with the very limitations that help to define the human condition. He no longer wants to be "but Faustus and a man"; he wants—expects—to be a "mighty god."

Irony (in the second sense above) operates, then, throughout most of the last scene. The great scholar who wanted all knowledge now wishes he had had none ("would I had never seen Wittenberg, never read book"); the man who expected to rule other men cannot even control his own tongue or raise his own hands; he who wanted to be a god now wishes he were only some "brutish beast." The effect is ironic again when Marlowe brings the satanic powers to a definitive test: can they prevent or even delay their spiritual consequences? The man who had thought to drop the moon "from her sphere" now tries to do so and to supplant it with the sun ("fair Nature's eye"), thus to avoid midnight, the hour of his doom, forever—or at least for "a year, a month, a week, a natural day." The man who had been told how to "turn thyself into what shape thou wilt" (Scene VI) now, in his desperate attempt to escape, tries to turn his body into air and his soul into water-drops. But he finds that the magic for which he sold his body and soul has no power to save them.

Marlowe also employs irony in the specifically dramatic sense of the first definition above. In the last scene, for example, Faustus says:

> The stars move still, time runs, the clock will strike,
> The Devil will come, and Faustus must be damned.

For him it is the simple, terrible truth; but for us it is more than that. As the clauses follow rapidly one upon the other, driving home the completeness of his despair and the degree to which he sees what is happening as inevitable, we remember that it was precisely (and now ironically) from the prison of the inevitable—"*Che sera sera*, what will be, shall be"—that he was (he claimed) trying to escape when he first rejected the ways of God. An even more vivid irony resides in the religious language that Faustus uses about Helen as he strains to find some joy to equal the lost joys of Heaven. You will wish, I think, to dwell (perhaps to the point of writing a paragraph or two) on the deep ironic effect when he speaks of the "*heavenly* Helen" and says, "make me *immortal* with a kiss," and then rhapsodizes:

> Her lips suck forth my soul; see where it flies!
> Come, Helen, come, give me my soul again.
> Here will I dwell, for heaven be in these lips.

His use of this language of the soul about a matter of the flesh is quite conscious. But our understanding of the language differs enormously from that of Faustus, and it is in this difference, of course, that the irony appears.

What other examples of irony can you find in the play? What about the quotation from Ovid in the last scene? Or the visual contrast between the young, beautiful Helen and the Old Man throughout Scene XIII? Or the action of Scene VI: is it ironic, for example, that Faustus at the end of the scene enthusiastically accepts the Devil's flashy but superficial floor show when at the beginning he had vigorously demanded genuine answers to searching questions about the universe? Where else do you find Marlowe working with irony?

WHAT WE SEE AND HEAR

Marlowe's text lacks really helpful stage directions almost to the degree that *Agamemnon* does, and I have done nothing this time to remedy the situation. Many modern dramatists, aware that their plays are going to be read more often than seen and, furthermore, anxious to control productions as much as possible, provide almost as much explanation, description, and direction as if they were writing novels. But in *Doctor Faustus*, even at the most crucial and complicated moments, it is entirely we—actors, directors, or readers—who must decide about such matters as, say, dress, movement, gesture, facial expression (now that there are no masks), and tone of voice (an increasingly subtle problem, the smaller and more intimate the theater). We must simply learn to read with the required imaginative vigor.

For example: when Mephistophilis, watching Faustus write the contract in blood, says, "O, what will not I do to obtain his soul" how does he speak—sadly? cynically? ironically? joyfully? or none of these? Think before you answer; for the answer is both more important and less simple than it may at first seem, just as Mephistophilis himself is a far less simple character than he may at first seem. Sometimes a liar but often oddly truthful, usually anxious to trap Faustus but sometimes moved to warn him, for the most part a faithful servant to Lucifer but occasionally unable to conceal his longing for God, Mephistophilis demands close study before we can say with confidence exactly how he would speak at any given moment.

Take another speech, this time by Faustus. In Scene VI he has been trying to get some real astrological knowledge out of Mephistophilis but gets only "freshmen's suppositions." At last he says,

"Well, I am answered. Tell me who made the world." And Mephistophilis refuses, leading directly to the climax of the first six scenes —Faustus' turn to Christ and Lucifer's arrival. What, then, is Faustus' tone in the words I have quoted? Does the tone change from one sentence to the next? Is there a noticeable pause between the sentences? If so, what does it signify? What might Faustus be thinking? Does he already know the answer to his question? Does he expect to get an answer from Mephistophilis? Why does he ask the question? And—to repeat—*how* does he ask it? As you try to decide how, you will, I think, discover much about this important scene that you had not previously noticed.

Verbal tone is the actor's realm. But now suppose that you are the director and that you must thus solve the problems raised, let us say, by the presence of supernatural figures and events (which always, of course, create special difficulties on the stage). How would you handle the blood-writing passage in Scene V? With what, for example, does Faustus cut himself? Suppose you have Mephistophilis hand him a dagger—would such an action here enrich or detract from the action later when Mephistophilis gives him a dagger with which to kill himself? And *how* does Faustus cut his arm? When he says to Mephistophilis, "View here the blood," do you want the audience, too, to be able to see it? Does he let it drip into a container—perhaps a kind of ink bottle—so that he can "set it on" the chafer of coals? Is there really an inscription on his arm? If so, in what ink is it written? Should the audience be able to see it? Why? In what ways does the second blood-writing (Scene XIII) contrast with the first? What does the contrast mean? Can you think of any stage business that would support the meaning?

As director, you must also consider the devils—their appearance and actions. What kind of costume and makeup would you give to Mephistophilis on his first, terrifying entrance? And later to Lucifer? In the Elizabethan theater the devils probably would have come up out of trap doors in the stage, and the angels would have appeared on the upper stage. Would you want to keep some such arrangement? What kind of dance would you direct the devils in Scene V to perform? How would you make them up? Are they ugly or attractive? What should they do with the "crowns and rich apparel"? Would you perhaps want them to dress Faustus as a king while they dance around him? Why? What should be his reaction to it all: what should the actor do? Should the show be the kind that truly "delights" the "mind," as Mephistophilis claims, or should you so manipulate the action as to communicate some ironic disparity between it and the claim?

We could ask similar questions about the "Devil dressed like a woman" (what does she do with her fireworks?), about the Seven Deadly Sins (the success here depends almost entirely upon show, for the speeches are flat), and about the devils that attack first the Old Man and then Faustus (how do these two actions contrast?). And of course every moment of every play—whether the events are natural or supernatural, realistic or fantastic—creates such questions for the director and his actors.

FOR FURTHER THOUGHT

1. When Faustus rejects philosophy, medicine, law, and divinity, he gives what he sees as the limits of each. Put these limits in your own words. In each case, how does he err—if he does? Is it fair to say that the rest of the play then explicates the limits of the way he has chosen? Explain. In what way does the following remark by St. Augustine relate to your discussion: "Christ is the rock of our physics, our ethics, our logic."

2. Faustus does in fact find a way to exceed the limits of human power, yet at the end he regrets and dismisses all his accomplishments. What, then, is the degree and nature of his success and failure?

3. Faustus soon regrets the loss of heaven and fears the pains of hell, but the Devil has ways to combat both feelings: immediate joys to take the place of joys to come, immediate pain to overcome the fear of future pain. What is missing in Faustus that would be impervious to the Devil's attacks? (The soliloquy at the beginning of Scene V is especially helpful here.)

4. What are some of the most important differences between Agamemnon and Faustus? For example: in their attitude toward God (or the gods), in the nature of the challenges they present to God, in their attitudes toward human accomplishment, in their connections with a family and a nation, in their social status and function, and in the nature of their accomplishments. How do such differences affect the meanings of the two plays?

5. What are some of the most important differences between the Greek and the Elizabethan theaters, and how are these differences specifically revealed in the two plays we have read?

Saint Joan

GEORGE BERNARD SHAW

Shaw (1856–1950) was an Irishman who spent most of his long life in England. He was a brilliant and controversial writer not only of plays but of political and economic tracts, of music and drama criticism, and of novels. Some of his better-known plays are *Arms and the Man, Man and Superman, Heartbreak House, Candida, Pygmalion,* and *Major Barbara. Saint Joan* was first performed in New York in 1923.

FROM THE AUTHOR'S PREFACE

JOAN OF ARC, a village girl from the Vosges, was born about 1412; burnt for heresy, witchcraft, and sorcery in 1431; rehabilitated after a fashion in 1456; designated Venerable in 1904; declared Blessed in 1908; and finally canonized in 1920. She is the most notable Warrior Saint in the Christian calendar, and the queerest fish among the eccentric worthies of the Middle Ages. . . . At eighteen Joan's pretensions were beyond those of the proudest Pope or the haughtiest emperor. She claimed to be the ambassador and plenipotentiary of God, and to be, in effect, a member of the Church Triumphant whilst still in the flesh on earth. She patronized her own king, and summoned the English king to repentance and obedience to her commands. She lectured, talked down, and overruled statesmen and prelates. She pooh-poohed the plans of generals, leading their troops to victory on plans of her own. She had an unbounded and quite unconcealed contempt for official opinion, judgment, and authority, and for War Office tactics and strategy. Had she been a sage and monarch in whom the most venerable hierarchy and the most illustrious dynasty converged, her pretensions and proceedings would have been as trying to the official mind as the pretensions of Caesar were to Cassius. As her actual condition was pure upstart, there were only two opinions about her. One was that she was miraculous: the other that she was unbearable.

* * *

The rehabilitation of 1456, corrupt job as it was, really did produce evidence enough to satisfy all reasonable critics that Joan was not a common termagant, not a harlot, not a witch, not a blasphemer, no more an idolater than the Pope himself, and not ill conducted in any sense apart from her soldiering, her wearing of men's clothes, and her audacity, but on the contrary good-humored, an intact virgin, very pious, very temperate (we should call her meal of bread soaked in the common wine which is the drinking water of France ascetic), very kindly, and, though a brave and hardy soldier, unable to endure loose language or licentious conduct. She went to the stake without a stain on her character except the overweening presumption, the superbity as they called it, that led her thither. . . . The mud that was thrown at her has dropped off by this time so completely that there is no need for any modern writer to wash up after it. What is far more difficult to get rid of is the mud that is being thrown at her judges, and the whitewash which disfigures her beyond recognition. When Jingo scurrility had done its worst to her, sectarian scurrility (in this case Protestant scurrility) used her stake to beat the Roman Catholic Church and the Inquisition. The easiest way to make these institutions the villains of a melodrama was to make The Maid its heroine. That melodrama may be dismissed as rubbish. Joan got a far fairer trial from the Church and the Inquisition than any prisoner of her type and in her situation gets nowadays in any official secular court; and the decision was strictly according to law. And she was not a melodramatic heroine: that is, a physically beautiful lovelorn parasite on an equally beautiful hero, but a genius and a saint, about as completely the opposite of a melodramatic heroine as it is possible for a human being to be.

. . .

What then is the modern view of Joan's voices and visions and messages from God? The nineteenth century said that they were delusions, but that as she was a pretty girl, and had been abominably illtreated and finally done to death by a superstitious rabble of medieval priests hounded on by a corrupt political bishop, it must be assumed that she was the innocent dupe of these delusions. The twentieth century finds this explanation too vapidly commonplace, and demands something more mystic. I think the twentieth century is right, because an explanation which amounts to Joan being mentally defective instead of, as she obviously was, mentally excessive, will not wash. I cannot believe, nor, if I could, could I expect all my readers to believe, as Joan did, that three ocularly visible well dressed persons, named respectively Saint Catherine, Saint Margaret, and Saint Michael, came down from heaven and gave her certain instructions with which they were charged by God for her. Not that such a belief would be more improbable or fantastic than some modern beliefs which we all swallow; but there are fashions and family habits in belief, and it happens that, my fashion being Victorian and my family habit Protestant, I find myself unable to attach any such objective validity to the form of Joan's visions.

But that there are forces at work which use individuals for purposes far transcending the purpose of keeping these individuals alive and prosperous and respectable and safe and happy in the middle station in life, which is all any good bourgeois can reasonably require, is established by the fact that men will, in the pursuit of knowledge and of social readjustments for which they will not be a penny the better, and are indeed often many pence the worse, face poverty, infamy, exile, imprisonment, dreadful hardship, and death. Even the selfish pursuit of personal power does not nerve men to the efforts and sacrifices which are eagerly made in pursuit of extensions of our power over nature, though these extensions may not touch the personal life of the seeker at any point. There is no more mystery about this appetite for knowledge and power than about the appetite for food: both are known as facts and as facts only, the difference between them being that the appetite for food is necessary to the life of the hungry man and is therefore a personal appetite, whereas the other is an appetite for evolution, and therefore a superpersonal need.

. . .

It is important to everyone nowadays to understand this, because modern science is making short work of the hallucinations without regard to the vital importance of the things they symbolize. If Joan were reborn today she would be sent, first to a convent school in which she would be mildly taught to connect inspiration and conscience with St Catherine and St Michael exactly as she was in the fifteenth century, and then finished up with a very energetic training in the gospel of Saints Louis Pasteur and Paul Bert, who would tell her (possibly in visions but more probably in pamphlets) not to be a superstitious little fool, and to empty out St Catherine and the rest of the Catholic hagiology as an obsolete iconography of exploded myths. It would be rubbed into her that Galileo was a martyr, and his persecutors incorrigible ignoramuses, and that St Teresa's hormones had gone astray and left her incurably hyperpituitary or hyperadrenal or hysteroid or epileptoid or anything but asteroid. She would have been convinced by precept and experiment that baptism and receiving the body of her Lord were contemptible superstitions, and that vaccination and vivisection were enlightened practices. Behind her new Saints Louis and Paul there would be not only Science purifying Religion and being purified by it, but hypochondria, melancholia, cowardice, stupidity, cruelty, muckraking curiosity, knowledge without wisdom, and everything that the eternal soul in Nature loathes, instead of the virtues of which St Catherine was the figure head. As to the new rites, which would be the saner Joan? the one who carried little children to be baptized of water and the spirit, or the one who sent the police to force their parents to have the most villainous racial poison we know thrust into their veins? the one who told them the story of the angel and Mary, or the one who questioned them as to their experiences of the Edipus complex? the one to whom the consecrated wafer was the very body of the virtue that was her salvation, or the one who looked forward to a precise and convenient regulation of her health and her desires by a nicely calculated diet of thyroid extract, adrenalin, thymin, pituitrin, and insulin, with pick-me-ups of hormone stimulants, the blood being first carefully fortified with antibodies against all possible infections by inoculations of infected bacteria and serum from infected animals, and against old age by surgical extirpation of the reproductive ducts or weekly doses of monkey gland?

It is true that behind all these quackeries there is a certain body of genuine scientific physiology. But was there any the less a certain body of genuine psychology behind St Catherine and the Holy Ghost? And which is the healthier mind? the saintly mind or the monkey gland mind? Does not the present cry of Back to the Middle Ages, which has been incubating ever since the pre-Raphaelite movement began, mean that it is no longer our Academy pictures that are intolerable, but our credulities that have not the excuse of being superstitions, our cruelties that have not the excuse of barbarism, our persecutions that have not the excuse of religious faith, our shameless substitution of successful swindlers and scoundrels and quacks for saints as objects of worship, and our deafness and blindness to the calls and visions of the inexorable power that made us, and will destroy us if we disregard it?

• • •

To see [Joan] in her proper perspective you must understand Christendom and the Catholic Church, the Holy Roman Empire and the Feudal System, as they existed and were understood in the Middle Ages. If you confuse the Middle Ages with the Dark Ages, and are in the habit of ridiculing your aunt for wearing 'medieval clothes,' meaning those in vogue in the eighteen-nineties, and are quite convinced that the world has progressed enormously, both morally and mechanically, since Joan's time, then you will never understand why Joan was burnt, much less feel that you might have voted for burning her yourself if you had been a member of the court that tried her; and until you feel that you know nothing essential about her.

• • •

Joan's trial was not . . . a national political trial. Ecclesiastical courts and the courts of the Inquisition (Joan was tried by a combination of the two) were Courts Christian: that is, international courts;

and she was tried, not as a traitress, but as a heretic, blasphemer, sorceress and idolater. Her alleged offences were not political offences against England, nor against the Burgundian faction in France, but against God and against the common morality of Christendom.

• • •

Her attachment to the Church was very different from the Bishop's, and does not, in fact, bear close examination from his point of view She delighted in the solaces the Church offers to sensitive souls: to her, confession and communion were luxuries beside which the vulgar pleasures of the senses were trash. Her prayers were wonderful conversations with her three saints. Her piety seemed superhuman to the formally dutiful people whose religion was only a task to them. But when the Church was not offering her her favorite luxuries, but calling on her to accept its interpretation of God's will, and to sacrifice her own, she flatly refused, and made it clear that her notion of a Catholic Church was one in which the Pope was Pope Joan. How could the Church tolerate that, when it had just destroyed Hus, and had watched the career of Wycliffe with a growing anger that would have brought him, too, to the stake, had he not died a natural death before the wrath fell on him in his grave? Neither Hus nor Wycliffe was as bluntly defiant as Joan: both were reformers of the Church like Luther; whilst Joan, like Mrs Eddy, was quite prepared to supersede St Peter as the rock on which the Church was built, and, like Mahomet, was always ready with a private relevation from God to settle every question and fit every occasion.

• • •

In the Catholic Church, far more than in law, there is no wrong without a remedy. It does not defer to Joanesque private judgment as such, the supremacy of private judgment for the individual being the quintessence of Protestantism; nevertheless it finds a place for private judgment *in excelsis* by admitting that the highest wisdom may come as a divine revelation to an individual. On sufficient evidence it will declare that individual a saint. Thus, as revelation may come by way of an enlightenment of the private judgment no less than by the words of a celestial personage appearing in a vision, a saint may be defined as a person of heroic virtue whose private judgment is privileged. Many innovating saints, notably Francis and Clare, have been in conflict with the Church during their lives, and have thus raised the question whether they were heretics or saints. Francis might have gone to the stake had he lived longer. It is therefore by no means im-

possible for a person to be excommunicated as a heretic, and on further consideration canonized as a saint. Excommunication by a
provincial ecclesiastical court is not one of the acts for which the
Church claims infallibility.

Still, there was a great wrong done to Joan and to the conscience
of the world by her burning. *Tout comprendre, c'est tout pardonner*,
which is the Devil's sentimentality, cannot excuse it. When we have
admitted that the tribunal was not only honest and legal, but excep-
tionally merciful in respect of sparing Joan the torture which was
customary when she was obdurate as to taking the oath, and that
Cauchon was far more self-disciplined and conscientious both as
priest and lawyer than any English judge ever dreams of being in a
political case in which his party and class prejudices are involved, the
human fact remains that the burning of Joan of Arc was a horror,
and that a historian who would defend it would defend anything.

• • •

And so, if we admit, as we must, that the burning of Joan was a mistake, we must broaden Catholicism sufficiently to include her in its
charter. Our Churches must admit that no official organization of
mortal men whose vocation does not carry with it extraordinary men-
tal powers (and this is all that any Church Militant can in the face of
fact and history pretend to be), can keep pace with the private judgment of persons of genius except when, by a very rare accident, the
genius happens to be Pope, and not even then unless he is an exceed-
ingly overbearing Pope. The Churches must learn humility as well as
teach it. The Apostolic Succession cannot be secured or confined by
the laying on of hands: the tongues of fire have descended on hea-
thens and outcasts too often for that, leaving anointed Churchmen to
scandalize History as worldly rascals. When the Church Militant be-
haves as if it were already the Church Triumphant, it makes these
appalling blunders about Joan and Bruno and Galileo and the rest
which make it so difficult for a Freethinker to join it; and a Church
which has no place for Freethinkers: nay, which does not inculcate
and encourage freethinking with a complete belief that thought,
when really free, must by its own law take the path that leads to The
Church's bosom, not only has no future in modern culture, but obviously has no faith in the valid science of its own tenets, and is guilty
of the heresy that theology and science are two different and opposite
impulses, rivals for human allegiance.

I have before me the letter of a Catholic priest. 'In your play,' he writes, 'I see the dramatic presentation of the conflict of the Regal, sacerdotal, and Prophetical powers, in which Joan was crushed. To me it is not the victory of any one of them over the others that will bring peace and the Reign of the Saints in the Kingdom of God, but their fruitful interaction in a costly but noble state of tension.' The Pope himself could not put it better; nor can I. We must accept the tension, and maintain it nobly without letting ourselves be tempted to relieve it by burning the thread. This is Joan's lesson to The Church; and its formulation by the hand of a priest emboldens me to claim that her canonization was a magnificently Catholic gesture as the canonization of a Protestant saint by the Church of Rome. But its special value and virtue cannot be apparent until it is known and understood as such. If any simple priest for whom this is too hard a saying tells me that it was not so intended, I shall remind him that the Church is in the hands of God, and not, as simple priests imagine, God in the hands of the Church; so if he answers too confidently for God's intentions he may be asked 'Hast thou entered into the springs of the sea? or hast thou walked in the recesses of the deep?' And Joan's own answer is also the answer of old: 'Though He slay me, yet will I trust in Him; *but I will maintain my own ways before Him.*'

When Joan maintained her own ways she claimed, like Job, that there was not only God and the Church to be considered, but the Word made Flesh: that is, the unaveraged individual, representing life possibly at its highest actual human evolution and possibly at its lowest, but never at its merely mathematical average. Now there is no deification of the democratic average in the theory of the Church: it is an avowed hierarchy in which the members are sifted until at the end of the process an individual stands supreme as the Vicar of Christ. But when the process is examined it appears that its successive steps of selection and election are of the superior by the inferior (the cardinal vice of democracy), with the result that great popes are as rare and accidental as great kings, and that it has sometimes been safer for an aspirant to the Chair and the Keys to pass as a moribund dotard than as an energetic saint. At best very few popes have been canonized, or could be without letting down the standard of sanctity set by the self-elected saints.

No other result could have been reasonably expected; for it is not possible that an official organization of the spiritual needs of millions of men and women, mostly poor and ignorant, should compete successfully in the selection of its principals with the direct choice of the

Holy Ghost as it flashes with unerring aim upon the individual. Nor can any College of Cardinals pray effectively that its choice may be inspired. The conscious prayer of the inferior may be that his choice may light on a greater than himself; but the sub-conscious intention of his self-preserving individuality must be to find a trustworthy servant for his own purposes. The saints and prophets, though they may be accidentally in this or that official position or rank, are always really self-selected, like Joan. And since neither Church nor State, by the secular necessities of its constitution, can guarantee even the recognition of such self-chosen missions, there is nothing for us but to make it a point of honor to privilege heresy to the last bearable degree on the simple ground that all evolution in thought and conduct must at first appear as heresy and misconduct. In short, though all society is founded on intolerance, all improvement is founded on tolerance, or the recognition of the fact that the law of evolution is Ibsen's law of change. And as the law of God in any sense of the word which can now command a faith proof against science is a law of evolution, it follows that the law of God is a law of change, and that when the Churches set themselves against change as such, they are setting themselves against the law of God.

• • •

At first sight we are disposed to repeat that Joan should have been excommunicated and then left to go her own way, though she would have protested vehemently against so cruel a deprivation of her spiritual food; for confession, absolution, and the body of her Lord were first necessaries of life to her. Such a spirit as Joan's might have got over that difficulty as the Church of England got over the Bulls of Pope Leo, by making a Church of her own, and affirming it to be the temple of the true and original faith from which her persecutors had strayed. But as such a proceeding was, in the eyes of both Church and State at that time, a spreading of damnation and anarchy, its toleration involved a greater strain on faith in freedom than political and ecclesiastical human nature could bear. It is easy to say that the Church should have waited for the alleged evil results instead of assuming that they would occur, and what they would be. That sounds simple enough; but if a modern Public Health Authority were to leave people entirely to their own devices in the matter of sanitation, saying, 'We have nothing to do with drainage or your views about drainage; but if you catch smallpox or typhus we will prosecute you and have you punished very severely like the authorities in Butler's

Erewhon,' it would either be removed to the County Asylum or reminded that A's neglect of sanitation may kill the child of B two miles off, or start an epidemic in which the most conscientious sanitarians may perish.

We must face the fact that society is founded on intolerance. There are glaring cases of the abuse of intolerance; but they are quite as characteristic of our own age as of the Middle Ages. The typical modern example and contrast is compulsory inoculation replacing what was virtually compulsory baptism. But compulsion to inoculate is objected to as a crudely unscientific and mischievous anti-sanitary quackery, not in the least because we think it wrong to compel people to protect their children from disease. Its opponents would make it a crime, and will probably succeed in doing so; and that will be just as intolerant as making it compulsory. Neither the Pasteurians nor their opponents the Sanitarians would leave parents free to bring up their children naked, though that course also has some plausible advocates. We may prate of toleration as we will; but society must always draw a line somewhere between allowable conduct and insanity or crime, in spite of the risk of mistaking sages for lunatics and saviors for blasphemers. We must persecute, even to the death; and all we can do to mitigate the danger of persecution is, first, to be very careful what we persecute, and second, to bear in mind that unless there is a large liberty to shock conventional people, and a well informed sense of the value of originality, individuality, and eccentricity, the result will be apparent stagnation covering a repression of evolutionary forces which will eventually explode with extravagant and probably destructive violence.

• • •

With all this in mind, consider the career of Joan. She was a village girl, in authority over sheep and pigs, dogs and chickens, and to some extent over her father's hired laborers when he hired any, but over no one else on earth. Outside the farm she had no authority, no prestige, no claim to the smallest deference. Yet she ordered everybody about, from her uncle to the king, the archbishop, and the military General Staff. Her uncle obeyed her like a sheep, and took her to the castle of the local commander, who, on being ordered about, tried to assert himself, but soon collapsed and obeyed. And so on up to the king, as we have seen. This would have been unbearably irritating even if her orders had been offered as rational solutions of the desperate difficulties in which her social superiors found themselves just then. But they were not so offered. Nor were they offered as the expression of Joan's arbitrary will. It was never 'I say so,' but always 'God says so.'

Leaders who take that line have no trouble with some people, and no end of trouble with others. They need never fear a lukewarm reception. Either they are messengers of God, or they are blasphemous impostors. In the Middle Ages the general belief in witchcraft greatly intensified this contrast, because when an apparent miracle happened (as in the case of the wind changing at Orleans) it proved the divine mission to the credulous, and proved a contract with the devil to the sceptical. All through, Joan had to depend on those who accepted her as an incarnate angel against those who added to an intense resentment of her presumption a bigoted abhorrence of her as a witch. To this abhorrence we must add the extreme irritation of those who did not believe in the voices, and regarded her as a liar and impostor. It is hard to conceive anything more infuriating to a statesman or a military commander, or to a court favorite, than to be overruled at every turn, or to be robbed of the ear of the reigning sovereign, by an impudent young upstart practising on the credulity of the populace and the vanity and silliness of an immature prince by exploiting a few of those lucky coincidences which pass as miracles with uncritical people. Not only were the envy, snobbery, and competitive ambition of the baser natures exacerbated by Joan's success, but among the friendly ones that were clever enough to be critical a quite reasonable scepticism and mistrust of her ability, founded on a fair observation of her obvious ignorance and temerity, were at work against her. And as she met all remonstrances and all criticisms, not with arguments or persuasion, but with a flat appeal to the authority of God and a claim to be in God's special confidence, she must have seemed, to all who were not infatuated by her, so insufferable that nothing but an unbroken chain of overwhelming successes in the military and political field could have saved her from the wrath that finally destroyed her.

· · ·

But even in its simplicity, the faith demanded by Joan is one which the anti-metaphysical temper of nineteenth century civilization, which remains powerful in England and America, and is tyrannical in France, contemptuously refuses her. We do not, like her contemporaries, rush to the opposite extreme in a recoil from her as from a witch self-sold to the devil, because we do not believe in the devil nor in the possibility of commercial contracts with him. Our credulity, though enormous, is not boundless; and our stock of it is quite used up by our mediums, clairvoyants, hand readers, slate writers, Christian Scientists, psycho-analysts, electronic vibration diviners, therapeutists of all schools registered and unregistered, astrologers, astronomers who tell us that the sun is nearly a hundred million miles away and that Betelgeuse is ten times as big as the whole universe, physicists who balance Betelgeuse by describing the incredible smallness of the atom, and a host of other marvel mongers whose credulity would have dissolved the Middle Ages in a roar of sceptical merriment. In the Middle Ages people believed that the earth was flat, for which they had at least the evidence of their senses: we believe it to be round, not because as many as one per cent of us could give the physical reasons for so quaint a belief, but because modern science has convinced us that nothing that is obvious is true, and that everything that is magical, improbable, extraordinary, gigantic, microscopic, heartless, or outrageous is scientific.

I must not, by the way, be taken as implying that the earth is flat, or that all or any of our amazing credulities are delusions or impostures. I am only defending my own age against the charge of being less imaginative than the Middle Ages. I affirm that the nineteenth century, and still more the twentieth, can knock the fifteenth into a cocked hat in point of susceptibility to marvels and saints and prophets and magicians and monsters and fairy tales of all kinds. The proportion of marvel to immediately credible statement in the latest edition of the Encyclopædia Britannica is enormously greater than in the Bible. The medieval doctors of divinity who did not pretend to settle how many angels could dance on the point of a needle cut a very poor figure as far as romantic credulity is concerned beside the modern physicists who have settled to the billionth of a millimetre every movement and position in the dance of the electrons. Not for worlds would I question the precise accuracy of these calculations or the existence of electrons (whatever they may be). The fate of Joan is a warning to me against such heresy. But why the men who believe in electrons should regard themselves as less credulous than the men who believed in angels is not apparent to me. If they refuse to believe, with the Rouen assessors of 1431, that Joan was a witch, it is not because that explanation is too marvellous, but because it is not marvellous enough.

Saint Joan

SCENE I

A fine spring morning on the river Meuse, between Lorraine and Champagne, in the year 1429 A.D., in the castle of Vaucouleurs.

CAPTAIN ROBERT DE BAUDRICOURT, *a military squire, handsome and physically energetic, but with no will of his own, is disguising that defect in his usual fashion by storming terribly at his* STEWARD, *a trodden worm, scanty of flesh, scanty of hair, who might be any age from 18 to 55, being the sort of man whom age cannot wither because he has never bloomed.*

The two are in a sunny stone chamber on the first floor of the castle. At a plain strong oak table, seated in chair to match, the CAPTAIN *presents his left profile. The* STEWARD *stands facing him at the other side of the table, if so deprecatory a stance as his can be called standing. The mullioned thirteenth-century window is open behind him. Near it in the corner is a turret with a narrow arched doorway leading to a winding stair which descends to the courtyard. There is a stout four-legged stool under the table, and a wooden chest under the window.*

ROBERT. No eggs! No eggs!! Thousand thunders, man, what do you mean by no eggs?

STEWARD. Sir: it is not my fault. It is the act of God.

ROBERT. Blasphemy. You tell me there are no eggs; and you blame your Maker for it.

STEWARD. Sir: what can I do? I cannot lay eggs.

ROBERT. [*Sarcastic.*] Ha! You jest about it.

STEWARD. No, sir, God knows. We all have to go without eggs just as you have, sir. The hens will not lay.

ROBERT. Indeed! [*Rising.*] Now listen to me, you.

STEWARD. [*Humbly.*] Yes, sir.

ROBERT. What am I?

STEWARD. What are you, sir?

ROBERT. [*Coming at him.*] Yes: what am I? Am I Robert, squire of Baudricourt and captain of this castle of Vaucouleurs; or am I a cowboy?

STEWARD. Oh, sir, you know you are a greater man here than the king himself.

ROBERT. Precisely. And now, do you know what you are?

STEWARD. I am nobody, sir, except that I have the honor to be your steward.

ROBERT. [*Driving him to the wall, adjective by adjective.*] You have not only the honor of being my steward, but the privilege of being the worst, most incompetent, drivelling snivelling jibbering jabbering idiot of a steward in France. [*He strides back to the table.*]

STEWARD. [*Cowering on the chest.*] Yes, sir: to a great man like you I must seem like that.

ROBERT. [*Turning.*] My fault, I suppose. Eh?

STEWARD. [*Coming to him deprecatingly.*] Oh, sir: you always give my most innocent words such a turn!

ROBERT. I will give your neck a turn if you dare tell me when I ask you how many eggs there are that you cannot lay any.

STEWARD. [*Protesting.*] Oh sir, oh sir—

ROBERT. No: not oh sir, oh sir, but no sir, no sir. My three Barbary hens and the black are the best layers in Champagne. And you come and tell me that there are no eggs! Who stole them? Tell me that, before I kick you out through the castle gate for a liar and a seller of my goods to thieves. The milk was short yesterday, too: do not forget that.

STEWARD. [*Desperate.*] I know, sir. I know only too well. There is no milk: there are no eggs: tomorrow there will be nothing.

ROBERT. Nothing! You will steal the lot: eh?

STEWARD. No, sir: nobody will steal anything. But there is a spell on us: we are bewitched.

ROBERT. That story is not good enough for me. Robert de Baudricourt burns witches and hangs thieves. Go. Bring me four dozen eggs and two gallons of milk here in this room before noon, or Heaven have mercy on your bones! I will teach you to make a fool of me. [*He resumes his seat with an air of finality.*]

STEWARD. Sir: I tell you there are no eggs. There will be none—not if you were to kill me for it—as long as The Maid is at the door.

ROBERT. The Maid! What maid? What are you talking about?

STEWARD. The girl from Lorraine, sir. From Domrémy.

ROBERT. [*Rising in fearful wrath.*] Thirty thousand thunders! Fifty thousand devils! Do you mean to say that that girl, who had the impudence to ask to see me two days ago, and whom I told you to send back to her father with my orders that he was to give her a good hiding, is here still?

STEWARD. I have told her to go, sir. She wont.

ROBERT. I did not tell you to tell her to go: I told you to throw her out. You have fifty men-at-arms and a dozen lumps of able-bodied servants to carry out my orders. Are they afraid of her?

STEWARD. She is so positive, sir.

ROBERT. [*Seizing him by the scruff of the neck.*] Positive! Now see here. I am going to throw you downstairs.

STEWARD. No, sir. Please.

ROBERT. Well, stop me by being positive. It's quite easy: any slut of a girl can do it.

STEWARD. [*Hanging limp in his hands.*] Sir, sir: you cannot get rid of her by throwing me out. [ROBERT *has to let him drop. He squats on his knees on the floor, contemplating his master resignedly.*] You see, sir, you are much more positive than I am. But so is she.

ROBERT. I am stronger than you are, you fool.

STEWARD. No, sir: it isnt that: it's your strong character, sir. She is weaker than we are: she is only a slip of a girl; but we cannot make her go.

ROBERT. You parcel of curs: you are afraid of her.

STEWARD. [*Rising cautiously.*] No, sir: we are afraid of you; but she puts courage into us. She really doesnt seem to be afraid of anything. Perhaps you could frighten her, sir.

ROBERT. [*Grimly.*] Perhaps. Where is she now?

STEWARD. Down in the courtyard, sir, talking to the soldiers as usual. She is always talking to the soldiers except when she is praying.

ROBERT. Praying! Ha! You believe she prays, you idiot. I know the sort of girl that is always talking to soldiers. She shall talk to me a bit. [*He goes to the window and shouts fiercely through it.*] Hallo, you there!

A GIRL'S VOICE. [*Bright, strong and rough.*] Is it me, sir?

ROBERT. Yes, you.

THE VOICE. Be you captain?

ROBERT. Yes, damn your impudence, I be captain. Come up here. [*To the soldiers in the yard.*] Shew her the way, you. And shove her along quick. [*He leaves the window, and returns to his place at the table, where he sits magisterially.*]

STEWARD. [*Whispering.*] She wants to go and be a soldier herself. She wants you to give her soldier's clothes. Armor, sir! And a sword! Actually! [*He steals behind* ROBERT.]

JOAN *appears in the turret doorway. She is an ablebodied country girl of 17 or 18, respectably dressed in red, with an uncommon face; eyes very wide apart and bulging as they often do in very imaginative people, a long well-shaped nose with wide nostrils, a short upper lip, resolute but full-lipped mouth, and handsome fighting chin. She comes eagerly to the table, delighted at having penetrated to* BAUDRICOURT'S *presence at last, and full of hope as to the results. His scowl does not check or frighten her in the least. Her voice is normally a hearty coaxing voice, very confident, very appealing, very hard to resist.*

JOAN. [*Bobbing a curtsey.*] Good morning, captain squire. Captain: you are to give me a horse and armor and some soldiers, and send me to the Dauphin. Those are your orders from my Lord.

ROBERT. [*Outraged.*] Orders from your lord! And who the devil may your lord be? Go back to him, and tell him that I am neither duke nor peer at his orders: I am squire of Baudricourt; and I take no orders except from the king.

JOAN. [*Reassuringly.*] Yes, squire: that is all right. My Lord is the King of Heaven.

ROBERT. Why, the girl's mad. [*To the* STEWARD.] Why didnt you tell me so, you blockhead?

STEWARD. Sir: do not anger her: give her what she wants.

JOAN. [*Impatient, but friendly.*] They all say I am mad until I talk to them, squire. But you see that it is the will of God that you are to do what He has put into my mind.

ROBERT. It is the will of God that I shall send you back to your father with orders to put you under lock and key and thrash the madness out of you. What have you to say to that?

JOAN. You think you will, squire; but you will find it all coming quite different. You said you would not see me; but here I am.

STEWARD. [*Appealing.*] Yes, sir. You see, sir.

ROBERT. Hold your tongue, you.

STEWARD. [*Abjectly.*] Yes, sir.

ROBERT. [*To* JOAN, *with a sour loss of confidence.*] So you are presuming on my seeing you, are you?

JOAN. [*Sweetly.*] Yes, squire.

ROBERT. [*Feeling that he has lost ground, brings down his two fists squarely on the table, and inflates his chest imposingly to cure the unwelcome and only too familiar sensation.*] Now listen to me. I am going to assert myself.

JOAN. [*Busily.*] Please do, squire. The horse will cost sixteen francs. It is a good deal of money: but I can save it on the armor. I can find a soldier's armor that will fit me well enough: I am very hardy; and I do not need beautiful armor made to my measure like you wear. I shall not want many soldiers: the Dauphin will give me all I need to raise the siege of Orleans.

ROBERT. [*Flabbergasted.*] To raise the siege of Orleans!

JOAN. [*Simply.*] Yes, squire: that is what God is sending me to do. Three men will be enough for you to send with me if they are good men and gentle to me. They have promised to come with me. Polly and Jack and—

ROBERT. Polly! You impudent baggage, do you dare call squire Bertrand de Poulengey Polly to my face?

JOAN. His friends call him so, squire: I did not know he had any other name. Jack—

ROBERT. That is Monsieur John of Metz, I suppose?

JOAN. Yes, Squire. Jack will come willingly: he is a very kind gentleman, and gives me money to give to the poor. I think John Godsave will come, and Dick the Archer, and their servants John of Hone-

court and Julian. There will be no trouble for you, squire: I have
arranged it all: you have only to give the order.

ROBERT. [*Contemplating her in a stupor of amazement.*] Well, I am
damned!

JOAN. [*With unruffled sweetness.*] No, squire: God is very merciful;
and the blessed saints Catherine and Margaret, who speak to me
every day [*he gapes*], will intercede for you. You will go to paradise;
and your name will be remembered for ever as my first helper.

ROBERT. [*To the* STEWARD, *still much bothered, but changing his tone
as he pursues a new clue.*] Is this true about Monsieur de Poulengey?

STEWARD. [*Eagerly.*] Yes, sir, and about Monsieur de Metz too. They
both want to go with her.

ROBERT. [*Thoughtful.*] Mf! [*He goes to the window, and shouts into
the courtyard.*] Hallo! You there: send Monsieur de Poulengey to
me, will you? [*He turns to Joan.*] Get out; and wait in the yard.

JOAN. [*Smiling brightly at him.*] Right, squire. [*She goes out.*]

ROBERT. [*To the* STEWARD.] Go with her, you, you dithering imbecile.
Stay within call; and keep your eye on her. I shall have her up here
again.

STEWARD. Do so in God's name, sir. Think of those hens, the best
layers in Champagne; and—

ROBERT. Think of my boot; and take your backside out of reach of it.

The STEWARD *retreats hastily and finds himself confronted in the
doorway by* BERTRAND DE POULENGEY, *a lymphatic French gentle-
man-at-arms, aged 36 or thereabout, employed in the department
of the provost-marshal, dreamily absent-minded, seldom speaking
unless spoken to, and then slow and obstinate in reply; altogether
in contrast to the self-assertive, loud-mouthed, superficially energetic, fundamentally will-less* ROBERT. *The* STEWARD *makes way for
him, and vanishes.*

POULENGEY *salutes, and stands awaiting orders.*

ROBERT. [*Genially.*] It isnt service, Polly. A friendly talk. Sit down.
[*He hooks the stool from under the table with his instep.*]

POULENGEY, *relaxing, comes into the room: places the stool between the table and the window: and sits down ruminatively.* ROB-
ERT, *half sitting on the end of the table, begins the friendly talk.*

ROBERT. Now listen to me, Polly. I must talk to you like a father.

POULENGEY *looks up at him gravely for a moment, but says nothing.*

ROBERT. It's about this girl you are interested in. Now, I have seen
her. I have talked to her. First, she's mad. That doesnt matter. Second, she's not a farm wench. She's a bourgeoise. That matters a
good deal. I know her class exactly. Her father came here last year
to represent his village in a lawsuit: he is one of their notables. A

farmer. Not a gentleman farmer: he makes money by it, and lives by it. Still, not a laborer. Not a mechanic. He might have a cousin a lawyer, or in the Church. People of this sort may be of no account socially; but they can give a lot of bother to the authorities. That is to say, to me. Now no doubt it seems to you a very simple thing to take this girl away, humbugging her into the belief that you are taking her to the Dauphin. But if you get her into trouble, you may get me into no end of a mess, as I am her father's lord, and responsible for her protection. So friends or no friends, Polly, hands off her.

POULENGEY. [*With deliberate impressiveness.*] I should as soon think of the Blessed Virgin herself in that way, as of this girl.

ROBERT. [*Coming off the table.*] But she says you and Jack and Dick have offered to go with her. What for? You are not going to tell me that you take her crazy notion of going to the Dauphin seriously, are you?

POULENGEY. [*Slowly.*] There is something about her. They are pretty foulmouthed and foulminded down there in the guardroom, some of them. But there hasnt been a word that has anything to do with her being a woman. They have stopped swearing before her. There is something. Something. It may be worth trying.

ROBERT. Oh, come, Polly! pull yourself together. Commonsense was never your strong point; but this is a little too much. [*He retreats disgustedly.*]

POULENGEY. [*Unmoved.*] What is the good of commonsense? If we had any commonsense we should join the Duke of Burgundy and the English king. They hold half the country, right down to the Loire. They have Paris. They have this castle: you know very well that we had to surrender it to the Duke of Bedford, and that you are only holding it on parole. The Dauphin is in Chinon, like a rat in a corner, except that he wont fight. We dont even know that he is the Dauphin: his mother says he isnt; and she ought to know. Think of that! the queen denying the legitimacy of her own son!

ROBERT. Well, she married her daughter to the English king. Can you blame the woman?

POULENGEY. I blame nobody. But thanks to her, the Dauphin is down and out; and we may as well face it. The English will take Orleans: the Bastard will not be able to stop them.

ROBERT. He beat the English the year before last at Montargis. I was with him.

POULENGEY. No matter: his men are cowed now; and he cant work miracles. And I tell you that nothing can save our side now but a miracle.

ROBERT. Miracles are all right, Polly. The only difficulty about them is that they dont happen nowadays.

POULENGEY. I used to think so. I am not so sure now. [*Rising, and moving ruminatively towards the window.*] At all events this is not a time to leave any stone unturned. There is something about the girl.

ROBERT. Oh! You think the girl can work miracles, do you?

POULENGEY. I think the girl herself is a bit of a miracle. Anyhow, she is the last card left in our hand. Better play her than throw up the game. [*He wanders to the turret.*]

ROBERT. [*Wavering.*] You really think that?

POULENGEY. [*Turning.*] Is there anything else left for us to think?

ROBERT. [*Going to him.*] Look here, Polly. If you were in my place would you let a girl like that do you out of sixteen francs for a horse?

POULENGEY. I will pay for the horse.

ROBERT. You will!

POULENGEY. Yes: I will back my opinion.

ROBERT. You will really gamble on a forlorn hope to the tune of sixteen francs?

POULENGEY. It is not a gamble.

ROBERT. What else is it?

POULENGEY. It is a certainty. Her words and her ardent faith in God have put fire into me.

ROBERT. [*Giving him up.*] Whew! You are as mad as she is.

POULENGEY. [*Obstinately.*] We want a few mad people now. See where the sane ones have landed us!

ROBERT. [*His irresoluteness now openly swamping his affected decisiveness.*] I shall feel like a precious fool. Still, if you feel sure—?

POULENGEY. I feel sure enough to take her to Chinon—unless you stop me.

ROBERT. This is not fair. You are putting the responsibility on me.

POULENGEY. It is on you whichever way you decide.

ROBERT. Yes: thats just it. Which way am I to decide? You dont see how awkward this is for me. [*Snatching at a dilatory step with an unconscious hope that* JOAN *will make up his mind for him.*] Do you think I ought to have another talk to her?

POULENGEY. [*Rising.*] Yes. [*He goes to the window and calls.*] Joan!

JOAN'S VOICE. Will he let us go, Polly?

POULENGEY. Come up. Come in. [*Turning to* ROBERT.] Shall I leave you with her?

ROBERT. No: stay here; and back me up.

POULENGEY *sits down on the chest.* ROBERT *goes back to his magisterial chair, but remains standing to inflate himself more imposingly.* JOAN *comes in, full of good news.*

JOAN. Jack will go halves for the horse.

ROBERT. Well!! [*He sits, deflated.*]

POULENGEY. [*Gravely.*] Sit down, Joan.

JOAN. [*Checked a little, and looking to* ROBERT.] May I?

ROBERT. Do what you are told.

> JOAN *curtsies and sits down on the stool between them.* ROBERT
> *outfaces his perplexity with his most peremptory air.*

ROBERT. What is your name?

JOAN. [*Chattily.*] They always call me Jenny in Lorraine. Here in France I am Joan. The soldiers call me The Maid.

ROBERT. What is your surname?

JOAN. Surname? What is that? My father sometimes calls himself d'Arc; but I know nothing about it. You met my father. He—

ROBERT. Yes, yes; I remember. You come from Domrémy in Lorraine, I think.

JOAN. Yes; but what does it matter? we all speak French.

ROBERT. Dont ask questions: answer them. How old are you?

JOAN. Seventeen: so they tell me. It might be nineteen. I dont remember.

ROBERT. What did you mean when you said that St Catherine and St Margaret talked to you every day?

JOAN. They do.

ROBERT. What are they like?

JOAN. [*Suddenly obstinate.*] I will tell you nothing about that: they have not given me leave.

ROBERT. But you actually see them; and they talk to you just as I am talking to you?

JOAN. No: it is quite different. I cannot tell you: you must not talk to me about my voices.

ROBERT. How do you mean? voices?

JOAN. I hear voices telling me what to do. They come from God.

ROBERT. They come from your imagination.

JOAN. Of course. That is how the messages of God come to us.

POULENGEY. Checkmate.

ROBERT. No fear! [*To* JOAN.] So God says you are to raise the siege of Orleans?

JOAN. And to crown the Dauphin in Rheims Cathedral.

ROBERT. [*Gasping.*] Crown the D—! Gosh!

JOAN. And to make the English leave France.

ROBERT. [*Sarcastic.*] Anything else?

JOAN. [*Charming.*] Not just at present, thank you, squire.

ROBERT. I suppose you think raising a siege is as easy as chasing a cow out of a meadow. You think soldiering is anybody's job?

JOAN. I do not think it can be very difficult if God is on your side, and you are willing to put your life in His hand. But many soldiers are very simple.

ROBERT. [*Grimly.*] Simple! Did you ever see English soldiers fighting?

JOAN. They are only men. God made them just like us; but He gave them their own country and their own language; and it is not His will that they should come into our country and try to speak our language.

ROBERT. Who has been putting such nonsense into your head? Dont you know that soldiers are subject to their feudal lord, and that it is nothing to them or to you whether he is the duke of Burgundy or the king of England or the king of France? What has their language to do with it?

JOAN. I do not understand that a bit. We are all subject to the King of Heaven; and He gave us our countries and our languages, and meant us to keep to them. If it were not so it would be murder to kill an Englishman in battle; and you, squire, would be in great danger of hell fire. You must not think about your duty to your feudal lord, but about your duty to God.

POULENGEY. It's no use, Robert: she can choke you like that every time.

ROBERT. Can she, by Saint Dennis! We shall see. [*To* JOAN.] We are not talking about God: we are talking about practical affairs. I ask you again, girl, have you ever seen English soldiers fighting? Have you ever seen them plundering, burning, turning the countryside into a desert? Have you heard no tales of their Black Prince who was blacker than the devil himself, or of the English king's father?

JOAN. You must not be afraid, Robert—

ROBERT. Damn you, I am not afraid. And who gave you leave to call me Robert?

JOAN. You were called so in church in the name of our Lord. All the other names are your father's or your brother's or anybody's.

ROBERT. Tcha!

JOAN. Listen to me, squire. At Domrémy we had to fly to the next village to escape from the English soldiers. Three of them were left behind, wounded. I came to know these three poor goddams quite well. They had not half my strength.

ROBERT. Do you know why they are called goddams?

JOAN. No. Everyone calls them goddams.

ROBERT. It is because they are always calling on their God to condemn their souls to perdition. That is what goddam means in their language. How do you like it?

JOAN. God will be merciful to them; and they will act like His good children when they go back to the country He made for them, and made them for. I have heard the tales of the Black Prince. The moment he touched the soil of our country the devil entered into him, and made him a black fiend. But at home, in the place made for him by God, he was good. It is always so. If I went into England against the will of God to conquer England, and tried to live there and speak its language, the devil would enter into me; and when I was old I should shudder to remember the wickedness I did.

ROBERT. Perhaps. But the more devil you were the better you might fight. That is why the goddams will take Orleans. And you cannot stop them, nor ten thousand like you.

JOAN. One thousand like me can stop them. Ten like me can stop them with God on our side. [*She rises impetuously, and goes at him, unable to sit quiet any longer.*] You do not understand, squire. Our soldiers are always beaten because they are fighting only to save their skins; and the shortest way to save your skin is to run away. Our knights are thinking only of the money they will make in ransoms: it is not kill or be killed with them, but pay or be paid. But I will teach them all to fight that the will of God may be done in France; and then they will drive the poor goddams before them like sheep. You and Polly will live to see the day when there will not be an English soldier on the soil of France; and there will be but one king there: not the feudal English king, but God's French one.

ROBERT. [*To* POULENGEY.] This may be all rot, Polly; but the troops might swallow it, though nothing that we can say seems able to put any fight into them. Even the Dauphin might swallow it. And if she can put fight into him, she can put it into anybody.

POULENGEY. I can see no harm in trying. Can you? And there is something about the girl—

ROBERT. [*Turning to* JOAN.] Now listen you to me; and [*desperately*] dont cut in before I have time to think.

JOAN. [*Plumping down on the stool again, like an obedient schoolgirl.*] Yes, Squire.

ROBERT. Your orders are, that you are to go to Chinon under the escort of this gentleman and three of his friends.

JOAN. [*Radiant, clasping her hands.*] Oh, squire! Your head is all circled with light, like a saint's.

POULENGEY. How is she to get into the royal presence?

ROBERT. [*Who has looked up for his halo rather apprehensively.*] I dont know: how did she get into my presence? If the Dauphin can keep her out he is a better man than I take him for. [*Rising.*] I will send her to Chinon; and she can say I sent her. Then let come what may: I can do no more.

JOAN. And the dress? I may have a soldier's dress, maynt I, squire?

ROBERT. Have what you please. I wash my hands of it.

JOAN. [*Wildly excited by her success.*] Come, Polly. [*She dashes out.*]

ROBERT. [*Shaking* POULENGEY's *hand.*] Goodbye, old man, I am taking a big chance. Few other men would have done it. But as you say, there is something about her.

POULENGEY. Yes: there is something about her. Goodbye. [*He goes out.*]

 ROBERT, *still very doubtful whether he has not been made a fool of by a crazy female, and a social inferior to boot, scratches his head and slowly comes back from the door.*

The STEWARD *runs in with a basket.*

STEWARD. Sir, sir—

ROBERT. What now?

STEWARD. The hens are laying like mad, sir. Five dozen eggs!

ROBERT. [*Stiffens convulsively: crosses himself: and forms with his pale lips the words.*] Christ in heaven! [*Aloud but breathless.*] She did come from God.

SCENE II

Chinon, in Touraine. An end of the throne room in the castle, curtained off to make an antechamber. The ARCHBISHOP OF RHEIMS, *close on 50, a full-fed prelate with nothing of the ecclesiastic about him except his imposing bearing, and the* LORD CHAMBERLAIN, MONSEIGNEUR DE LA TRÉMOUILLE, *a monstrous arrogant wineskin of a man, are waiting for the* DAUPHIN. *There is a door in the wall to the right of the two men. It is late in the afternoon on the 8th of March, 1429. The* ARCHBISHOP *stands with dignity whilst the* CHAMBERLAIN, *on his left, fumes about in the worst of tempers.*

LA TRÉMOUILLE. What the devil does the Dauphin mean by keeping us waiting like this? I dont know how you have the patience to stand there like a stone idol.

THE ARCHBISHOP. You see, I am an archbishop; and an archbishop is a sort of idol. At any rate he has to learn to keep still and suffer fools patiently. Besides, my dear Lord Chamberlain, it is the Dauphin's royal privilege to keep you waiting, is it not?

LA TRÉMOUILLE. Dauphin be damned! saving your reverence. Do you know how much money he owes me?

THE ARCHBISHOP. Much more than he owes me, I have no doubt, because you are a much richer man. But I take it he owes you all you could afford to lend him. That is what he owes me.

LA TRÉMOUILLE. Twenty-seven thousand: that was his last haul. A cool twenty-seven thousand!

THE ARCHBISHOP. What becomes of it all? He never has a suit of clothes that I would throw to a curate.

LA TRÉMOUILLE. He dines on a chicken or a scrap of mutton. He borrows my last penny; and there is nothing to shew for it. [*A* PAGE *appears in the doorway.*] At last!

THE PAGE. No, my lord: it is not His Majesty. Monsieur de Rais is approaching.

LA TRÉMOUILLE. Young Bluebeard! Why announce him?

THE PAGE. Captain La Hire is with him. Something has happened, I think.

GILLES DE RAIS, *a young man of 25, very smart and self-possessed, and sporting the extravagance of a little curled beard dyed blue at a clean-shaven court, comes in. He is determined to make himself agreeable, but lacks natural joyousness, and is not really pleasant. In fact when he defies the Church some eleven years later he is accused of trying to extract pleasure from horrible cruelties, and hanged. So far, however, there is no shadow of the gallows on him. He advances gaily to the* ARCHBISHOP. *The* PAGE *withdraws.*

BLUEBEARD. Your faithful lamb, Archbishop. Good day, my lord. Do you know what has happened to La Hire?

LA TRÉMOUILLE. He has sworn himself into a fit, perhaps.

BLUEBEARD. No: just the opposite. Foul Mouthed Frank, the only man in Tourain who could beat him at swearing, was told by a soldier that he shouldnt use such language when he was at the point of death.

THE ARCHBISHOP. Nor at any other point. But was Foul Mouthed Frank on the point of death?

BLUEBEARD. Yes: he has just fallen into a well and been drowned. La Hire is frightened out of his wits.

CAPTAIN LA HIRE *comes in: a war dog with no court manners and pronounced camp ones.*

BLUEBEARD. I have just been telling the Chamberlain and the Archbishop. The Archbishop says you are a lost man.

LA HIRE. [*Striding past* BLUEBEARD, *and planting himself between the* ARCHBISHOP *and* LA TRÉMOUILLE.] This is nothing to joke about. It is worse than we thought. It was not a soldier, but an angel dressed as a soldier.

THE ARCHBISHOP.

THE CHAMBERLAIN. } [*Exclaiming all together.*] An angel!

BLUEBEARD.

LA HIRE. Yes, an angel. She has made her way from Champagne with half a dozen men through the thick of everything: Burgundians, Goddams, deserters, robbers, and Lord knows who; and they never met a soul except the country folk. I know one of them: de Poulengey. He says she's an angel. If ever I utter an oath again may my soul be blasted to eternal damnation!

THE ARCHBISHOP. A very pious beginning, Captain.

BLUEBEARD *and* LA TRÉMOUILLE *laugh at him. The* PAGE *returns.*

THE PAGE. His Majesty.

They stand perfunctorily at court attention. The DAUPHIN, *aged 26, really* KING CHARLES THE SEVENTH *since the death of his father, but as yet uncrowned, comes in through the curtains with a paper in his hands. He is a poor creature physically; and the current fashion of shaving closely, and hiding every scrap of hair under the*

*headcovering or headdress, both by women and men, makes the
worst of his appearance. He has little narrow eyes, near together, a
long pendulous nose that droops over his thick short upper lip, and
the expression of a young dog accustomed to be kicked, yet incorrigible and irrepressible. But he is neither vulgar nor stupid; and he
has a cheeky humor which enables him to hold his own in conversation. Just at present he is excited, like a child with a new toy. He
comes to the* ARCHBISHOP's *left hand.* BLUEBEARD *and* LA HIRE *re-
tire towards the curtains.*

CHARLES. Oh, Archbishop, do you know what Robert de Baudricourt
is sending me from Vaucouleurs?

THE ARCHBISHOP. [*Contemptuously.*] I am not interested in the new-
est toys.

CHARLES. [*Indignantly.*] It isnt a toy. [*Sulkily.*] However, I can get on
very well without your interest.

THE ARCHBISHOP. Your Highness is taking offence very unnecessarily.

CHARLES. Thank you. You are always ready with a lecture, arnt you?

LA TRÉMOUILLE. [*Roughly.*] Enough grumbling. What have you got
there?

CHARLES. What is that to you?

LA TRÉMOUILLE. It is my business to know what is passing between
you and the garrison at Vaucouleurs. [*He snatches the paper from
the* DAUPHIN's *hand, and begins reading it with some difficulty, following the words with his finger and spelling them out syllable by
syllable.*]

CHARLES. [*Mortified.*] You all think you can treat me as you please because I owe you money, and because I am no good at fighting. But
I have the blood royal in my veins.

THE ARCHBISHOP. Even that has been questioned, your Highness. One
hardly recognizes in you the grandson of Charles the Wise.

CHARLES. I want to hear no more of my grandfather. He was so wise
that he used up the whole family stock of wisdom for five genera-
tions, and left me the poor fool I am, bullied and insulted by all of
you.

THE ARCHBISHOP. Control yourself, sir. These outbursts of petulance
are not seemly.

CHARLES. Another lecture! Thank you. What a pity it is that though
you are an archbishop saints and angels dont come to see you!

THE ARCHBISHOP. What do you mean?

CHARLES. Aha! Ask that bully there [*pointing to* LA TRÉMOUILLE].

LA TRÉMOUILLE. [*Furious.*] Hold your tongue. Do you hear?

CHARLES. Oh, I hear. You neednt shout. The whole castle can hear.
Why dont you go and shout at the English, and beat them for me?

LA TRÉMOUILLE. [*Raising his fist.*] You young—

CHARLES. [*Running behind the* ARCHBISHOP.] Dont you raise your hand to me. It's high treason.

LA HIRE. Steady, Duke! Steady!

THE ARCHBISHOP. [*Resolutely.*] Come, come! this will not do. My Lord Chamberlain: please! please! we must keep some sort of order. [*To the* DAUPHIN.] And you, sir: if you cannot rule your kingdom, at least try to rule yourself.

CHARLES. Another lecture! Thank you.

LA TRÉMOUILLE. [*Handing over the paper to the* ARCHBISHOP.] Here: read the accursed thing for me. He has sent the blood boiling into my head: I cant distinguish the letters.

CHARLES. [*Coming back and peering round* LA TRÉMOUILLE's *left shoulder.*] I will read it for you if you like. I can read, you know.

LA TRÉMOUILLE. [*With intense contempt, not at all stung by the taunt.*] Yes: reading is about all you are fit for. Can you make it out, Archbishop?

THE ARCHBISHOP. I should have expected more commonsense from De Baudricourt. He is sending some cracked country lass here—

CHARLES. [*Interrupting.*] No: he is sending a saint: an angel. And she is coming to me: to me, the king, and not to you, Archbishop, holy as you are. She knows the blood royal if you dont. [*He struts up to the curtains between* BLUEBEARD *and* LA HIRE.]

THE ARCHBISHOP. You cannot be allowed to see this crazy wench.

CHARLES. [*Turning.*] But I am the king; and I will.

LA TRÉMOUILLE. [*Brutally.*] Then she cannot be allowed to see you. Now!

CHARLES. I tell you I will. I am going to put my foot down—

BLUEBEARD. [*Laughing at him.*] Naughty! What would your wise grandfather say?

CHARLES. That just shews your ignorance, Bluebeard. My grandfather had a saint who used to float in the air when she was praying, and told him everything he wanted to know. My poor father had two saints, Marie de Maillé and the Gasque of Avignon. It is in our family; and I dont care what you say: I will have my saint too.

THE ARCHBISHOP. This creature is not a saint. She is not even a respectable woman. She does not wear women's clothes. She is dressed like a soldier, and rides round the country with soldiers. Do you suppose such a person can be admitted to your Highness's court?

LA HIRE. Stop. [*Going to the* ARCHBISHOP.] Did you say a girl in armor, like a soldier?

THE ARCHBISHOP. So De Baudricourt describes her.

LA HIRE. But by all the devils in hell—Oh, God forgive me, what am I saying?—by Our Lady and all the saints, this must be the angel that struck Foul Mouthed Frank dead for swearing.

CHARLES. [*Triumphant.*] You see! A miracle!

LA HIRE. She may strike the lot of us dead if we cross her. For Heaven's sake, Archbishop, be careful what you are doing.

THE ARCHBISHOP. [*Severely.*] Rubbish! Nobody has been struck dead. A drunken blackguard who has been rebuked a hundred times for swearing has fallen into a well, and been drowned. A mere coincidence.

LA HIRE. I do not know what a coincidence is. I do know that the man is dead, and that she told him he was going to die.

THE ARCHBISHOP. We are all going to die, Captain.

LA HIRE. [*Crossing himself.*] I hope not. [*He backs out of the conversation.*]

BLUEBEARD. We can easily find out whether she is an angel or not. Let us arrange when she comes that I shall be the Dauphin, and see whether she will find me out.

CHARLES. Yes: I agree to that. If she cannot find the blood royal I will have nothing to do with her.

THE ARCHBISHOP. It is for the Church to make saints: let De Baudricourt mind his own business, and not dare usurp the function of his priest. I say the girl shall not be admitted.

BLUEBEARD. But, Archbishop—

THE ARCHBISHOP. [*Sternly.*] I speak in the Church's name. [*To the* DAUPHIN.] Do you dare say she shall?

CHARLES. [*Intimidated but sulky.*] Oh, if you make it an excommunication matter, I have nothing more to say, of course. But you havnt read the end of the letter. De Baudricourt says she will raise the siege of Orleans, and beat the English for us.

LA TRÉMOUILLE. Rot!

CHARLES. Well, will you save Orleans for us, with all your bullying?

LA TRÉMOUILLE. [*Savagely.*] Do not throw that in my face again: do you hear? I have done more fighting than you ever did or ever will. But I cannot be everywhere.

THE DAUPHIN. Well, thats something.

BLUEBEARD. [*Coming between the* ARCHBISHOP *and* CHARLES.] You have Jack Dunois at the head of your troops in Orleans: the brave Dunois, the handsome Dunois, the wonderful invincible Dunois, the darling of all the ladies, the beautiful bastard. Is it likely that the country lass can do what he cannot do?

CHARLES. Why doesnt he raise the siege, then?

LA HIRE. The wind is against him.

BLUEBEARD. How can the wind hurt him at Orleans? It is not on the Channel.

LA HIRE. It is on the river Loire; and the English hold the bridgehead. He must ship his men across the river and upstream, if he is to take them in the rear. Well, he cannot, because there is a devil of a wind blowing the other way. He is tired of paying the priests to pray for a west wind. What he needs is a miracle. You tell me that what the girl did to Foul Mouthed Frank was no miracle. No matter: it finished Frank. If she changes the wind for Dunois, that may not be a miracle either; but it may finish the English. What harm is there in trying?

THE ARCHBISHOP. [*Who has read the end of the letter and become more thoughtful.*] It is true that De Baudricourt seems extraordinarily impressed.

LA HIRE. De Baudricourt is a blazing ass; but he is a soldier; and if he thinks she can beat the English, all the rest of the army will think so too.

LA TRÉMOUILLE. [*To the* ARCHBISHOP, *who is hesitating.*] Oh, let them have their way. Dunois' men will give up the town in spite of him if somebody does not put some fresh spunk into them.

THE ARCHBISHOP. The Church must examine the girl before anything decisive is done about her. However, since his Highness desires it, let her attend the Court.

LA HIRE. I will find her and tell her. [*He goes out.*]

CHARLES. Come with me, Bluebeard; and let us arrange so that she will not know who I am. You will pretend to be me. [*He goes out through the curtains.*]

BLUEBEARD. Pretend to be that thing! Holy Michael! [*He follows the* DAUPHIN.]

LA TRÉMOUILLE. I wonder will she pick him out!

THE ARCHBISHOP. Of course she will.

LA TRÉMOUILLE. Why? How is she to know?

THE ARCHBISHOP. She will know what everybody in Chinon knows: that the Dauphin is the meanest-looking and worst-dressed figure in the Court, and that the man with the blue beard is Gilles de Rais.

LA TRÉMOUILLE. I never thought of that.

THE ARCHBISHOP. You are not so accustomed to miracles as I am. It is part of my profession.

LA TRÉMOUILLE. [*Puzzled and a little scandalized.*] But that would not be a miracle at all.

THE ARCHBISHOP. [*Calmly.*] Why not?

LA TRÉMOUILLE. Well, come! what is a miracle?

THE ARCHBISHOP. A miracle, my friend, is an event which creates faith. That is the purpose and nature of miracles. They may seem very wonderful to the people who witness them, and very simple to those who perform them. That does not matter: if they confirm or create faith they are true miracles.

LA TRÉMOUILLE. Even when they are frauds, do you mean?

THE ARCHBISHOP. Frauds deceive. An event which creates faith does not deceive: therefore it is not a fraud, but a miracle.

LA TRÉMOUILLE. [*Scratching his neck in his perplexity.*] Well, I suppose as you are an archbishop you must be right. It seems a bit fishy to me. But I am no churchman, and dont understand these matters.

THE ARCHBISHOP. You are not a churchman; but you are a diplomatist and a soldier. Could you make our citizens pay war taxes, or our soldiers sacrifice their lives, if they knew what is really happening instead of what seems to them to be happening?

LA TRÉMOUILLE. No, by Saint Dennis: the fat would be in the fire before sundown.

THE ARCHBISHOP. Would it not be quite easy to tell them the truth?

LA TRÉMOUILLE. Man alive, they wouldnt believe it.

THE ARCHBISHOP. Just so. Well, the Church has to rule men for the good of their souls as you have to rule them for the good of their bodies. To do that, the Church must do as you do: nourish their faith by poetry.

LA TRÉMOUILLE. Poetry! I should call it humbug.

THE ARCHBISHOP. You would be wrong, my friend. Parables are not lies because they describe events that have never happened. Miracles are not frauds because they are often—I do not say always—very simple and innocent contrivances by which the priest fortifies the faith of his flock. When this girl picks out the Dauphin among his courtiers, it will not be a miracle for me, because I shall know how it has been done, and my faith will not be increased. But as for the others, if they feel the thrill of the supernatural, and forget their sinful clay in a sudden sense of the glory of God, it will be a miracle and a blessed one. And you will find that the girl herself will be more affected than anyone else. She will forget how she really picked him out. So, perhaps, will you.

LA TRÉMOUILLE. Well, I wish I were clever enough to know how much of you is God's archbishop and how much the most artful fox in Touraine. Come on, or we shall be late for the fun; and I want to see it, miracle or no miracle.

THE ARCHBISHOP. [*Detaining him a moment.*] Do not think that I am a lover of crooked ways. There is a new spirit rising in men: we are at the dawning of a wider epoch. If I were a simple monk, and had not to rule men, I should seek peace for my spirit with Aristotle and Pythagoras rather than with the saints and their miracles.

LA TRÉMOUILLE. And who the deuce was Pythagoras?

THE ARCHBISHOP. A sage who held that the earth is round, and that it moves round the sun.

LA TRÉMOUILLE. What an utter fool! Couldnt he use his eyes?

They go out together through the curtains, which are presently withdrawn, revealing the full depth of the throne room with the Court assembled. On the right are two Chairs of State on a dais. BLUEBEARD *is standing theatrically on the dais, playing the king, and, like the courtiers, enjoying the joke rather obviously. There is a curtained arch in the wall behind the dais; but the main door, guarded by men-at-arms, is at the other side of the room; and a clear path across is kept and lined by the courtiers.* CHARLES *is in this path in the middle of the room.* LA HIRE *is on his right. The* ARCHBISHOP, *on his left, has taken his place by the dais:* LA TRÉMOUILLE *at the other side of it. The* DUCHESS DE LA TRÉ- MOUILLE, *pretending to be the Queen, sits in the Consort's chair, with a group of ladies in waiting close by, behind the* ARCHBISHOP.

The chatter of the courtiers makes such a noise that nobody no- tices the appearance of the page at the door.

THE PAGE. The Duke of—[*Nobody listens.*] The Duke of—[*The chatter continues. Indignant at his failure to command a hearing, he snatches the halberd of the nearest man-at-arms, and thumps the floor with it. The chatter ceases; and everybody looks at him in silence.*] Attention! [*He restores the halberd to the man-at-arms.*] The Duke of Vendôme presents Joan the Maid to his Majesty.

CHARLES. [*Putting his finger on his lip.*] Ssh! [*He hides behind the nearest courtier, peering out to see what happens.*]

BLUEBEARD. [*Majestically.*] Let her approach the throne.

JOAN, *dressed as a soldier, with her hair bobbed and hanging thickly round her face, is led in by a bashful and speechless noble- man, from whom she detaches herself to stop and look round ea- gerly for the* DAUPHIN.

THE DUCHESS. [*To the nearest lady in waiting.*] My dear! Her hair!

All the ladies explode in uncontrollable laughter.

BLUEBEARD. [*Trying not to laugh, and waving his hand in depreca- tion of their merriment.*] Ssh—ssh! Ladies! Ladies!!

JOAN. [*Not at all embarrassed.*] I wear it like this because I am a soldier. Where be Dauphin?

A titter runs through the Court as she walks to the dais.

BLUEBEARD. [*Condescendingly.*] You are in the presence of the Dau- phin.

JOAN *looks at him sceptically for a moment, scanning him hard up and down to make sure. Dead silence, all watching her. Fun dawns in her face.*

JOAN. Coom, Bluebeard! Thou canst not fool me. Where be Dau- phin?

A roar of laughter breaks out as GILLES, *with a gesture of sur- render, joins in the laugh, and jumps down from the dais beside* LA TRÉMOUILLE. JOAN, *also on the broad grin, turns back, searching along the row of courtiers, and presently makes a dive, and drags out* CHARLES *by the arm.*

JOAN. [*Releasing him and bobbing him a little curtsey.*] Gentle little Dauphin, I am sent to you to drive the English away from Orleans and from France, and to crown you king in the cathedral at Rheims, where all true kings of France are crowned.

CHARLES. [*Triumphant, to the Court.*] You see, all of you: she knew the blood royal. Who dare say now that I am not my father's son? [*To* JOAN.] But if you want me to be crowned at Rheims you must talk to the Archbishop, not to me. There he is! [*He is standing behind her.*]

JOAN. [*Turning quickly, overwhelmed with emotion.*] Oh, my lord! [*She falls on both knees before him, with bowed head, not daring to look up.*] My lord: I am only a poor country girl; and you are filled with the blessedness and glory of God Himself; but you will touch me with your hands, and give me your blessing, wont you?

BLUEBEARD. [*Whispering to* LA TRÉMOUILLE.] The old fox blushes.

LA TRÉMOUILLE. Another miracle!

THE ARCHBISHOP. [*Touched, putting his hand on her head.*] Child: you are in love with religion.

JOAN. [*Startled: looking up at him.*] Am I? I never thought of that. Is there any harm in it?

THE ARCHBISHOP. There is no harm in it, my child. But there is danger.

JOAN. [*Rising, with a sunflush of reckless happiness irradiating her face.*] There is always danger, except in heaven. Oh, my lord, you have given me such strength, such courage. It must be a most wonderful thing to be Archbishop.

The Court smiles broadly: even titters a little.

THE ARCHBISHOP. [*Drawing himself up sensitively.*] Gentlemen: your levity is rebuked by this maid's faith. I am, God help me, all unworthy; but your mirth is a deadly sin.

Their faces fall. Dead silence.

BLUEBEARD. My lord: we were laughing at her, not at you.

THE ARCHBISHOP. What? Not at my unworthiness but at her faith! Gilles de Rais: this maid prophesied that the blasphemer should be drowned in his sin—

JOAN. [*Distressed.*] No!

THE ARCHBISHOP. [*Silencing her by a gesture.*] I prophesy now that you will be hanged in yours if you do not learn when to laugh and when to pray.

BLUEBEARD. My lord: I stand rebuked. I am sorry: I can say no more. But if you prophesy that I shall be hanged, I shall never be able to resist temptation, because I shall always be telling myself that I may as well be hanged for a sheep as a lamb.

The courtiers take heart at this. There is more tittering.

JOAN. [*Scandalized.*] You are an idle fellow, Bluebeard; and you have great impudence to answer the Archbishop.

LA HIRE. [*With a huge chuckle.*] Well said, lass! Well said!

JOAN. [*Impatiently to the* ARCHBISHOP.] Oh, my lord, will you send all these silly folks away so that I may speak to the Dauphin alone?

LA HIRE. [*Goodhumoredly.*] I can take a hint. [*He salutes; turns on his heel; and goes out.*]

THE ARCHBISHOP. Come, gentlemen. The Maid comes with God's blessing, and must be obeyed.

The courtiers withdraw, some through the arch, others at the opposite side. The ARCHBISHOP *marches across to the door, followed by the* DUCHESS *and* LA TRÉMOUILLE. *As the* ARCHBISHOP *passes* JOAN, *she falls on her knees, and kisses the hem of his robe fervently. He shakes his head in instinctive remonstrance; gathers the robe from her; and goes out. She is left kneeling directly in the* DUCHESS'S *way.*

THE DUCHESS. [*Coldly.*] Will you allow me to pass, please?

JOAN. [*Hastily rising, and standing back.*] Beg pardon, maam, I am sure.

The DUCHESS *passes on.* JOAN *stares after her; then whispers to the* DAUPHIN.

JOAN. Be that Queen?

CHARLES. No. She thinks she is.

JOAN. [*Again staring after the* DUCHESS.] Oo-oo-ooh! [*Her awe-struck amazement at the figure cut by the magnificently dressed lady is not wholly complimentary.*]

LA TRÉMOUILLE. [*Very surly.*] I'll trouble your Highness not to gibe at my wife. [*He goes out. The others have already gone.*]

JOAN. [*To the* DAUPHIN.] Who be old Gruff-and-Grum?

CHARLES. He is the Duke de la Trémouille.

JOAN. What be his job?

CHARLES. He pretends to command the army. And whenever I find a friend I can care for, he kills him.

JOAN. Why dost let him?

CHARLES. [*Petulantly moving to the throne side of the room to escape from her magnetic field.*] How can I prevent him? He bullies me. They all bully me.

JOAN. Art afraid?

CHARLES. Yes: I am afraid. It's no use preaching to me about it. It's all very well for these big men with their armor that is too heavy for me, and their swords that I can hardly lift, and their muscle and their shouting and their bad tempers. They like fighting: most of them are making fools of themselves all the time they are not fighting; but I am quiet and sensible; and I dont want to kill people: I only want to be left alone to enjoy myself in my own way. I never asked to be a king: it was pushed on me. So if you are going to say 'Son of St Louis: gird on the sword of your ancestors, and lead us to victory' you may spare your breath to cool your porridge; for I cannot do it. I am not built that way; and there is an end of it.

JOAN. [*Trenchant and masterful.*] Blethers! We are all like that to begin with. I shall put courage into thee.

CHARLES. But I dont want to have courage put into me. I want to sleep in a comfortable bed, and not live in continual terror of being killed or wounded. Put courage into the others, and let them have their bellyful of fighting; but let me alone.

JOAN. It's no use, Charlie: thou must face what God puts on thee. If thou fail to make thyself king, thoult be a beggar: what else art fit for? Come! Let me see thee sitting on the throne. I have looked forward to that.

CHARLES. What is the good of sitting on the throne when the other fellows give all the orders? However! [*He sits enthroned, a piteous figure.*] here is the king for you! Look your fill at the poor devil.

JOAN. Thourt not king yet, lad: thourt but Dauphin. Be not led away by them around thee. Dressing up dont fill empty noddle. I know the people: the real people that make thy bread for thee; and I tell thee they count no man king of France until the holy oil has been poured on his hair, and himself consecrated and crowned in Rheims Cathedral. And thou needs new clothes, Charlie. Why does not Queen look after thee properly?

CHARLES. We're too poor. She wants all the money we can spare to put on her own back. Besides, I like to see her beautifully dressed; and I dont care what I wear myself: I should look ugly anyhow.

JOAN. There is some good in thee, Charlie; but it is not yet a king's good.

CHARLES. We shall see. I am not such a fool as I look. I have my eyes open; and I can tell you that one good treaty is worth ten good fights. These fighting fellows lose all on the treaties that they gain on the fights. If we can only have a treaty, the English are sure to have the worst of it, because they are better at fighting than at thinking.

JOAN. If the English win, it is they that will make the treaty: and then God help poor France! Thou must fight, Charlie, whether thou will or no. I will go first to hearten thee. We must take our courage in both hands: aye, and pray for it with both hands too.

CHARLES. [*Descending from his throne and again crossing the room to escape from her dominating urgency.*] Oh do stop talking about God and praying. I cant bear people who are always praying. Isnt it bad enough to have to do it at the proper times?

JOAN. [*Pitying him.*] Thou poor child, thou hast never prayed in thy life. I must teach thee from the beginning.

CHARLES. I am not a child: I am a grown man and a father; and I will not be taught any more.

JOAN. Aye, you have a little son. He that will be Louis the Eleventh when you die. Would you not fight for him?

CHARLES. No: a horrid boy. He hates me. He hates everybody, selfish little beast! I dont want to be bothered with children. I dont want to be a father; and I dont want to be a son: especially a son of St Louis. I dont want to be any of these fine things you all have your heads full of: I want to be just what I am. Why cant you mind your own business, and let me mind mine?

JOAN. [*Again contemptuous.*] Minding your own business is like minding your own body: it's the shortest way to make yourself sick. What is my business? Helping mother at home. What is thine? Petting lapdogs and sucking sugarsticks. I call that muck. I tell thee it is God's business we are here to do: not our own. I have a message to thee from God; and thou must listen to it, though thy heart break with the terror of it.

CHARLES. I dont want a message; but can you tell me any secrets? Can you do any cures? Can you turn lead into gold, or anything of that sort?

JOAN. I can turn thee into a king, in Rheims Cathedral; and that is a miracle that will take some doing, it seems.

CHARLES. If we go to Rheims, and have a coronation, Anne will want new dresses. We cant afford them. I am all right as I am.

JOAN. As you are! And what is that? Less than my father's poorest shepherd. Thourt not lawful owner of thy own land of France till thou be consecrated.

CHARLES. But I shall not be lawful owner of my own land anyhow. Will the consecration pay off my mortgages? I have pledged my last acre to the Archbishop and that fat bully. I owe money even to Bluebeard.

JOAN. [*Earnestly.*] Charlie: I come from the land, and have gotten my strength working on the land; and I tell thee that the land is thine to rule righteously and keep God's peace in, and not to pledge at the pawnshop as a drunken woman pledges her children's clothes. And I come from God to tell thee to kneel in the cathedral and solemnly give thy kingdom to Him for ever and ever, and become the greatest king in the world as His steward and His bailiff, His soldier and His servant. The very clay of France will become holy: her soldiers will be the soldiers of God: the rebel dukes will be rebels against God: the English will fall on their knees and beg thee let them return to their lawful homes in peace. Wilt be a poor little Judas, and betray me and Him that sent me?

CHARLES. [*Tempted at last.*] Oh, if I only dare!

JOAN. I shall dare, dare, and dare again, in God's name! Art for or against me?

CHARLES. [*Excited.*] I'll risk it, I warn you I shant be able to keep it up; but I'll risk it. You shall see. [*Running to the main door and shouting.*] Hallo! Come back, everybody. [*To* JOAN, *as he runs back to the arch opposite.*] Mind you stand by and dont let me be bullied. [*Through the arch.*] Come along, will you: the whole Court. [*He sits down in the royal chair as they all hurry in to their former places, chattering and wondering.*] Now I'm in for it; but no matter: here goes! [*To the* PAGE.] Call for silence, you little beast, will you?

THE PAGE. [*Snatching a halberd as before and thumping with it repeatedly.*] Silence for His Majesty the King. The King speaks. [*Peremptorily.*] Will you be silent there? [*Silence.*]

CHARLES. [*Rising.*] I have given the command of the army to The Maid. The Maid is to do as she likes with it. [*He descends from the dais.*]

General amazement. LA HIRE, *delighted, slaps his steel thigh-piece with his gauntlet.*

LA TRÉMOUILLE. [*Turning threateningly towards* CHARLES.] What is this? I command the army.

JOAN *quickly puts her hand on* CHARLES'S *shoulder as he instinctively recoils.* CHARLES, *with a grotesque effort culminating in an extravagant gesture, snaps his fingers in the* CHAMBERLAIN'S *face.*

JOAN. Thou'rt answered, old Gruff-and-Grum. [*Suddenly flashing out her sword as she divines that her moment has come.*] Who is for God and His Maid? Who is for Orleans with me?

LA HIRE. [*Carried away, drawing also.*] For God and His Maid! To Orleans!

ALL THE KNIGHTS. [*Following his lead with enthusiasm.*] To Orleans!

JOAN, *radiant, falls on her knees in thanksgiving to God. They all kneel, except the* ARCHBISHOP, *who gives his benediction with a sigh, and* LA TRÉMOUILLE, *who collapses, cursing.*

SCENE III

Orleans, April 29th, 1429. DUNOIS, *aged 26, is pacing up and down a patch of ground on the south bank of the silver Loire, commanding a long view of the river in both directions. He has had his lance stuck up with a pennon, which streams in a strong east wind. His shield with its bend sinister lies beside it. He has his commander's baton in his hand. He is well built, carrying his armor easily. His broad brow and pointed chin give him an equilaterally triangular face, already marked by active service and responsibility, with the expression of a good-natured and capable man who has no affectations and no foolish illusions. His* PAGE *is sitting on the ground, elbows on knees, cheeks on fists, idly watching the water. It is evening; and both man and boy are affected by the loveliness of the Loire.*

DUNOIS. [*Halting for a moment to glance up at the streaming pennon and shake his head wearily before he resumes his pacing.*] West wind, west wind, west wind. Strumpet: steadfast when you should be wanton, wanton when you should be steadfast. West wind on the silver Loire: what rhymes to Loire? [*He looks again at the pennon, and shakes his fist at it.*] Change, curse you, change, English harlot of a wind, change. West, west, I tell you. [*With a growl he resumes his march in silence, but soon begins again.*] West wind, wanton wind, wilful wind, womanish wind, false wind from over the water, will you never blow again?

THE PAGE. [*Bounding to his feet.*] See! There! There she goes!

DUNOIS. [*Startled from his reverie: eagerly.*] Where? Who? The Maid?

THE PAGE. No: the kingfisher. Like blue lightning. She went into that bush.

DUNOIS. [*Furiously disappointed.*] Is that all? You infernal young idiot: I have a mind to pitch you into the river.

THE PAGE. [*Not afraid, knowing his man.*] It looked frightfully jolly, that flash of blue. Look! There goes the other!

DUNOIS. [*Running eagerly to the river brim.*] Where? Where?

THE PAGE. [*Pointing.*] Passing the reeds.

DUNOIS. [*Delighted.*] I see.

They follow the flight till the bird takes cover.

THE PAGE. You blew me up because you were not in time to see them yesterday.

DUNOIS. You knew I was expecting The Maid when you set up your yelping. I will give you something to yelp for next time.

THE PAGE. Arnt they lovely? I wish I could catch them.

DUNOIS. Let me catch you trying to trap them, and I will put you in the iron cage for a month to teach you what a cage feels like. You are an abominable boy.

THE PAGE. [*Laughs, and squats down as before.*]!

DUNOIS. [*Pacing.*] Blue bird, blue bird, since I am friend to thee, change thou the wind for me. No: it does not rhyme. He who has sinned for thee: thats better. No sense in it, though. [*He finds himself close to the page.*] You abominable boy! [*He turns away from him.*] Mary in the blue snood, kingfisher color: will you grudge me a west wind?

A SENTRY'S VOICE WESTWARD. Halt! Who goes there?

JOAN'S VOICE. The Maid.

DUNOIS. Let her pass. Hither, Maid! To me!

JOAN, *in splendid armor, rushes in in a blazing rage. The wind drops; and the pennon flaps idly down the lance; but* DUNOIS *is too much occupied with* JOAN *to notice it.*

JOAN. [*Bluntly.*] Be you Bastard of Orleans?

DUNOIS. [*Cool and stern, pointing to his shield.*] You see the bend sinister. Are you Joan the Maid?

JOAN. Sure.

DUNOIS. Where are your troops?

JOAN. Miles behind. They have cheated me. They have brought me to the wrong side of the river.

DUNOIS. I told them to.

JOAN. Why did you? The English are on the other side!

DUNOIS. The English are on both sides.

JOAN. But Orleans is on the other side. We must fight the English there. How can we cross the river?

DUNOIS. [*Grimly.*] There is a bridge.

JOAN. In God's name, then, let us cross the bridge, and fall on them.

DUNOIS. It seems simple; but it cannot be done.

JOAN. Who says so?

DUNOIS. I say so; and older and wiser heads than mine are of the same opinion.

JOAN. [*Roundly.*] Then your older and wiser heads are fatheads: they have made a fool of you; and now they want to make a fool of me too, bringing me to the wrong side of the river. Do you not know that I bring you better help than ever came to any general or any town?

DUNOIS. [*Smiling patiently.*] Your own?

JOAN. No: the help and counsel of the King of Heaven. Which is the way to the bridge?

DUNOIS. You are impatient, Maid.

JOAN. Is this a time for patience? Our enemy is at our gates; and here we stand doing nothing. Ah, why are you not fighting? Listen to me; I will deliver you from fear. I—

DUNOIS. [*Laughing heartily, and waving her off.*] No, no, my girl: if you delivered me from fear I should be a good knight for a story book, but a very bad commander of the army. Come! let me begin to make a soldier of you. [*He takes her to the water's edge.*] Do you see those two forts at this end of the bridge? the big ones?

JOAN. Yes. Are they ours or the goddams'?

DUNOIS. Be quiet, and listen to me. If I were in either of those forts with only ten men I could hold it against an army. The English have more than ten times ten goddams in those forts to hold them against us.

JOAN. They cannot hold them against God. God did not give them the land under those forts: they stole it from Him. He gave it to us. I will take those forts.

DUNOIS. Single-handed?

JOAN. Our men will take them. I will lead them.

DUNOIS. Not a man will follow you.

JOAN. I will not look back to see whether anyone is following me.

DUNOIS. [*Recognizing her mettle, and clapping her heartily on the shoulder.*] Good. You have the makings of a soldier in you. You are in love with war.

JOAN. [*Startled.*] Oh! And the Archbishop said I was in love with religion.

DUNOIS. I, God forgive me, am a little in love with war myself, the ugly devil! I am like a man with two wives. Do you want to be like a woman with two husbands?

JOAN. [*Matter-of-fact.*] I will never take a husband. A man in Toul took an action against me for breach of promise; but I never promised him. I am a soldier: I do not want to be thought of as a woman. I will not dress as a woman. I do not care for the things women care for. They dream of lovers, and of money. I dream of leading a charge, and of placing the big guns. You soldiers do not know how to use the big guns: you think you can win battles with a great noise and smoke.

DUNOIS. [*With a shrug.*] True. Half the time the artillery is more trouble than it is worth.

JOAN. Aye, lad; but you cannot fight stone walls with horses: you must have guns, and much bigger guns too.

DUNOIS. [*Grinning at her familiarity, and echoing it.*] Aye, lass; but a good heart and a stout ladder will get over the stoniest wall.

JOAN. I will be first up the ladder when we reach the fort, Bastard. I dare you to follow me.

DUNOIS. You must not dare a staff officer, Joan: only company officers are allowed to indulge in displays of personal courage. Besides, you must know that I welcome you as a saint, not as a soldier. I have daredevils enough at my call, if they could help me.

JOAN. I am not a daredevil: I am a servant of God. My sword is sacred: I found it behind the altar in the church of St Catherine, where God hid it for me; and I may not strike a blow with it. My heart is full of courage, not of anger. I will lead; and your men will follow: that is all I can do. But I must do it: you shall not stop me.

DUNOIS. All in good time. Our men cannot take those forts by a sally across the bridge. They must come by water, and take the English in the rear on this side.

JOAN. [*Her military sense asserting itself.*] Then make rafts and put big guns on them; and let your men cross to us.

DUNOIS. The rafts are ready; and the men are embarked. But they must wait for God.

JOAN. What do you mean? God is waiting for them.

DUNOIS. Let Him send us a wind then. My boats are downstream: they cannot come up against both wind and current. We must wait until God changes the wind. Come: let me take you to the church.

JOAN. No. I love church; but the English will not yield to prayers: they understand nothing but hard knocks and slashes. I will not go to church until we have beaten them.

DUNOIS. You must: I have business for you there.

JOAN. What business?

DUNOIS. To pray for a west wind. I have prayed; and I have given two silver candlesticks; but my prayers are not answered. Yours may be: you are young and innocent.

JOAN. Oh yes: you are right. I will pray: I will tell St Catherine: she will make God give me a west wind. Quick: shew me the way to the church.

THE PAGE. [*Sneezes violently.*] At-cha!!!

JOAN. God bless you, child! Coom, Bastard.

> *They go out. The* PAGE *rises to follow. He picks up the shield, and is taking the spear as well when he notices the pennon, which is now streaming eastward.*

THE PAGE. [*Dropping the shield and calling excitedly after them.*] Seigneur! Seigneur! Mademoiselle!

DUNOIS. [*Running back.*] What is it? The kingfisher? [*He looks eagerly for it up the river.*]

JOAN. [*Joining them.*] Oh, a kingfisher! Where?

THE PAGE. No: the wind, the wind, the wind [*pointing to the pennon*]: that is what made me sneeze.

DUNOIS. [*Looking at the pennon.*] The wind has changed. [*He crosses himself.*] God has spoken. [*Kneeling and handing his baton to* JOAN.] You command the king's army. I am your soldier.

THE PAGE. [*Looking down the river.*] The boats have put off. They are ripping upstream like anything.

DUNOIS. [*Rising.*] Now for the forts. You dared me to follow. Dare you lead?

JOAN. [*Bursting into tears and flinging her arms round* DUNOIS, *kissing him on both cheeks.*] Dunois, dear comrade in arms, help me. My eyes are blinded with tears. Set my foot on the ladder, and say 'Up, Joan.'

DUNOIS. [*Dragging her out.*] Never mind the tears: make for the flash of the guns.

JOAN. [*In a blaze of courage.*] Ah!

DUNOIS. [*Dragging her along with him.*] For God and Saint Dennis!

THE PAGE. [*Shrilly.*] The Maid! The Maid! God and The Maid! Hurray-ay-ay! [*He snatches up the shield and lance, and capers out after them, mad with excitement.*]

SCENE IV

A *tent in the English camp.* A *bullnecked English* CHAPLAIN *of 50 is sitting on a stool at a table, hard at work writing. At the other side of the table an imposing* NOBLEMAN, *aged 46, is seated in a handsome chair turning over the leaves of an illuminated Book of Hours. The* NOBLEMAN *is enjoying himself: the* CHAPLAIN *is struggling with suppressed wrath. There is an unoccupied leather stool on the* NOBLEMAN's *left. The table is on his right.*

THE NOBLEMAN. Now this is what I call workmanship. There is nothing on earth more exquisite than a bonny book, with well-placed columns of rich black writing in beautiful borders, and illuminated pictures cunningly inset. But nowadays, instead of looking at books, people read them. A book might as well be one of those orders for bacon and bran that you are scribbling.

THE CHAPLAIN. I must say, my lord, you take our situation very coolly. Very coolly indeed.

THE NOBLEMAN. [*Supercilious.*] What is the matter?

THE CHAPLAIN. The matter, my lord, is that we English have been defeated.

THE NOBLEMAN. That happens, you know. It is only in history books and ballads that the enemy is always defeated.

THE CHAPLAIN. But we are being defeated over and over again. First, Orleans—

THE NOBLEMAN. [*Poohpoohing.*] Oh, Orleans!

THE CHAPLAIN. I know what you are going to say, my lord: that was a clear case of witchcraft and sorcery. But we are still being defeated. Jargeau, Meung, Beaugency, just like Orleans. And now we have been butchered at Patay, and Sir John Talbot taken prison. [*He throws down his pen, almost in tears.*] I feel it, my lord: I feel it very deeply. I cannot bear to see my countrymen defeated by a parcel of foreigners.

THE NOBLEMAN. Oh! you are an Englishman, are you?

THE CHAPLAIN. Certainly not, my lord: I am a gentleman. Still, like your lordship, I was born in England; and it makes a difference.

THE NOBLEMAN. You are attached to the soil, eh?

THE CHAPLAIN. It pleases your lordship to be satirical at my expense: your greatness privileges you to be so with impunity. But your lordship knows very well that I am not attached to the soil in a vulgar manner, like a serf. Still, I have a feeling about it; [*with growing agitation*] and I am not ashamed of it; and [*rising wildly*] by God, if this goes on any longer I will fling my cassock to the devil, and take arms myself, and strangle the accursed witch with my own hands.

THE NOBLEMAN. [*Laughing at him goodnaturedly.*] So you shall, chaplain: so you shall, if we can do nothing better. But not yet, not quite yet.

The CHAPLAIN *resumes his seat very sulkily.*

THE NOBLEMAN. [*Airily.*] I should not care very much about the witch —you see, I have made my pilgrimage to the Holy Land; and the Heavenly Powers, for their own credit, can hardly allow me to be worsted by a village sorceress—but the Bastard of Orleans is a harder nut to crack; and as he has been to the Holy Land too, honors are easy between us as far as that goes.

THE CHAPLAIN. He is only a Frenchman, my lord.

THE NOBLEMAN. A Frenchman! Where did you pick up that expression? Are these Burgundians and Bretons and Picards and Gascons beginning to call themselves Frenchmen, just as our fellows are beginning to call themselves Englishmen? They actually talk of France and England as their countries. Theirs, if you please! What is to become of me and you if that way of thinking comes into fashion?

THE CHAPLAIN. Why, my lord? Can it hurt us?

THE NOBLEMAN. Men cannot serve two masters. If this cant of serving their country once takes hold of them, goodbye to the authority of their feudal lords, and goodbye to the authority of the Church. That is, goodbye to you and me.

THE CHAPLAIN. I hope I am a faithful servant of the Church; and there are only six cousins between me and the barony of Stogumber, which was created by the Conqueror. But is that any reason why I should stand by and see Englishmen beaten by a French bastard and a witch from Lousy Champagne?

THE NOBLEMAN. Easy, man, easy: we shall burn the witch and beat the bastard all in good time. Indeed I am waiting at present for the Bishop of Beauvais, to arrange the burning with him. He has been turned out of his diocese by her faction.

THE CHAPLAIN. You have first to catch her, my lord.

THE NOBLEMAN. Or buy her. I will offer a king's ransom.

THE CHAPLAIN. A king's ransom! For that slut!

THE NOBLEMAN. One has to leave a margin. Some of Charles's people will sell her to the Burgundians; the Burgundians will sell her to us; and there will probably be three or four middlemen who will expect their little commissions.

THE CHAPLAIN. Monstrous. It is all those scoundrels of Jews: they get in every time money changes hands. I would not leave a Jew alive in Christendom if I had my way.

THE NOBLEMAN. Why not? The Jews generally give value. They make you pay; but they deliver the goods. In my experience the men who want something for nothing are invariably Christians.

A PAGE *appears.*

THE PAGE. The Right Reverend the Bishop of Beauvais: Monseigneur Cauchon.

> CAUCHON, *aged about 60, comes in. The* PAGE *withdraws. The two Englishmen rise.*

THE NOBLEMAN. [*With effusive courtesy.*] My dear Bishop, how good of you to come! Allow me to introduce myself: Richard de Beauchamp, Earl of Warwick, at your service.

CAUCHON. Your lordship's fame is well known to me.

WARWICK. This reverend cleric is Master John de Stogumber.

THE CHAPLAIN. [*Glibly.*] John Bowyer Spenser Neville de Stogumber, at your service, my lord: Bachelor of Theology, and Keeper of the Private Seal to His Eminence the Cardinal of Winchester.

WARWICK. [*To* CAUCHON.] You call him the Cardinal of England, I believe. Our king's uncle.

CAUCHON. Messire John de Stogumber: I am always the very good friend of His Eminence. [*He extends his hand to the* CHAPLAIN, *who kisses his ring.*]

WARWICK. Do me the honor to be seated. [*He gives* CAUCHON *his chair, placing it at the head of the table.*]

> CAUCHON *accepts the place of honor with a grave inclination.* WARWICK *fetches the leather stool carelessly, and sits in his former place. The* CHAPLAIN *goes back to his chair.*
>
> *Though* WARWICK *has taken second place in calculated deference to the* BISHOP, *he assumes the lead in opening the proceedings as a matter of course. He is still cordial and expansive; but there is a new note in his voice which means that he is coming to business.*

WARWICK. Well, my Lord Bishop, you find us in one of our unlucky moments. Charles is to be crowned at Rheims, practically by the young woman from Lorraine; and—I must not deceive you, nor flatter your hopes—we cannot prevent it. I suppose it will make a great difference to Charles's position.

CAUCHON. Undoubtedly. It is a masterstroke of The Maid's.

THE CHAPLAIN. [*Again agitated.*] We were not fairly beaten, my lord. No Englishman is ever fairly beaten.

> CAUCHON *raises his eyebrow slightly, then quickly composes his face.*

WARWICK. Our friend here takes the view that the young woman is a sorceress. It would, I presume, be the duty of your reverend lordship to denounce her to the Inquisition, and have her burnt for that offence.

CAUCHON. If she were captured in my diocese: yes.

WARWICK. [*Feeling that they are getting on capitally.*] Just so. Now I suppose there can be no reasonable doubt that she is a sorceress.

THE CHAPLAIN. Not the least. An arrant witch.

WARWICK. [*Gently reproving the interruption.*] We are asking for the Bishop's opinion, Messire John.

CAUCHON. We shall have to consider not merely our own opinions here, but the opinions—the prejudices, if you like—of a French court.

WARWICK. [*Correcting.*] A Catholic court, my lord.

CAUCHON. Catholic courts are composed of mortal men, like other courts, however sacred their function and inspiration may be. And if the men are Frenchmen, as the modern fashion calls them, I am afraid the bare fact that an English army has been defeated by a French one will not convince them that there is any sorcery in the matter.

THE CHAPLAIN. What! Not when the famous Sir Talbot himself has been defeated and actually taken prisoner by a drab from the ditches of Lorraine!

CAUCHON. Sir John Talbot, we all know, is a fierce and formidable soldier, Messire; but I have yet to learn that he is an able general. And though it pleases you to say that he has been defeated by this girl, some of us may be disposed to give a little of the credit to Dunois.

THE CHAPLAIN. [*Contemptuously.*] The Bastard of Orleans!

CAUCHON. Let me remind—

WARWICK. [*Interposing.*] I know what you are going to say, my lord. Dunois defeated me at Montargis.

CAUCHON. [*Bowing.*] I take that as evidence that the Seigneur Dunois is a very able commander indeed.

WARWICK. Your lordship is the flower of courtesy. I admit, on our side, that Talbot is a mere fighting animal, and that it probably served him right to be taken at Patay.

THE CHAPLAIN. [*Chafing.*] My lord: at Orleans this woman had her throat pierced by an English arrow, and was seen to cry like a child from the pain of it. It was a death wound; yet she fought all day; and when our men had repulsed all her attacks like true Englishmen, she walked alone to the wall of our fort with a white banner in her hand; and our men were paralyzed, and could neither shoot nor strike whilst the French fell on them and drove them on to the bridge, which immediately burst into flames and crumbled under them, letting them down into the river, where they were drowned in heaps. Was this your bastard's generalship? or were those flames the flames of hell, conjured up by witchcraft?

WARWICK. You will forgive Messire John's vehemence, my lord; but he has put our case. Dunois is a great captain, we admit; but why could he do nothing until the witch came?

CAUCHON. I do not say that there were no supernatural powers on her side. But the names on that white banner were not the names of

Satan and Beelzebub, but the blessed names of our Lord and His holy mother. And your commander who was drowned—Clahz-da I think you call him—

WARWICK. Glasdale. Sir William Glasdale.

CAUCHON. Glass-dell, thank you. He was no saint; and many of our people think that he was drowned for his blasphemies against The Maid.

WARWICK. [*Beginning to look very dubious.*] Well, what are we to infer from all this, my lord? Has The Maid converted you?

CAUCHON. If she had, my lord, I should have known better than to have trusted myself here within your grasp.

WARWICK. [*Blandly deprecating.*] Oh! oh! My lord!

CAUCHON. If the devil is making use of this girl—and I believe he is—

WARWICK. [*Reassured.*] Ah! You hear, Messire John? I knew your lordship would not fail us. Pardon my interruption. Proceed.

CAUCHON. If it be so, the devil has longer views than you give him credit for.

WARWICK. Indeed? In what way? Listen to this, Messire John.

CAUCHON. If the devil wanted to damn a country girl, do you think so easy a task would cost him the winning of half a dozen battles? No, my lord: any trumpery imp could do that much if the girl could be damned at all. The Prince of Darkness does not condescend to such cheap drudgery. When he strikes, he strikes at the Catholic Church, whose realm is the whole spiritual world. When he damns, he damns the souls of the entire human race. Against that dreadful design The Church stands ever on guard. And it is as one of the instruments of that design that I see this girl. She is inspired, but diabolically inspired.

THE CHAPLAIN. I told you she was a witch.

CAUCHON. [*Fiercely.*] She is not a witch. She is a heretic.

THE CHAPLAIN. What difference does that make?

CAUCHON. You, a priest, ask me that! You English are strangely blunt in the mind. All these things that you call witchcraft are capable of a natural explanation. The woman's miracles would not impose on a rabbit: she does not claim them as miracles herself. What do her victories prove but that she has a better head on her shoulders than your swearing Glass-dells and mad bull Talbots, and that the courage of faith, even though it be a false faith, will always outstay the courage of wrath?

THE CHAPLAIN. [*Hardly able to believe his ears.*] Does your lordship compare Sir John Talbot, three times Governor of Ireland, to a mad bull?!!!

WARWICK. It would not be seemly for you to do so, Messire John, as you are still six removes from a barony. But as I am an earl, and Talbot is only a knight, I may make bold to accept the comparison.

[*To the* BISHOP.] My lord: I wipe the slate as far as the witchcraft goes. None the less, we must burn the woman.

CAUCHON. I cannot burn her. The Church cannot take life. And my first duty is to seek this girl's salvation.

WARWICK. No doubt. But you do burn people occasionally.

CAUCHON. No. When The Church cuts off an obstinate heretic as a dead branch from the tree of life, the heretic is handed over to the secular arm. The Church has no part in what the secular arm may see fit to do.

WARWICK. Precisely. And I shall be the secular arm in this case. Well, my lord, hand over your dead branch; and I will see that the fire is ready for it. If you will answer for The Church's part, I will answer for the secular part.

CAUCHON. [*With smouldering anger.*] I can answer for nothing. You great lords are too prone to treat The Church as a mere political convenience.

WARWICK. [*Smiling and propitiatory.*] Not in England, I assure you.

CAUCHON. In England more than anywhere else. No, my lord: the soul of this village girl is of equal value with yours or your king's before the throne of God; and my first duty is to save it. I will not suffer your lordship to smile at me as if I were repeating a meaningless form of words, and it were well understood between us that I should betray the girl to you. I am no mere political bishop: my faith is to me what your honor is to you; and if there be a loophole through which this baptized child of God can creep to her salvation, I shall guide her to it.

THE CHAPLAIN. [*Rising in a fury.*] You are a traitor.

CAUCHON. [*Springing up.*] You lie, priest. [*Trembling with rage.*] If you dare do what this woman has done—set your country above the holy Catholic Church—you shall go to the fire with her.

THE CHAPLAIN. My lord: I—I went too far. I—[*He sits down with a submissive gesture.*]

WARWICK. [*Who has risen apprehensively.*] My lord: I apologize to you for the word used by Messire John de Stogumber. It does not mean in England what it does in France. In your language traitor means betrayer: one who is perfidious, treacherous, unfaithful, disloyal. In our country it means simply one who is not wholly devoted to our English interests.

CAUCHON. I am sorry: I did not understand. [*He subsides into his chair with dignity.*]

WARWICK. [*Resuming his seat, much relieved.*] I must apologize on my own account if I have seemed to take the burning of this poor girl too lightly. When one has seen whole countrysides burnt over and over again as mere items in military routine, one has to grow a very thick skin. Otherwise one might go mad: at all events, I should. May I venture to assume that your lordship also, having to see so many heretics burned from time to time, is compelled to take —shall I say a professional view of what would otherwise be a very horrible incident?

CAUCHON. Yes: it is a painful duty: even, as you say, a horrible one. But in comparison with the horror of heresy it is less than nothing. I am not thinking of this girl's body, which will suffer for a few moments only, and which must in any event die in some more or less painful manner, but of her soul, which may suffer to all eternity.

WARWICK. Just so; and God grant that her soul may be saved! But the practical problem would seem to be how to save her soul without saving her body. For we must face it, my lord: if this cult of The Maid goes on, our cause is lost.

THE CHAPLAIN. [*His voice broken like that of a man who has been crying.*] May I speak, my lord?

WARWICK. Really, Messire John, I had rather you did not, unless you can keep your temper.

THE CHAPLAIN. It is only this. I speak under correction; but The Maid is full of deceit: she pretends to be devout. Her prayers and confessions are endless. How can she be accused of heresy when she neglects no observance of a faithful daughter of The Church?

CAUCHON. [*Flaming up.*] A faithful daughter of The Church! The Pope himself at his proudest dare not presume as this woman presumes. She acts as if she herself were The Church. She brings the message of God to Charles; and The Church must stand aside. She will crown him in the cathedral of Rheims: she, not The Church! She sends letters to the king of England giving him God's command through her to return to his island on pain of God's vengeance, which she will execute. Let me tell you that the writing of such letters was the practice of the accursed Mahomet, the anti-Christ. Has she ever in all her utterances said one word of The Church? Never. It is always God and herself.

WARWICK. What can you expect? A beggar on horseback! Her head is turned.

CAUCHON. Who has turned it? The devil. And for a mighty purpose. He is spreading this heresy everywhere. The man Hus, burnt only thirteen years ago at Constance, infected all Bohemia with it. A man named WcLeef, himself an anointed priest, spread the pestilence in England; and to your shame you let him die in his bed. We have such people here in France too: I know the breed. It is cancerous; if it be not cut out, stamped out, burnt out, it will not stop until it has brought the whole body of human society into sin and corruption, into waste and ruin. By it an Arab camel driver drove Christ and His Church out of Jerusalem, and ravaged his way west like a wild beast until at last there stood only the Pyrenees and

God's mercy between France and damnation. Yet what did the camel driver do at the beginning more than this shepherd girl is doing? He had his voices from the angel Gabriel: she has her voices from St Catherine and St Margaret and the Blessed Michael. He declared himself the messenger of God, and wrote in God's name to the kings of the earth. Her letters to them are going forth daily. It is not the Mother of God now to whom we must look for intercession, but to Joan the Maid. What will the world be like when The Church's accumulated wisdom and knowledge and experience, its councils of learned, venerable pious men, are thrust into the kennel by every ignorant laborer or dairymaid whom the devil can puff up with the monstrous self-conceit of being directly inspired from heaven? It will be a world of blood, of fury, of devastation, of each man striving for his own hand: in the end a world wrecked back into barbarism. For now you have only Mahomet and his dupes, and the Maid and her dupes; but what will it be when every girl thinks herself a Joan and every man a Mahomet? I shudder to the very marrow of my bones when I think of it. I have fought it all my life; and I will fight it to the end. Let all this woman's sins be forgiven her except only this sin; for it is the sin against the Holy Ghost; and if she does not recant in the dust before the world, and submit herself to the last inch of her soul to her Church, to the fire she shall go if she once falls into my hand.

WARWICK. [*Unimpressed.*] You feel strongly about it, naturally.

CAUCHON. Do not you?

WARWICK. I am a soldier, not a churchman. As a pilgrim I saw something of the Mahometans. They were not so ill-bred as I had been led to believe. In some respects their conduct compared favorably with ours.

CAUCHON. [*Displeased.*] I have noticed this before. Men go to the East to convert the infidels. And the infidels pervert them. The Crusader comes back more than half a Saracen. Not to mention that all Englishmen are born heretics.

THE CHAPLAIN. Englishmen heretics!!! [*Appealing to* WARWICK.] My lord: must we endure this? His lordship is beside himself. How can what an Englishman believes be heresy? It is a contradiction in terms.

CAUCHON. I absolve you, Messire de Stogumber, on the ground of invincible ignorance. The thick air of your country does not breed theologians.

WARWICK. You would not say so if you heard us quarrelling about religion, my lord! I am sorry you think I must be either a heretic or a blockhead because, as a travelled man, I know that the followers of Mahomet profess great respect for our Lord, and are more ready to forgive St Peter for being a fisherman than your lordship is to forgive Mahomet for being a camel driver. But at least we can proceed in this matter without bigotry.

CAUCHON. When men call the zeal of the Christian Church bigotry I know what to think.

WARWICK. They are only east and west views of the same thing.

CAUCHON. [*Bitterly ironical.*] Only east and west! Only!!

WARWICK. Oh, my Lord Bishop, I am not gainsaying you. You will carry The Church with you; but you have to carry the nobles also. To my mind there is a stronger case against The Maid than the one you have so forcibly put. Frankly, I am not afraid of this girl becoming another Mahomet, and superseding The Church by a great heresy. I think you exaggerate that risk. But have you noticed that in these letters of hers, she proposes to all the kings of Europe, as she has already pressed on Charles, a transaction which would wreck the whole social structure of Christendom?

CAUCHON. Wreck The Church. I tell you so.

WARWICK. [*Whose patience is wearing out.*] My lord: pray get The Church out of your head for a moment; and remember that there are temporal institutions in the world as well as spiritual ones. I and my peers represent the feudal aristocracy as you represent The Church. We are the temporal power. Well, do you not see how this girl's idea strikes at us?

CAUCHON. How does her idea strike at you, except as it strikes at all of us, through The Church?

WARWICK. Her idea is that the kings should give their realms to God, and then reign as God's bailiffs.

CAUCHON. [*Not interested.*] Quite sound theologically, my lord. But the king will hardly care, provided he reign. It is an abstract idea: a mere form of words.

WARWICK. By no means. It is a cunning device to supersede the aristocracy, and make the king sole and absolute autocrat. Instead of the king being merely the first among his peers, he becomes their master. That we cannot suffer: we call no man master. Nominally we hold our lands and dignities from the king, because there must be a keystone to the arch of human society; but we hold our lands in our own hands, and defend them with our own swords and those of our own tenants. Now by The Maid's doctrine the king will take our lands—our lands!—and make them a present to God; and God will then vest them wholly in the king.

CAUCHON. Need you fear that? You are the makers of kings after all. York or Lancaster in England, Lancaster or Valois in France: they reign according to your pleasure.

WARWICK. Yes; but only as long as the people follow their feudal lords, and know the king only as a travelling show, owning nothing but the highway that belongs to everybody. If the people's thoughts and hearts were turned to the king, and their lords became only the king's servants in their eyes, the king could break us across his knee one by one; and then what should we be but liveried courtiers in his halls?

CAUCHON. Still you need not fear, my lord. Some men are born kings; and some are born statesmen. The two are seldom the same. Where would the king find counsellors to plan and carry out such policy for him?

WARWICK. [*With a not too friendly smile.*] Perhaps in the Church, my lord.

    CAUCHON, *with an equally sour smile, shrugs his shoulders, and does not contradict him.*

WARWICK. Strike down the barons; and the cardinals will have it all their own way.

CAUCHON. [*Conciliatory, dropping his polemical tone.*] My lord: we shall not defeat The Maid if we strive against one another. I know well that there is a Will to Power in the world. I know that while it lasts there will be a struggle between the Emperor and the Pope, between the dukes and the political cardinals, between the barons and the kings. The devil divides us and governs. I see you are no friend to The Church: you are an earl first and last, as I am a churchman first and last. But can we not sink our differences in the face of a common enemy? I see now that what is in your mind is not that this girl has never once mentioned The Church, and thinks only of God and herself, but that she has never once mentioned the peerage, and thinks only of the king and herself.

WARWICK. Quite so. These two ideas of hers are the same idea at bottóm. It goes deep, my lord. It is the protest of the individual soul against the interference of priest or peer between the private man and his God. I should call it Protestantism if I had to find a name for it.

CAUCHON. [*Looking hard at him.*] You understand it wonderfully well, my lord. Scratch an Englishman, and find a Protestant.

WARWICK. [*Playing the pink of courtesy.*] I think you are not entirely void of sympathy with The Maid's secular heresy, my lord. I leave you to find a name for it.

CAUCHON. You mistake me, my lord. I have no sympathy with her political presumptions. But as a priest I have gained a knowledge of the minds of the common people; and there you will find yet another most dangerous idea. I can express it only by such phrases as France for the French, England for the English, Italy for the Italians, Spain for the Spanish, and so forth. It is sometimes so narrow and bitter in country folk that it surprises me that this country girl can rise above the idea of her village for its villagers. But she can. She does. When she threatens to drive the English from the soil of

France she is undoubtedly thinking of the whole extent of country in which French is spoken. To her the French-speaking people are what the Holy Scriptures describe as a nation. Call this side of her heresy Nationalism if you will: I can find you no better name for it. I can only tell you that it is essentially anti-Catholic and anti-Christian; for the Catholic Church knows only one realm, and that is the realm of Christ's kingdom. Divide that kingdom into nations, and you dethrone Christ. Dethrone Christ, and who will stand between our throats and the sword? The world will perish in a welter of war.

WARWICK. Well, if you will burn the Protestant, I will burn the Nationalist, though perhaps I shall not carry Messire John with me there. England for the English will appeal to him.

THE CHAPLAIN. Certainly England for the English goes without saying: it is the simple law of nature. But this woman denies to England her legitimate conquests, given her by God because of her peculiar fitness to rule over less civilized races for their own good. I do not understand what your lordships mean by Protestant and Nationalist: you are too learned and subtle for a poor clerk like myself. But I know as a matter of plain commonsense that the woman is a rebel; and that is enough for me. She rebels against Nature by wearing man's clothes, and fighting. She rebels against The Church by usurping the divine authority of the Pope. She rebels against God by her damnable league with Satan and his evil spirits against our army. And all these rebellions are only excuses for her great rebellion against England. That is not to be endured. Let her perish. Let her burn. Let her not infect the whole flock. It is expedient that one woman die for the people.

WARWICK. [*Rising.*] My lord: we seem to be agreed.

CAUCHON. [*Rising also, but in protest.*] I will not imperil my soul. I will uphold the justice of the Church. I will strive to the utmost for this woman's salvation.

WARWICK. I am sorry for the poor girl. I hate these severities. I will spare her if I can.

THE CHAPLAIN. [*Implacably.*] I would burn her with my own hands.

CAUCHON. [*Blessing him.*] Sancta simplicitas!

SCENE V

The ambulatory in the cathedral of Rheims, near the door of the vestry. A pillar bears one of the stations of the cross. The organ is playing the people out of the nave after the coronation. JOAN *is kneeling in prayer before the station. She is beautifully dressed, but still in male attire. The organ ceases as* DUNOIS, *also splendidly arrayed, comes into the ambulatory from the vestry.*

DUNOIS. Come, Joan! you have had enough praying. After that fit of crying you will catch a chill if you stay here any longer. It is all over: the cathedral is empty; and the streets are full. They are calling for The Maid. We have told them you are staying here alone to pray; but they want to see you again.

JOAN. No: let the king have all the glory.

DUNOIS. He only spoils the show, poor devil. No, Joan: you have crowned him; and you must go through with it.

JOAN. [*Shakes her head reluctantly.*]

DUNOIS. [*Raising her.*] Come come! it will be over in a couple of hours. It's better than the bridge at Orleans: eh?

JOAN. Oh, dear Dunois, how I wish it were the bridge at Orleans again! We lived at that bridge.

DUNOIS. Yes, faith, and died too: some of us.

JOAN. Isnt it strange, Jack? I am such a coward: I am frightened beyond words before a battle; but it is so dull afterwards when there is no danger: oh, so dull! dull! dull!

DUNOIS. You must learn to be abstemious in war, just as you are in your food and drink, my little saint.

JOAN. Dear Jack: I think you like me as a soldier likes his comrade.

DUNOIS. You need it, poor innocent child of God. You have not many friends at court.

JOAN. Why do all these courtiers and knights and churchmen hate me? What have I done to them? I have asked nothing for myself except that my village shall not be taxed; for we cannot afford war taxes. I have brought them luck and victory: I have set them right when they were doing all sorts of stupid things: I have crowned Charles and made him a real king; and all the honors he is handing out have gone to them. Then why do they not love me?

DUNOIS. [*Rallying her.*] Sim-ple-ton! Do you expect stupid people to love you for shewing them up? Do blundering old military dug-outs love the successful young captains who supersede them? Do ambitious politicians love the climbers who take the front seats from them? Do archbishops enjoy being played off their own altars, even by saints? Why, I should be jealous of you myself if I were ambitious enough.

JOAN. You are the pick of the basket here, Jack: the only friend I have among all these nobles. I'll wager your mother was from the country. I will go back to the farm when I have taken Paris.

DUNOIS. I am not so sure that they will let you take Paris.

JOAN. [*Startled.*] What!

DUNOIS. I should have taken it myself before this if they had all been sound about it. Some of them would rather Paris took you, I think. So take care.

JOAN. Jack: the world is too wicked for me. If the goddams and the

Burgundians do not make an end of me, the French will. Only for
my voices I should lose all heart. That is why I had to steal away to
pray here alone after the coronation. I'll tell you something, Jack. It
is in the bells I hear my voices. Not to-day, when they all rang: that
was nothing but jangling. But here in this corner, where the bells
come down from heaven, and the echoes linger, or in the fields,
where they come from a distance through the quiet of the countryside, my voices are in them. [*The cathedral clock chimes the
quarter.*] Hark! [*She becomes rapt.*] Do you hear? 'Dear-child-
of-God': just what you said. At the half-hour they will say 'Be-
brave-go-on'. At the three-quarters they will say 'I-am-thy-Help'.
But it is at the hour, when the great bell goes after 'God-will-save-
France': it is then that St Margaret and St Catherine and sometimes even the blessed Michael will say things that I cannot tell
beforehand. Then, oh then—

DUNOIS. [*Interrupting her kindly but not sympathetically.*] Then,
Joan, we shall hear whatever we fancy in the booming of the bell.
You make me uneasy when you talk about your voices: I should
think you were a bit cracked if I hadnt noticed that you give me
very sensible reasons for what you do, though I hear you telling
others you are only obeying Madame Saint Catherine.

JOAN. [*Crossly.*] Well, I have to find reasons for you, because you do
not believe in my voices. But the voices come first; and I find the
reasons after: whatever you may choose to believe.

DUNOIS. Are you angry, Joan?

JOAN. Yes. [*Smiling.*] No: not with you. I wish you were one of the
village babies.

DUNOIS. Why?

JOAN. I could nurse you for awhile.

DUNOIS. You are a bit of a woman after all.

JOAN. No: not a bit: I am a soldier and nothing else. Soldiers always
nurse children when they get a chance.

DUNOIS. That is true. [*He laughs.*]

   KING CHARLES, *with* BLUEBEARD *on his left and* LA HIRE *on his
right, comes from the vestry, where he has been disrobing.* JOAN
shrinks away behind the pillar. DUNOIS *is left between* CHARLES *and*
LA HIRE.

DUNOIS. Well, your Majesty is an anointed king at last. How do you
like it?

CHARLES. I would not go through it again to be emperor of the sun
and moon. The weight of those robes! I thought I should have
dropped when they loaded that crown on to me. And the famous
holy oil they talked so much about was rancid: phew! The Archbishop must be nearly dead: his robes must have weighed a ton:
they are stripping him still in the vestry.

DUNOIS. [*Drily.*] Your majesty should wear armor oftener. That would accustom you to heavy dressing.

CHARLES. Yes: the old jibe! Well, I am not going to wear armor: fighting is not my job. Where is The Maid?

JOAN. [*Coming forward between* CHARLES *and* BLUEBEARD, *and falling on her knee.*] Sire: I have made you king: my work is done. I am going back to my father's farm.

CHARLES. [*Surprised, but relieved.*] Oh, are you? Well, that will be very nice.

JOAN *rises, deeply discouraged.*

CHARLES. [*Continuing heedlessly.*] A healthy life, you know.

DUNOIS. But a dull one.

BLUEBEARD. You will find the petticoats tripping you up after leaving them off for so long.

LA HIRE. You will miss the fighting. It's a bad habit, but a grand one, and the hardest of all to break yourself of.

CHARLES. [*Anxiously.*] Still, we dont want you to stay if you would really rather go home.

JOAN. [*Bitterly.*] I know well that none of you will be sorry to see me go. [*She turns her shoulder to* CHARLES *and walks past him to the more congenial neighborhood of* DUNOIS *and* LA HIRE.]

LA HIRE. Well, I shall be able to swear when I want to. But I shall miss you at times.

JOAN. La Hire: in spite of all your sins and swears we shall meet in heaven; for I love you as I love Pitou, my old sheep dog. Pitou could kill a wolf. You will kill the English wolves until they go back to their country and become good dogs of God, will you not?

LA HIRE. You and I together: yes.

JOAN. No: I shall last only a year from the beginning.

ALL THE OTHERS. What!

JOAN. I know it somehow.

DUNOIS. Nonsense!

JOAN. Jack: do you think you will be able to drive them out?

DUNOIS. [*With quiet conviction.*] Yes: I shall drive them out. They beat us because we thought battles were tournaments and ransom markets. We played the fool while the goddams took war seriously. But I have learnt my lesson, and taken their measure. They have no roots here. I have beaten them before; and I shall beat them again.

JOAN. You will not be cruel to them, Jack?

DUNOIS. The goddams will not yield to tender handling. We did not begin it.

JOAN. [*Suddenly.*] Jack: before I go home, let us take Paris.

CHARLES. [*Terrified.*] Oh no no. We shall lose everything we have gained. Oh dont let us have any more fighting. We can make a very good treaty with the Duke of Burgundy.

JOAN. *Treaty! [She stamps with impatience.]*

CHARLES. Well, why not, now that I am crowned and anointed? Oh, that oil!

The ARCHBISHOP *comes from the vestry, and joins the group between* CHARLES *and* BLUEBEARD.

CHARLES. Archbishop: The Maid wants to start fighting again.

THE ARCHBISHOP. Have we ceased fighting, then? Are we at peace?

CHARLES. No: I suppose not; but let us be content with what we have done. Let us make a treaty. Our luck is too good to last; and now is our chance to stop before it turns.

JOAN. Luck! God has fought for us; and you call it luck! And you would stop while there are still Englishmen on this holy earth of dear France!

THE ARCHBISHOP. *[Sternly.]* Maid: the king addressed himself to me, not to you. You forget yourself. You very often forget yourself.

JOAN. *[Unabashed, and rather roughly.]* Then speak, you; and tell him that it is not God's will that he should take his hand from the plough.

THE ARCHBISHOP. If I am not so glib with the name of God as you are, it is because I interpret His will with the authority of the Church and of my sacred office. When you first came you respected it, and would not have dared to speak as you are now speaking. You came clothed with the virtue of humility; and because God blessed your enterprises accordingly, you have stained yourself with the sin of pride. The old Greek tragedy is rising among us. It is the chastisement of hubris.

CHARLES. Yes: she thinks she knows better than everyone else.

JOAN. *[Distressed, but naïvely incapable of seeing the effect she is producing.]* But I do know better than any of you seem to. And I am not proud: I never speak unless I know I am right.

BLUEBEARD. ⎱ *[Exclaiming* ⎰ Ha ha!
CHARLES. ⎰ *together.]* ⎱ Just so.

THE ARCHBISHOP. How do you know you are right?

JOAN. I always know. My voices—

CHARLES. Oh, your voices, your voices. Why dont the voices come to me? I am king, not you.

JOAN. They do come to you; but you do not hear them. You have not sat in the field in the evening listening for them. When the angelus rings you cross yourself and have done with it; but if you prayed from your heart, and listened to the thrilling of the bells in the air after they stop ringing, you would hear the voices as well as I do. *[Turning brusquely from him.]* But what voices do you need to tell you what the blacksmith can tell you: that you must strike while the iron is hot? I tell you we must make a dash at Compiègne and relieve it as we relieved Orleans. Then Paris will open its gates; or if not, we will break through them. What is your crown worth without your capital?

LA HIRE. That is what I say too. We shall go through them like a red hot shot through a pound of butter. What do you say, Bastard?

DUNOIS. If our cannon balls were all as hot as your head, and we had enough of them, we should conquer the earth, no doubt. Pluck and impetuosity are good servants in war, but bad masters: they have delivered us into the hands of the English every time we have trusted to them. We never know when we are beaten: that is our great fault.

JOAN. You never know when you are victorious: that is a worse fault. I shall have to make you carry looking-glasses in battle to convince you that the English have not cut off all your noses. You would have been besieged in Orleans still, you and your councils of war, if I had not made you attack. You should always attack; and if you only hold on long enough the enemy will stop first. You dont know how to begin a battle; and you dont know how to use your cannons. And I do.

She squats down on the flags with crossed ankles, pouting.

DUNOIS. I know what you think of us, General Joan.

JOAN. Never mind that, Jack. Tell them what you think of me.

DUNOIS. I think that God was on your side; for I have not forgotten how the wind changed, and how our hearts changed when you came; and by my faith I shall never deny that it was in your sign that we conquered. But I tell you as a soldier that God is no man's daily drudge, and no maid's either. If you are worthy of it He will sometimes snatch you out of the jaws of death and set you on your feet again; but that is all: once on your feet you must fight with all your might and all your craft. For He has to be fair to your enemy too: dont forget that. Well, He set us on our feet through you at Orleans; and the glory of it has carried us through a few good battles here to the coronation. But if we presume on it further, and trust to God to do the work we should do ourselves, we shall be defeated; and serve us right!

JOAN. But—

DUNOIS. Sh! I have not finished. Do not think, any of you, that these victories of ours were won without generalship. King Charles: you have said no word in your proclamations of my part in this campaign; and I make no complaint of that; for the people will run after The Maid and her miracles and not after the Bastard's hard work finding troops for her and feeding them. But I know exactly how much God did for us through The Maid, and how much He left me to do by my own wits; and I tell you that your little hour of miracles is over, and that from this time on he who plays the war game best will win—if the luck is on his side.

JOAN. Ah! if, if, if, if! If ifs and ans were pots and pans there'd be no need of tinkers. [*Rising impetuously.*] I tell you, Bastard, your art of war is no use, because your knights are no good for real fighting. War is only a game to them, like tennis and all their other games: they make rules as to what is fair and what is not fair, and heap armor on themselves and on their poor horses to keep out the arrows; and when they fall they cant get up, and have to wait for their squires to come and lift them to arrange about the ransom with the man that has poked them off their horse. Cant you see that all the like of that is gone by and done with? What use is armor against gunpowder? And if it was, do you think men that are fighting for France and for God will stop to bargain about ransoms, as half your knights live by doing? No: they will fight to win; and they will give up their lives out of their own hand into the hand of God when they go into battle, as I do. Common folks understand this. They cannot afford armor and cannot pay ransoms; but they followed me half naked into the moat and up the ladder and over the wall. With them it is my life or thine, and God defend the right! You may shake your head, Jack; and Bluebeard may twirl his billygoat's beard and cock his nose at me; but remember the day your knights and captains refused to follow me to attack the English at Orleans! You locked the gates to keep me in; and it was the townsfolk and the common people that followed me, and forced the gate, and shewed you the way to fight in earnest.

BLUEBEARD. [*Offended.*] Not content with being Pope Joan, you must be Caesar and Alexander as well.

THE ARCHBISHOP. Pride will have a fall, Joan.

JOAN. Oh, never mind whether it is pride or not: is it true? is it commonsense?

LA HIRE. It is true. Half of us are afraid of having our handsome noses broken; and the other half are out for paying off their mortgages. Let her have her way, Dunois: she does not know everything; but she has got hold of the right end of the stick. Fighting is not what it was; and those who know least about it often make the best job of it.

DUNOIS. I know all that. I do not fight in the old way: I have learnt the lesson of Agincourt, of Poitiers and Crecy. I know how many lives any move of mine will cost; and if the move is worth the cost I make it and pay the cost. But Joan never counts the cost at all: she goes ahead and trusts to God: she thinks she has God in her pocket. Up to now she has had the numbers on her side; and she has won. But I know Joan; and I see that some day she will go ahead when she has only ten men to do the work of a hundred. And then she will find that God is on the side of the big battalions. She will be taken by the enemy. And the lucky man that makes the capture will receive sixteen thousand pounds from the Earl of Ouareek.

JOAN. [*Flattered.*] Sixteen thousand pounds! Eh, laddie, have they offered that for me? There cannot be so much money in the world.

DUNOIS. There is, in England. And now tell me, all of you, which of you will lift a finger to save Joan once the English have got her? I speak first, for the army. The day after she has been dragged from her horse by a goddam or a Burgundian, and he is not struck dead: the day after she is locked in a dungeon, and the bars and bolts do not fly open at the touch of St Peter's angel: the day when the enemy finds out that she is as vulnerable as I am and not a bit more invincible, she will not be worth the life of a single soldier to us; and I will not risk that life, much as I cherish her as a companion-in-arms.

JOAN. I dont blame you, Jack: you are right. I am not worth one soldier's life if God lets me be beaten; but France may think me worth my ransom after what God has done for her through me.

CHARLES. I tell you I have no money; and this coronation, which is all your fault, has cost me the last farthing I can borrow.

JOAN. The Church is richer than you. I put my trust in the Church.

THE ARCHBISHOP. Woman: they will drag you through the streets, and burn you as a witch.

JOAN. [*Running to him.*] Oh, my lord, do not say that. It is impossible. I a witch!

THE ARCHBISHOP. Peter Cauchon knows his business. The University of Paris has burnt a woman for saying that what you have done was well done, and according to God.

JOAN. [*Bewildered.*] But why? What sense is there in it?. What I have done is according to God. They could not burn a woman for speaking the truth.

THE ARCHBISHOP. They did.

JOAN. But you know that she was speaking the truth. You would not let them burn me.

THE ARCHBISHOP. How could I prevent them?

JOAN. You would speak in the name of the Church. You are a great prince of the Church. I would go anywhere with your blessing to protect me.

THE ARCHBISHOP. I have no blessing for you while you are proud and disobedient.

JOAN. Oh, why will you go on saying things like that? I am not proud and disobedient. I am a poor girl, and so ignorant that I do not know A from B. How could I be proud? And how can you say that I am disobedient when I always obey my voices, because they come from God.

THE ARCHBISHOP. The voice of God on earth is the voice of the Church Militant; and all the voices that come to you are the echoes of your own wilfulness.

JOAN. It is not true.

THE ARCHBISHOP. [*Flushing angrily.*] You tell the Archbishop in his cathedral that he lies; and yet you say you are not proud and disobedient.

JOAN. I never said you lied. It was you that as good as said my voices lied. When have they ever lied? If you will not believe in them: even if they are only the echoes of my own commonsense, are they not always right? and are not your earthly counsels always wrong?

THE ARCHBISHOP. [*Indignantly.*] It is waste of time admonishing you.

CHARLES. It always comes back to the same thing. She is right; and everyone else is wrong.

THE ARCHBISHOP. Take this as your last warning. If you perish through setting your private judgment above the instructions of your spiritual directors, the Church disowns you, and leaves you to whatever fate your presumption may bring upon you. The Bastard has told you that if you persist in setting up your military conceit above the counsels of your commanders—

DUNOIS. [*Interposing.*] To put it quite exactly, if you attempt to relieve the garrison in Compiègne without the same superiority in numbers you had at Orleans—

THE ARCHBISHOP. The army will disown you, and will not rescue you. And His Majesty the King has told you that the throne has not the means of ransoming you.

CHARLES. Not a penny.

THE ARCHBISHOP. You stand alone: absolutely alone, trusting to your own conceit, your own ignorance, your own headstrong presumption, your own impiety in hiding all these sins under the cloak of a trust in God. When you pass through these doors into the sunlight, the crowd will cheer you. They will bring you their little children and their invalids to heal: they will kiss your hands and feet, and do what they can, poor simple souls, to turn your head, and madden you with the self-confidence that is leading you to your destruction. But you will be none the less alone; they cannot save you. We and we only can stand between you and the stake at which our enemies have burnt that wretched woman in Paris.

JOAN. [*Her eyes skyward.*] I have better friends and better counsel than yours.

THE ARCHBISHOP. I see that I am speaking in vain to a hardened heart. You reject our protection, and are determined to turn us all against you. In future, then, fend for yourself; and if you fail, God have mercy on your soul.

DUNOIS. That is the truth, Joan. Heed it.

JOAN. Where would you all have been now if I had heeded that sort of truth? There is no help, no counsel, in any of you. Yes: I am alone on earth: I have always been alone. My father told my brothers to drown me if I would not stay to mind his sheep while France was bleeding to death: France might perish if only our lambs were safe. I thought France would have friends at the court of the king of France; and I find only wolves fighting for pieces of her poor torn body. I thought God would have friends everywhere, because He is the friend of everyone; and in my innocence I believed that you who now cast me out would be like strong towers to keep harm from me. But I am wiser now; and nobody is any the worse for being wiser. Do not think you can frighten me by telling me that I am alone. France is alone; and God is alone; and what is my loneliness before the loneliness of my country and my God? I see now that the loneliness of God is His strength: what would He be if He listened to your jealous little counsels? Well, my loneliness shall be my strength too; it is better to be alone with God; His friendship will not fail me, nor His counsel, nor His love. In His strength I will dare, and dare, and dare, until I die. I will go out now to the common people, and let the love in their eyes comfort me for the hate in yours. You will all be glad to see me burnt; but if I go through the fire I shall go through it to their hearts for ever and ever. And so, God be with me!

She goes from them. They stare after her in glum silence for a moment. Then GILLES DE RAIS *twirls his beard.*

BLUEBEARD. You know, the woman is quite impossible. I dont dislike her, really; but what are you to do with such a character?

DUNOIS. As God is my judge, if she fell into the Loire I would jump in in full armor to fish her out. But if she plays the fool at Compiègne, and gets caught, I must leave her to her doom.

LA HIRE. Then you had better chain me up; for I could follow her to hell when the spirit rises in her like that.

THE ARCHBISHOP. She disturbs my judgment too: there is a dangerous power in her outbursts. But the pit is open at her feet; and for good or evil we cannot turn her from it.

CHARLES. If only she would keep quiet, or go home!

They follow her dispiritedly.

SCENE VI

Rouen, 30th May 1431. A great stone hall in the castle, arranged for a trial-at-law, but not a trial-by-jury, the court being the BISHOP's *court with the Inquisition participating: hence there are two raised chairs side by side for the* BISHOP *and the* INQUISITOR *as judges. Rows of chairs radiating from them at an obtuse angle are for the canons, the doctors of law and theology, and the Dominican monks, who act as assessors. In the angle is a table for the scribes, with stools. There is also a heavy rough wooden stool for the prisoner. All these are at the inner end of the hall. The further end is open to the courtyard through a row of arches. The court is shielded from the weather by screens and curtains.*

Looking down the great hall from the middle of the inner end, the judicial chairs and scribes' table are to the right. The prisoner's stool is to the left. There are arched doors right and left. It is a fine sunshiny May morning.

WARWICK *comes in through the arched doorway on the judges' side, followed by his* PAGE.

THE PAGE. [*Pertly.*] I suppose your lordship is aware that we have no business here. This is an ecclesiastical court; and we are only the secular arm.

WARWICK. I am aware of that fact. Will it please your impudence to find the Bishop of Beauvais for me, and give him a hint that he can have a word with me here before the trial, if he wishes?

THE PAGE. [*Going.*] Yes, my lord.

WARWICK. And mind you behave yourself. Do not address him as Pious Peter.

THE PAGE. No, my lord. I shall be kind to him, because, when The Maid is brought in, Pious Peter will have to pick a peck of pickled pepper.

CAUCHON *enters through the same door with a* DOMINICAN MONK *and a* CANON, *the latter carrying a brief.*

THE PAGE. The Right Reverend his lordship the Bishop of Beauvais. And two other reverend gentlemen.

WARWICK. Get out; and see that we are not interrupted.

THE PAGE. Right, my lord. [*He vanishes airily.*]

CAUCHON. I wish your lordship good-morrow.

WARWICK. Good-morrow to your lordship. Have I had the pleasure of meeting your friends before? I think not.

CAUCHON. [*Introducing the* MONK, *who is on his right.*] This, my lord, is Brother John Lemaître, of the order of St Dominic. He is acting as deputy for the Chief Inquisitor into the evil of heresy in France. Brother John: the Earl of Warwick.

WARWICK. Your Reverence is most welcome. We have no Inquisitor in England, unfortunately; though we miss him greatly, especially on occasions like the present.

The INQUISITOR *smiles patiently, and bows. He is a mild elderly gentleman, but has evident reserves of authority and firmness.*

CAUCHON. [*Introducing the* CANON, *who is on his left.*] This gentleman is Canon John D'Estivet, of the Chapter of Bayeux. He is acting as Promoter.

WARWICK. Promoter?

CAUCHON. Prosecutor, you would call him in civil law.

WARWICK. Ah! prosecutor. Quite, quite. I am very glad to make your acquaintance, Canon D'Estivet.

D'ESTIVET *bows.* [*He is on the young side of middle age, well mannered, but vulpine beneath his veneer.*]

WARWICK. May I ask what stage the proceedings have reached? It is now more than nine months since The Maid was captured at Compiègne by the Burgundians. It is fully four months since I bought her from the Burgundians for a very handsome sum, solely that she might be brought to justice. It is very nearly three months since I delivered her up to you, my Lord Bishop, as a person suspected of heresy. May I suggest that you are taking a rather unconscionable time to make up your minds about a very plain case? Is this trial never going to end?

THE INQUISITOR. [*Smiling.*] It has not yet begun, my lord.

WARWICK. Not yet begun! Why, you have been at it eleven weeks!

CAUCHON. We have not been idle, my lord. We have held fifteen examinations of The Maid: six public and nine private.

THE INQUISITOR. [*Always patiently smiling.*] You see, my lord, I have been present at only two of these examinations. They were proceedings of the Bishop's court solely, and not of the Holy Office. I have only just decided to associate myself—that is, to associate the Holy Inquisition—with the Bishop's court. I did not at first think that this was a case of heresy at all. I regarded it as a political case, and The Maid as a prisoner of war. But having now been present at two of the examinations, I must admit that this seems to be one of the gravest cases of heresy within my experience. Therefore everything is now in order, and we proceed to trial this morning. [*He moves towards the judicial chairs.*]

CAUCHON. This moment, if your lordship's convenience allows.

WARWICK. [*Graciously.*] Well, that is good news, gentlemen. I will not attempt to conceal from you that our patience was becoming strained.

CAUCHON. So I gathered from the threats of your soldiers to drown those of our people who favor The Maid.

WARWICK. Dear me! At all events their intentions were friendly to you, my lord.

CAUCHON. [*Sternly.*] I hope not. I am determined that the woman shall have a fair hearing. The justice of the Church is not a mockery, my lord.

THE INQUISITOR. [*Returning.*] Never has there been a fairer examination within my experience, my lord. The Maid needs no lawyers to take her part: she will be tried by her most faithful friends, all ardently desirous to save her soul from perdition.

D'ESTIVET. Sir: I am the Promoter; and it has been my painful duty to present the case against the girl; but believe me, I would throw up my case today and hasten to her defence if I did not know that men far my superiors in learning and piety, in eloquence and persuasiveness, have been sent to reason with her, to explain to her the danger she is running, and the ease with which she may avoid it. [*Suddenly bursting into forensic eloquence, to the disgust of* CAUCHON *and the* INQUISITOR, *who have listened to him so far with patronizing approval.*] Men have dared to say that we are acting from hate; but God is our witness that they lie. Have we tortured her? No. Have we ceased to exhort her; to implore her to have pity on herself; to come to the bosom of her Church as an erring but beloved child? Have we—

CAUCHON. [*Interrupting drily.*] Take care, Canon. All that you say is true; but if you make his lordship believe it I will not answer for your life, and hardly for my own.

WARWICK. [*Deprecating, but by no means denying.*] Oh, my lord, you are very hard on us poor English. But we certainly do not share your pious desire to save The Maid: in fact I tell you now plainly that her death is a political necessity which I regret but cannot help. If the Church lets her go—

CAUCHON. [*With fierce and menacing pride.*] If the Church lets her go, woe to the man, were he the Emperor himself, who dares lay a finger on her! The Church is not subject to political necessity, my lord.

THE INQUISITOR. [*Interposing smoothly.*] You need have no anxiety about the result, my lord. You have an invincible ally in the matter: one who is far more determined than you that she shall burn.

WARWICK. And who is this very convenient partisan, may I ask?

THE INQUISITOR. The Maid herself. Unless you put a gag in her mouth you cannot prevent her from convicting herself ten times over every time she opens it.

D'ESTIVET. That is perfectly true, my lord. My hair bristles on my head when I hear so young a creature utter such blasphemies.

WARWICK. Well, by all means do your best for her if you are quite sure it will be of no avail. [*Looking hard at* CAUCHON.] I should be sorry to have to act without the blessing of the Church.

CAUCHON. [*With a mixture of cynical admiration and contempt.*] And yet they say Englishmen are hypocrites! You play for your side, my lord, even at the peril of your soul. I cannot but admire such devotion; but I dare not go so far myself. I fear damnation.

WARWICK. If we feared anything we could never govern England, my lord. Shall I send your people in to you?

CAUCHON. Yes: it will be very good of your lordship to withdraw and allow the court to assemble.

WARWICK *turns on his heel, and goes out through the courtyard.* CAUCHON *takes one of the judicial seats; and* D'ESTIVET *sits at the scribes' table, studying his brief.*

CAUCHON. [*Casually, as he makes himself comfortable.*] What scoundrels these English nobles are!

THE INQUISITOR. [*Taking the other judicial chair on* CAUCHON's *left.*] All secular power makes men scoundrels. They are not trained for the work; and they have not the Apostolic Succession. Our own nobles are just as bad.

The BISHOP'S ASSESSORS *hurry into the hall, headed by* CHAPLAIN DE STOGUMBER *and* CANON DE COURCELLES, *a young priest of 30. The scribes sit at the table, leaving a chair vacant opposite* D'ESTIVET. *Some of the assessors take their seats: other stand chatting, waiting for the proceedings to begin formally.* DE STOGUMBER, *aggrieved and obstinate, will not take his seat: neither will the* CANON, *who stands on his right.*

CAUCHON. Good morning, Master de Stogumber. [*To the* INQUISITOR.] Chaplain to the Cardinal of England.

THE CHAPLAIN. [*Correcting him.*] Of Winchester, my lord. I have to make a protest, my lord.

CAUCHON. You make a great many.

THE CHAPLAIN. I am not without support, my lord. Here is Master de Courcelles, Canon of Paris, who associates himself with me in my protest.

CAUCHON. Well, what is the matter?

THE CHAPLAIN. [*Sulkily.*] Speak you, Master de Courcelles, since I do not seem to enjoy his lordship's confidence. [*He sits down in dudgeon next to* CAUCHON, *on his right.*]

COURCELLES. My lord: we have been at great pains to draw up an indictment of The Maid on sixty-four counts. We are now told that they have been reduced, without consulting us.

THE INQUISITOR. Master de Courcelles: I am the culprit. I am overwhelmed with admiration for the zeal displayed in your sixty-four counts; but in accusing a heretic, as in other things, enough is enough. Also you must remember that all the members of the court are not so subtle and profound as you, and that some of your very great learning might appear to them to be very great nonsense. Therefore I have thought it well to have your sixty-four articles cut down to twelve—

COURCELLES. [*Thunderstruck.*] Twelve!!!

THE INQUISITOR. Twelve will, believe me, be quite enough for your purpose.

THE CHAPLAIN. But some of the most important points have been reduced almost to nothing. For instance, The Maid has actually declared that the blessed saints Margaret and Catherine, and the holy Archangel Michael, spoke to her in French. That is a vital point.

THE INQUISITOR. You think, doubtless, that they should have spoken in Latin?

CAUCHON. No: he thinks they should have spoken in English.

THE CHAPLAIN. Naturally, my lord.

THE INQUISITOR. Well, as we are all here agreed, I think, that these voices of The Maid are the voices of evil spirits tempting her to her damnation, it would not be very courteous to you, Master de Stogumber, or to the King of England, to assume that English is the devil's native language. So let it pass. The matter is not wholly omitted from the twelve articles. Pray take your places, gentlemen; and let us proceed to business.

All who have not taken their seats, do so.

THE CHAPLAIN. Well, I protest. That is all.

COURCELLES. I think it hard that all our work should go for nothing. It is only another example of the diabolical influence which this woman exercises over the court. [*He takes his chair, which is on the* CHAPLIN'S *right.*]

CAUCHON. Do you suggest that I am under diabolical influence?

COURCELLES. I suggest nothing, my lord. But it seems to me that there is a conspiracy here to hush up the fact that The Maid stole the Bishop of Senlis's horse.

CAUCHON. [*Keeping his temper with difficulty.*] This is not a police court. Are we to waste our time on such rubbish?

COURCELLES. [*Rising, shocked.*] My lord: do you call the Bishop's horse rubbish?

THE INQUISITOR. [*Blandly.*] Master de Courcelles: The Maid alleges that she paid handsomely for the Bishop's horse, and that if he did not get the money the fault was not hers. As that may be true, the point is one on which The Maid may well be acquitted.

COURCELLES. Yes, if it were an ordinary horse. But the Bishop's horse! how can she be acquitted for that? [*He sits down again, bewildered and discouraged.*]

THE INQUISITOR. I submit to you, with great respect, that if we persist in trying The Maid on trumpery issues on which we may have to declare her innocent, she may escape us on the great main issue of heresy, on which she seems so far to insist on her own guilt. I will ask you, therefore, to say nothing, when The Maid is brought before us, of these stealings of horses, and dancings round fairy trees with the village children, and prayings at haunted wells, and a dozen other things which you were diligently inquiring into until my arrival. There is not a village girl in France against whom you could not prove such things: they all dance round haunted trees, and pray at magic wells. Some of them would steal the Pope's horse if they got the chance. Heresy, gentlemen, heresy is the charge we have to try. The detection and suppression of heresy is my peculiar business: I am here as an inquisitor, not as an ordinary magistrate. Stick to the heresy, gentlemen; and leave the other matters alone.

CAUCHON. I may say that we have sent to the girl's village to make inquiries about her, and there is practically nothing serious against her.

THE CHAPLAIN. ⎫ [*Rising and* ⎧ Nothing serious, my lord—
COURCELLES. ⎬ *clamoring* ⎨ What! The fairy tree not—
⎭ *together.*] ⎩

CAUCHON. [*Out of patience.*] Be silent, gentlemen; or speak one at a time.

COURCELLES *collapses into his chair, intimidated.*

THE CHAPLAIN. [*Sulkily resuming his seat.*] That is what The Maid said to us last Friday.

CAUCHON. I wish you had followed her counsel, sir. When I say nothing serious, I mean nothing that men of sufficiently large mind to conduct an inquiry like this would consider serious. I agree with my colleague the Inquisitor that it is on the count of heresy that we must proceed.

LADVENU. [*A young but ascetically fine-drawn Dominican who is sitting next* COURCELLES, *on his right.*] But is there any great harm in the girl's heresy? Is it not merely her simplicity? Many saints have said as much as Joan.

THE INQUISITOR. [*Dropping his blandness and speaking very gravely.*] Brother Martin: if you had seen what I have seen of heresy, you would not think it a light thing even in its most apparently harmless and even lovable and pious origins. Heresy begins with people who are to all appearance better than their neighbors. A gentle and pious girl, or a young man who has obeyed the command of our Lord by giving all his riches to the poor, and putting on the garb of poverty, the life of austerity, and the rule of humility and charity, may be the founder of a heresy that will wreck both Church and Empire if not ruthlessly stamped out in time. The records of the Holy Inquisition are full of histories we dare not give to the world, because they are beyond the belief of honest men and innocent women; yet they all began with saintly simpletons. I have seen this again and again. Mark what I say: the woman who quarrels with her clothes, and puts on the dress of a man, is like the man who throws off his fur gown and dresses like John the Baptist: they are followed, as surely as the night follows the day, by bands of wild women and men who refuse to wear any clothes at all. When maids will neither marry nor take regular vows, and then reject marriage and exalt their lusts into divine inspirations, then, as surely as the summer follows the spring, they begin with polygamy, and end by incest. Heresy at first seems innocent and even laudable; but it ends in such a monstrous horror of unnatural wickedness that the most tender-hearted among you, if you saw it at work as I have seen it, would clamor against the mercy of the Church in dealing with it.

For two hundred years the Holy Office has striven with these diabolical madnesses; and it knows that they begin always by vain and
ignorant persons setting up their own judgment against the Church,
and taking it upon themselves to be the interpreters of God's will.
You must not fall into the common error of mistaking these simpletons for liars and hypocrites. They believe honestly and sincerely
that their diabolical inspiration is divine. Therefore you must be on
your guard against your natural compassion. You are all, I hope,
merciful men: how else could you have devoted your lives to the
service of our gentle Savior? You are going to see before you a
young girl, pious and chaste; for I must tell you, gentlemen, that
the things said of her by our English friends are supported by no
evidence, whilst there is abundant testimony that her excesses have
been excesses of religion and charity and not of worldliness and
wantonness. This girl is not one of those whose hard features are
the sign of hard hearts, and whose brazen looks and lewd demeanor
condemn them before they are accused. The devilish pride that has
led her into her present peril has left no mark on her countenance.
Strange as it may seem to you, it has even left no mark on her character outside those special matters in which she is proud; so that
you will see a diabolical pride and a natural humility seated side by
side in the selfsame soul. Therefore be on your guard. God forbid
that I should tell you to harden your hearts; for her punishment if
we condemn her will be so cruel that we should forfeit our own
hope of divine mercy were there one grain of malice against her in
our hearts. But if you hate cruelty—and if any man here does not
hate it I command him on his soul's salvation to quit this holy
court—I say, if you hate cruelty, remember that nothing is so cruel
in its consequences as the toleration of heresy. Remember also that
no court of law can be so cruel as the common people are to those
whom they suspect of heresy. The heretic in the hands of the Holy
Office is safe from violence, is assured of a fair trial, and cannot
suffer death, even when guilty, if repentance follows sin. Innumer-
able lives of heretics have been saved because the Holy Office has
taken them out of the hands of the people, and because the people
have yielded them up, knowing that the Holy Office would deal
with them. Before the Holy Inquisition existed, and even now
when its officers are not within reach, the unfortunate wretch suspected of heresy, perhaps quite ignorantly and unjustly, is stoned,
torn in pieces, drowned, burned in his house with all his innocent
children, without a trial, unshriven, unburied save as a dog is
buried: all of them deeds hateful to God and most cruel to man.
Gentlemen; I am compassionate by nature as well as by my profession; and though the work I have to do may seem cruel to those
who do not know how much more cruel it would be to leave it un-

done, I would go to the stake myself sooner than do it if I did not
know its righteousness, its necessity, its essential mercy. I ask you to
address yourself to this trial in that conviction. Anger is a bad coun-
sellor; cast out anger. Pity is sometimes worse: cast out pity. But do
not cast out mercy. Remember only that justice comes first. Have
you anything to say, my lord, before we proceed to trial?

CAUCHON. You have spoken for me, and spoken better than I could.
I do not see how any sane man could disagree with a word that has
fallen from you. But this I will add. The crude heresies of which
you have told us are horrible; but their horror is like that of the
black death: they rage for a while and then die out, because sound
and sensible men will not under any incitement be reconciled to
nakedness and incest and polygamy and the like. But we are confronted today throughout Europe with a heresy that is spreading
among men not weak in mind nor diseased in brain: nay, the
stronger the mind, the more obstinate the heretic. It is neither dis-
credited by fantastic extremes nor corrupted by the common lusts
of the flesh; but it, too, sets up the private judgment of the single
erring mortal against the considered wisdom and experience of the
Church. The mighty structure of Catholic Christendom will never
be shaken by naked madmen or by the sins of Moab and Ammon.
But it may be betrayed from within, and brought to barbarous ruin
and desolation, by this arch heresy which the English Commander
calls Protestantism.

THE ASSESSORS. [*Whispering.*] Protestantism! What was that? What
does the Bishop mean? Is it a new heresy? The English Commander, he said. Did you ever hear of Protestantism? etc., etc.

CAUCHON. [*Continuing.*] And that reminds me. What provision has
the Earl of Warwick made for the defence of the secular arm
should The Maid prove obdurate, and the people be moved to pity
her?

THE CHAPLAIN. Have no fear on that score, my lord. The noble earl
has eight hundred men-at-arms at the gates. She will not slip
through our English fingers even if the whole city be on her side.

CAUCHON. [*Revolted.*] Will you not add, God grant that she repent
and purge her sin?

THE CHAPLAIN. That does not seem to me to be consistent; but of
course I agree with your lordship.

CAUCHON. [*Giving him up with a shrug of contempt.*] The court sits.

THE INQUISITOR. Let the accused be brought in.

LADVENU. [*Calling.*] The accused. Let her be brought in.

   JOAN, *chained by the ankles, is brought in through the arched
   door behind the prisoner's stool by a guard of English soldiers.
   With them is the* EXECUTIONER *and his assistants. They lead her to
   the prisoner's stool, and place themselves behind it after taking off*

her chain. She wears a page's black suit. Her long imprisonment and the strain of the examinations which have preceded the trial have left their mark on her; but her vitality still holds; she confronts the court unabashed, without a trace of the awe which their formal solemnity seems to require for the complete success of its impressiveness.

THE INQUISITOR. [*Kindly.*] Sit down, Joan. [*She sits on the prisoner's stool.*] You look very pale today. Are you not well?

JOAN. Thank you kindly: I am well enough. But the Bishop sent me some carp; and it made me ill.

CAUCHON. I am sorry. I told them to see that it was fresh.

JOAN. You meant to be good to me, I know; but it is a fish that does not agree with me. The English thought you were trying to poison me—

CAUCHON. ⎫ [*Together.*] ⎰ What!
THE CHAPLAIN. ⎭ ⎱ No, my lord.

JOAN. [*Continuing.*] They are determined that I shall be burnt as a witch; and they sent their doctor to cure me; but he was forbidden to bleed me because the silly people believe that a witch's witchery leaves her if she is bled; so he only called me filthy names. Why do you leave me in the hands of the English? I should be in the hands of the Church. And why must I be chained by the feet to a log of wood? Are you afraid I will fly away?

D'ESTIVET. [*Harshly.*] Woman: it is not for you to question the court: it is for us to question you.

COURCELLES. When you were left unchained, did you not try to escape by jumping from a tower sixty feet high? If you cannot fly like a witch, how is it that you are still alive?

JOAN. I suppose because the tower was not so high then. It has grown higher every day since you began asking me questions about it.

D'ESTIVET. Why did you jump from the tower?

JOAN. How do you know that I jumped?

D'ESTIVET. You were found lying in the moat. Why did you leave the tower?

JOAN. Why would anybody leave a prison if they could get out?

D'ESTIVET. You tried to escape?

JOAN. Of course I did; and not for the first time either. If you leave the door of the cage open the bird will fly out.

D'ESTIVET. [*Rising.*] That is a confession of heresy. I call the attention of the court to it.

JOAN. Heresy, he calls it! Am I a heretic because I try to escape from prison?

D'ESTIVET. Assuredly, if you are in the hands of the Church, and you wilfully take yourself out of its hands, you are deserting the Church; and that is heresy.

JOAN. It is great nonsense. Nobody could be such a fool as to think that.

D'ESTIVET. You hear, my lord, how I am reviled in the execution of my duty by this woman. [*He sits down indignantly.*]

CAUCHON. I have warned you before, Joan, that you are doing yourself no good by these pert answers.

JOAN. But you will not talk sense to me. I am reasonable if you will be reasonable.

THE INQUISITOR. [*Interposing.*] This is not yet in order. You forget, Master Promoter, that the proceedings have not been formally opened. The time for questions is after she has sworn on the Gospels to tell us the whole truth.

JOAN. You say this to me every time. I have said again and again that I will tell you all that concerns this trial. But I cannot tell you the whole truth: God does not allow the whole truth to be told. You do not understand it when I tell it. It is an old saying that he who tells too much truth is sure to be hanged. I am weary of this argument: we have been over it nine times already. I have sworn as much as I will swear; and I will swear no more.

COURCELLES. My lord: she should be put to the torture.

THE INQUISITOR. You hear, Joan? That is what happens to the obdurate. Think before you answer. Has she been shewn the instruments?

THE EXECUTIONER. They are ready, my lord. She has seen them.

JOAN. If you tear me limb from limb until you separate my soul from my body you will get nothing out of me beyond what I have told you. What more is there to tell that you could understand? Besides I cannot bear to be hurt; and if you hurt me I will say anything you like to stop the pain. But I will take it all back afterwards; so what is the use of it?

LADVENU. There is much in that. We should proceed mercifully.

COURCELLES. But the torture is customary.

THE INQUISITOR. It must not be applied wantonly. If the accused will confess voluntarily, then its use cannot be justified.

COURCELLES. But this is unusual and irregular. She refuses to take the oath.

LADVENU. [*Disgusted.*] Do you want to torture the girl for the mere pleasure of it?

COURCELLES. [*Bewildered.*] But it is not a pleasure. It is the law. It is customary. It is always done.

THE INQUISITOR. That is not so, Master, except when the inquiries are carried on by people who do not know their legal business.

COURCELLES. But the woman is a heretic. I assure you it is always done.

CAUCHON. [*Decisively.*] It will not be done today if it is not necessary. Let there be an end of this. I will not have it said that we proceeded on forced confessions. We have sent our best preachers and doctors to this woman to exhort and implore her to save her soul and body from the fire: we shall not now send the executioner to thrust her into it.

COURCELLES. Your lordship is merciful, of course. But it is a great responsibility to depart from the usual practice.

JOAN. Thou art a rare noodle, Master. Do what was done last time is thy rule, eh?

COURCELLES. [*Rising.*] Thou wanton: dost thou dare call me noodle?

THE INQUISITOR. Patience, Master, patience: I fear you will soon be only too terribly avenged.

COURCELLES. [*Mutters.*] Noodle indeed! [*He sits down, much discontented.*]

THE INQUISITOR. Meanwhile, let us not be moved by the rough side of a shepherd lass's tongue.

JOAN. Nay: I am no shepherd lass, though I have helped with the sheep like anyone else. I will do a lady's work in the house—spin or weave—against any woman in Rouen.

THE INQUISITOR. This is not a time for vanity, Joan. You stand in great peril.

JOAN. I know it: have I not been punished for my vanity? If I had not worn my cloth of gold surcoat in battle like a fool, that Burgundian soldier would never have pulled me backwards off my horse; and I should not have been here.

THE CHAPLAIN. If you are so clever at woman's work why do you not stay at home and do it?

JOAN. There are plenty of other women to do it; but there is nobody to do my work.

CAUCHON. Come! we are wasting time on trifles. Joan: I am going to put a most solemn question to you. Take care how you answer; for your life and salvation are at stake on it. Will you for all you have said and done, be it good or bad, accept the judgment of God's Church on earth? More especially as to the acts and words that are imputed to you in this trial by the Promoter here, will you submit your case to the inspired interpretation of the Church Militant?

JOAN. I am a faithful child of the Church. I will obey the Church—

CAUCHON. [*Hopefully leaning forward.*] You will?

JOAN. —provided it does not command anything impossible.

CAUCHON *sinks back in his chair with a heavy sigh. The* INQUISITOR *purses his lips and frowns.* LADVENU *shakes his head pitifully.*

D'ESTIVET. She imputes to the Church the error and folly of commanding the impossible.

JOAN. If you command me to declare that all I have done and said, and all the visions and revelations I have had, were not from God, then that is impossible: I will not declare it for anything in the world. What God made me do I will never go back on; and what

He has commanded or shall command I will not fail to do in spite
of any man alive. That is what I mean by impossible. And in case
the Church should bid me do anything contrary to the command
I have from God, I will not consent to it, no matter what it may be.

THE ASSESSORS. [*Shocked and indignant.*] Oh! The Church contrary
to God! What do you say now? Flat heresy. This is beyond everything, etc., etc.

D'ESTIVET. [*Throwing down his brief.*] My lord: do you need anything
more than this?

CAUCHON. Woman: you have said enough to burn ten heretics. Will
you not be warned? Will you not understand?

THE INQUISITOR. If the Church Militant tells you that your revelations
and visions are sent by the devil to tempt you to your damnation,
will you not believe that the Church is wiser than you?

JOAN. I believe that God is wiser than I; and it is His commands that
I will do. All the things that you call my crimes have come to me by
the command of God. I say that I have done them by the order of
God: it is impossible for me to say anything else. If any Churchman says the contrary I shall not mind him: I shall mind God alone,
whose command I always follow.

LADVENU. [*Pleading with her urgently.*] You do not know what you
are saying, child. Do you want to kill yourself? Listen. Do you not
believe that you are subject to the Church of God on earth?

JOAN. Yes. When have I ever denied it?

LADVENU. Good. That means, does it not, that you are subject to our
Lord the Pope, to the cardinals, the archbishops, and the bishops
for whom his lordship stands here today?

JOAN. God must be served first.

D'ESTIVET. Then your voices command you not to submit yourself to
the Church Militant?

JOAN. My voices do not tell me to disobey the Church; but God must
be served first.

CAUCHON. And you, and not the Church, are to be the judge?

JOAN. What other judgment can I judge by but my own?

THE ASSESSORS. [*Scandalized.*] Oh! [*They cannot find words.*]

CAUCHON. Out of your own mouth you have condemned yourself. We
have striven for your salvation to the verge of sinning ourselves:
we have opened the door to you again and again; and you have shut
it in our faces and in the face of God. Dare you pretend, after what
you have said, that you are in a state of grace?

JOAN. If I am not, may God bring me to it: if I am, may God keep me
in it!

LADVENU. That is a very good reply, my lord.

COURCELLES. Were you in a state of grace when you stole the Bishop's
horse?

CAUCHON. [*Rising in a fury.*] Oh, devil take the Bishop's horse and you too! We are here to try a case of heresy; and no sooner do we come to the root of the matter than we are thrown back by idiots who understand nothing but horses. [*Trembling with rage, he forces himself to sit down.*]

THE INQUISITOR. Gentlemen, gentlemen: in clinging to these small issues you are The Maid's best advocates. I am not surprised that his lordship has lost patience with you. What does the Promoter say? Does he press these trumpery matters?

D'ESTIVET. I am bound by my office to press everything; but when the woman confesses a heresy that must bring upon her the doom of excommunication, of what consequence is it that she has been guilty also of offences which expose her to minor penances? I share the impatience of his lordship as to these minor charges. Only, with great respect, I must emphasize the gravity of two very horrible and blasphemous crimes which she does not deny. First, she has intercourse with evil spirits, and is therefore a sorceress. Second, she wears men's clothes, which is indecent, unnatural, and abominable; and in spite of our most earnest remonstrances and entreaties, she will not change them even to receive the sacrament.

JOAN. Is the blessed St Catherine an evil spirit? Is St Margaret? Is Michael the Archangel?

COURCELLES. How do you know that the spirit which appears to you is an archangel? Does he not appear to you as a naked man?

JOAN. Do you think God cannot afford clothes for him?

The ASSESSORS *cannot help smiling, especially as the joke is against* COURCELLES.

LADVENU. Well answered, Joan.

THE INQUISITOR. It is, in effect, well answered. But no evil spirit would be so simple as to appear to a young girl in a guise that would scandalize her when he meant her to take him for a messenger from the Most High. Joan: the Church instructs you that these apparitions are demons seeking your soul's perdition. Do you accept the instruction of the Church?

JOAN. I accept the messenger of God. How could any faithful believer in the Church refuse him?

CAUCHON. Wretched woman: again I ask you, do you know what you are saying?

THE INQUISITOR. You wrestle in vain with the devil for her soul, my lord: she will not be saved. Now as to this matter of the man's dress. For the last time, will you put off that impudent attire, and dress as becomes your sex?

JOAN. I will not.

D'ESTIVET. [*Pouncing.*] The sin of disobedience, my lord.

JOAN. [*Distressed.*] But my voices tell me I must dress as a soldier.

LADVENU. Joan, Joan: does not that prove to you that the voices are the voices of evil spirits? Can you suggest to us one good reason why an angel of God should give you such shameless advice?

JOAN. Why, yes: what can be plainer commonsense? I was a soldier living among soldiers. I am a prisoner guarded by soldiers. If I were to dress as a woman they would think of me as a woman; and then what would become of me? If I dress as a soldier they think of me as a soldier, and I can live with them as I do at home with my brothers. That is why St Catherine tells me I must not dress as a woman until she gives me leave.

COURCELLES. When will she give you leave?

JOAN. When you take me out of the hands of the English soldiers. I have told you that I should be in the hands of the Church, and not left night and day with four soldiers of the Earl of Warwick. Do you want me to live with them in petticoats?

LADVENU. My lord: what she says is, God knows, very wrong and shocking; but there is a grain of worldly sense in it such as might impose on a simple village maiden.

JOAN. If we were as simple in the village as you are in your courts and palaces, there would soon be no wheat to make bread for you.

CAUCHON. That is the thanks you get for trying to save her, Brother Martin.

LADVENU. Joan: we are all trying to save you. His lordship is trying to save you. The Inquisitor could not be more just to you if you were his own daughter. But you are blinded by a terrible pride and self-sufficiency.

JOAN. Why do you say that? I have said nothing wrong. I cannot understand.

THE INQUISITOR. The blessed St Athanasius has laid it down in his creed that those who cannot understand are damned. It is not enough to be simple. It is not enough even to be what simple people call good. The simplicity of a darkened mind is no better than the simplicity of a beast.

JOAN. There is great wisdom in the simplicity of a beast, let me tell you; and sometimes great foolishness in the wisdom of scholars.

LADVENU. We know that, Joan: we are not so foolish as you think us. Try to resist the temptation to make pert replies to us. Do you see that man who stands behind you [*he indicates the* EXECUTIONER]?

JOAN. [*Turning and looking at the man.*] Your torturer? But the Bishop said I was not to be tortured.

LADVENU. You are not to be tortured because you have confessed everything that is necessary to your condemnation. That man is not only the torturer: he is also the Executioner. Executioner: let The Maid hear your answers to my questions. Are you prepared for the burning of a heretic this day?

THE EXECUTIONER. Yes, Master.

LADVENU. Is the stake ready?

THE EXECUTIONER. It is. In the market-place. The English have built it too high for me to get near her and make the death easier. It will be a cruel death.

JOAN. [*Horrified.*] But you are not going to burn me now?

THE INQUISITOR. You realize it at last.

LADVENU. There are eight hundred English soldiers waiting to take you to the market-place the moment the sentence of excommunication has passed the lips of your judges. You are within a few short moments of that doom.

JOAN. [*Looking round desperately for rescue.*] Oh God!

LADVENU. Do not despair, Joan. The Church is merciful. You can save yourself.

JOAN. [*Hopefully.*] Yes: my voices promised me I should not be burnt. St Catherine bade me be bold.

CAUCHON. Woman: are you quite mad? Do you not yet see that your voices have deceived you?

JOAN. Oh no: that is impossible.

CAUCHON. Impossible! They have led you straight to your excommunication, and to the stake which is there waiting for you.

LADVENU. [*Pressing the point hard.*] Have they kept a single promise to you since you were taken at Compiègne? The devil has betrayed you. The Church holds out its arms to you.

JOAN. [*Despairing.*] Oh, it is true: it is true: my voices have deceived me. I have been mocked by devils: my faith is broken. I have dared and dared; but only a fool will walk into a fire: God, who gave me my commonsense, cannot will me to do that.

LADVENU. Now God be praised that He has saved you at the eleventh hour! [*He hurries to the vacant seat at the scribes' table, and snatches a sheet of paper, on which he sets to work writing eagerly.*]

CAUCHON. Amen!

JOAN. What must I do?

CAUCHON. You must sign a solemn recantation of your heresy.

JOAN. Sign? That means to write my name. I cannot write.

CAUCHON. You have signed many letters before.

JOAN. Yes; but someone held my hand and guided the pen. I can make my mark.

THE CHAPLAIN. [*Who has been listening with growing alarm and indignation.*] My lord: do you mean that you are going to allow this woman to escape us?

THE INQUISITOR. The law must take its course, Master de Stogumber. And you know the law.

THE CHAPLAIN. [*Rising, purple with fury.*] I know that there is no faith in a Frenchman. [*Tumult, which he shouts down.*] I know what my lord the Cardinal of Winchester will say when he hears of this. I know what the Earl of Warwick will do when he learns that you intend to betray him. There are eight hundred men at the gate who will see that this abominable witch is burnt in spite of your teeth.

THE ASSESSORS. [*Meanwhile.*] What is this? What did he say? He accuses us of treachery! This is past bearing. No faith in a Frenchman! Did you hear that? This is an intolerable fellow. Who is he? Is this what English Churchmen are like? He must be mad or drunk, etc., etc.

THE INQUISITOR. [*Rising.*] Silence, pray! Gentlemen: pray silence! Master Chaplain: bethink you a moment of your holy office: of what you are, and where you are. I direct you to sit down.

THE CHAPLAIN. [*Folding his arms doggedly, his face working convulsively.*] I will NOT sit down.

CAUCHON. Master Inquisitor: this man has called me a traitor to my face before now.

THE CHAPLAIN. So you are a traitor. You are all traitors. You have been doing nothing but begging this damnable witch on your knees to recant all through this trial.

THE INQUISITOR. [*Placidly resuming his seat.*] If you will not sit, you must stand: that is all.

THE CHAPLAIN. I will NOT stand. [*He flings himself back into his chair.*]

LADVENU. [*Rising with the paper in his hand.*] My lord: here is the form of recantation for The Maid to sign.

CAUCHON. Read it to her.

JOAN. Do not trouble. I will sign it.

THE INQUISITOR. Woman: you must know what you are putting your hand to. Read it to her, Brother Martin. And let all be silent.

LADVENU. [*Reading quietly.*] 'I, Joan, commonly called The Maid, a miserable sinner, do confess that I have most grievously sinned in the following articles. I have pretended to have revelations from God and the angels and the blessed saints, and perversely rejected the Church's warnings that these were temptations by demons. I have blasphemed abominably by wearing an immodest dress, contrary to the Holy Scripture and the canons of the Church. Also I have clipped my hair in the style of a man, and, against all the duties which have made my sex specially acceptable in heaven, have taken up the sword, even to the shedding of human blood, inciting men to slay each other, invoking evil spirits to delude them, and stubbornly and most blasphemously imputing these sins to Almighty God. I confess to the sin of sedition, to the sin of idolatry, to the sin of disobedience, to the sin of pride, and to the sin of heresy. All of which sins I now renounce and abjure and depart from, humbly thanking you Doctors and Masters who have brought me back to the truth and into the grace of our Lord. And I will never return to my errors but will remain in communion with our Holy Church and in obedience to our Holy Father the Pope of Rome. All this I swear by God Almighty and the Holy Gospels, in witness whereto I sign my name to this recantation.'

THE INQUISITOR. You understand this, Joan?

JOAN. [*Listless.*] It is plain enough, sir.

THE INQUISITOR. And it is true?

JOAN. It may be true. If it were not true, the fire would not be ready for me in the market-place.

LADVENU. [*Taking up his pen and a book, and going to her quickly lest she should compromise herself again.*] Come, child: let me guide your hand. Take the pen. [*She does so; and they begin to write, using the book as a desk.*] J.E.H.A.N.E. So. Now make your mark by yourself.

JOAN. [*Makes her mark, and gives him back the pen, tormented by the rebellion of her soul against her mind and body.*] There!

LADVENU. [*Replacing the pen on the table, and handing the recantation to* CAUCHON *with a reverence.*] Praise be to God, my brothers, the lamb has returned to the flock; and the shepherd rejoices in her more than in ninety and nine just persons. [*He returns to his seat.*]

THE INQUISITOR. [*Taking the paper from* CAUCHON.] We declare thee by this act set free from the danger of excommunication in which thou stoodest. [*He throws the paper down to the table.*]

JOAN. I thank you.

THE INQUISITOR. But because thou has sinned most presumptuously against God and the Holy Church, and that thou mayst repent thy errors in solitary contemplation, and be shielded from all temptation to return to them, we, for the good of thy soul, and for a penance that may wipe out thy sins and bring thee finally unspotted to the throne of grace, do condemn thee to eat the bread of sorrow and drink the water of affliction to the end of thy earthly days in perpetual imprisonment.

JOAN. [*Rising in consternation and terrible anger.*] Perpetual imprisonment! Am I not then to be set free?

LADVENU. [*Mildly shocked.*] Set free, child, after such wickedness as yours! What are you dreaming of?

JOAN. Give me that writing. [*She rushes to the table; snatches up the paper; and tears it into fragments.*] Light your fire: do you think I dread it as much as the life of a rat in a hole? My voices were right.

LADVENU. Joan! Joan!

JOAN. Yes: they told me you were fools [*the word gives great offence*], and that I was not to listen to your fine words nor trust to your charity. You promised me my life; but you lied [*indignant exclama-*

tions]. You think that life is nothing but not being stone dead. It is not the bread and water I fear: I can live on bread: when have I asked for more? It is no hardship to drink water if the water be clean. Bread has no sorrow for me, and water no affliction. But to shut me from the light of the sky and the sight of the fields and flowers; to chain my feet so that I can never again ride with the soldiers nor climb the hills; to make me breathe foul damp darkness, and keep from me everything that brings me back to the love of God when your wickedness and foolishness tempt me to hate Him: all this is worse than the furnace in the Bible that was heated seven times. I could do without my warhorse; I could drag about in a skirt; I could let the banners and the trumpets and the knights and soldiers pass me and leave me behind as they leave the other women, if only I could still hear the wind in the trees, the larks in the sunshine, the young lambs crying through the healthy frost, and the blessed blessed church bells that send my angel voices floating to me on the wind. But without these things I cannot live; and by your wanting to take them away from me, or from any human creature, I know that your counsel is of the devil, and that mine is of God.

THE ASSESSORS. [*In great commotion.*] Blasphemy! blasphemy! She is possessed. She said our counsel was of the devil. And hers of God. Monstrous! The devil is in our midst, etc., etc.

D'ESTIVET. [*Shouting above the din.*] She is a relapsed heretic, obstinate, incorrigible, and altogether unworthy of the mercy we have shewn her. I call for her excommunication.

THE CHAPLAIN. [*To the* EXECUTIONER.] Light your fire, man. To the stake with her.

The EXECUTIONER *and his assistants hurry out through the courtyard.*

LADVENU. You wicked girl: if your counsel were of God would He not deliver you?

JOAN. His ways are not your ways. He wills that I go through the fire to His bosom; for I am His child, and you are not fit that I should live among you. That is my last word to you.

The soldiers seize her.

CAUCHON. [*Rising.*] Not yet.

They wait. There is a dead silence. CAUCHON *turns to the* INQUISITOR *with an inquiring look. The* INQUISITOR *nods affirmatively. They rise solemnly, and intone the sentence antiphonally.*

CAUCHON. We decree that thou art a relapsed heretic.

THE INQUISITOR. Cast out from the unity of the Church.

CAUCHON. Sundered from her body.

THE INQUISITOR. Infected with the leprosy of heresy.

CAUCHON. A member of Satan.

THE INQUISITOR. We declare that thou must be excommunicate.

CAUCHON. And now we do cast thee out, segregate thee, and abandon thee to the secular power.

THE INQUISITOR. Admonishing the same secular power that it moderate its judgment of thee in respect of death and division of the limbs. [*He resumes his seat.*]

CAUCHON. And if any true sign of penitence appear in thee, to permit our Brother Martin to administer to thee the sacrament of penance.

THE CHAPLAIN. Into the fire with the witch. [*He rushes at her, and helps the soldiers to push her out.*]

JOAN *is taken away through the courtyard. The* ASSESSORS *rise in disorder, and follow the soldiers, except* LADVENU, *who has hidden his face in his hands.*

CAUCHON. [*Rising again in the act of sitting down.*] No, no: this is irregular. The representative of the secular arm should be here to receive her from us.

THE INQUISITOR. [*Also on his feet again.*] That man is an incorrigible fool.

CAUCHON. Brother Martin: see that everything is done in order.

LADVENU. My place is at her side, my Lord. You must exercise your own authority. [*He hurries out.*]

CAUCHON. These English are impossible: they will thrust her straight into the fire. Look!

He points to the courtyard, in which the glow and flicker of fire can now be seen reddening the May daylight. Only the BISHOP and the INQUISITOR are left in the court.

CAUCHON. [*Turning to go.*] We must stop that.

THE INQUISITOR. [*Calmly.*] Yes; but not too fast, my lord.

CAUCHON. [*Halting.*] But there is not a moment to lose.

THE INQUISITOR. We have proceeded in perfect order. If the English choose to put themselves in the wrong, it is not our business to put them in the right. A flaw in the procedure may be useful later on: one never knows. And the sooner it is over, the better for that poor girl.

CAUCHON. [*Relaxing.*] That is true. But I suppose we must see this dreadful thing through.

THE INQUISITOR. One gets used to it. Habit is everything. I am accustomed to the fire: it is soon over. But it is a terrible thing to see a young and innocent creature crushed between these mighty forces, the Church and the Law.

CAUCHON. You call her innocent!

THE INQUISITOR. Oh, quite innocent. What does she know of the Church and the Law? She did not understand a word we were saying. It is the ignorant who suffer. Come, or we shall be late for the end.

CAUCHON. [*Going with him.*] I shall not be sorry if we are: I am not so accustomed as you.

They are going out when WARWICK *comes in, meeting them.*

WARWICK. Oh, I am intruding. I thought it was all over. [*He makes a feint of retiring.*]

CAUCHON. Do not go, my lord. It is all over.

THE INQUISITOR. The execution is not in our hands, my lord; but it is desirable that we should witness the end. So by your leave—[*He bows, and goes out through the courtyard.*]

CAUCHON. There is some doubt whether your people have observed the forms of law, my lord.

WARWICK. I am told that there is some doubt whether your authority runs in this city, my lord. It is not in your diocese. However, if you will answer for that I will answer for the rest.

CAUCHON. It is to God that we both must answer. Good morning, my lord.

WARWICK. My lord: good morning.

They look at one another for a moment with unconcealed hostility. Then CAUCHON *follows the* INQUISITOR *out.* WARWICK *looks round. Finding himself alone, he calls for attendance.*

WARWICK. Hallo: some attendance here! [*Silence.*] Hallo, there! [*Silence.*] Hallo! Brian, you young blackguard, where are you? [*Silence.*] Guard! [*Silence.*] They have all gone to see the burning: even that child.

The silence is broken by someone frantically howling and sobbing.

WARWICK. What in the devil's name—?

The CHAPLAIN *staggers in from the courtyard like a demented creature, his face streaming with tears, making the piteous sounds that* WARWICK *has heard. He stumbles to the prisoner's stool, and throws himself upon it with heartrending sobs.*

WARWICK. [*Going to him and patting him on the shoulder.*] What is it, Master John? What is the matter?

THE CHAPLAIN. [*Clutching at his hand.*] My lord, my lord: for Christ's sake pray for my wretched guilty soul.

WARWICK. [*Soothing him.*] Yes, yes: of course I will. Calmly, gently—

THE CHAPLAIN. [*Blubbering miserably.*] I am not a bad man, my lord.

WARWICK. No, no: not at all.

THE CHAPLAIN. I meant no harm. I did not know what it would be like.

WARWICK. [*Hardening.*] Oh! You saw it, then?

THE CHAPLAIN. I did not know what I was doing. I am a hotheaded fool; and I shall be damned to all eternity for it.

WARWICK. Nonsense! Very distressing, no doubt; but it was not your doing.

THE CHAPLAIN. [*Lamentably.*] I let them do it. If I had known, I would have torn her from their hands. You dont know: you havnt seen: it is so easy to talk when you dont know. You madden yourself with words: you damn yourself because it feels grand to throw oil on the flaming hell of your own temper. But when it is brought home to you; when you see the thing you have done; when it is blinding your eyes, stifling your nostrils, tearing your heart, then—then—[*falling on his knees*] O God, take away this sight from me! O Christ, deliver me from this fire that is consuming me! She cried to Thee in the midst of it: Jesus! Jesus! Jesus! She is in Thy bosom; and I am in hell for evermore.

WARWICK. [*Summarily hauling him to his feet.*] Come come, man! you must pull yourself together. We shall have the whole town talking of this. [*He throws him not too gently into a chair at the table.*] If you have not the nerve to see these things, why do you not do as I do, and stay away?

THE CHAPLAIN. [*Bewildered and submissive.*] She asked for a cross. A soldier gave her two sticks tied together. Thank God he was an Englishman! I might have done it; but I did not: I am a coward, a mad dog, a fool. But he was an Englishman too.

WARWICK. The fool; they will burn him too if the priests get hold of him.

THE CHAPLAIN. [*Shaken with a convulsion.*] Some of the people laughed at her. They would have laughed at Christ. They were French people, my lord: I know they were French.

WARWICK. Hush! someone is coming. Control yourself.

LADVENU *comes back through the courtyard to* WARWICK's *right hand, carrying a bishop's cross which he has taken from a church. He is very grave and composed.*

WARWICK. I am informed that it is all over, Brother Martin.

LADVENU. [*Enigmatically.*] We do not know, my lord. It may have only just begun.

WARWICK. What does that mean, exactly?

LADVENU. I took this cross from the church for her that she might see it to the last: she had only two sticks that she put into her bosom. When the fire crept round us, and she saw that if I held the cross before her I should be burnt myself, she warned me to get down and save myself. My lord: a girl who could think of another's danger in such a moment was not inspired by the devil. When I had to snatch the cross from her sight, she looked up to heaven. And I do not believe that the heavens were empty. I firmly believe that her Savior appeared to her then in His tenderest glory. She called to Him and died. This is not the end for her, but the beginning.

WARWICK. I am afraid it will have a bad effect on the people.

LADVENU. It had, my lord, on some of them. I heard laughter. Forgive me for saying that I hope and believe it was English laughter.

THE CHAPLAIN. [*Rising frantically.*] No: it was not. There was only one Englishman there that disgraced his country; and that was the mad dog, de Stogumber. [*He rushes wildly out, shrieking.*] Let them torture him. Let them burn him. I will go pray among her ashes. I am no better than Judas: I will hang myself.

WARWICK. Quick, Brother Martin: follow him: he will do himself some mischief. After him, quick.

LADVENU *hurries out,* WARWICK *urging him. The* EXECUTIONER *comes in by the door behind the judges' chairs; and* WARWICK, *returning, finds himself face to face with him.*

WARWICK. Well, fellow: who are you?

THE EXECUTIONER. [*With dignity.*] I am not addressed as fellow, my lord. I am the Master Executioner of Rouen: it is a highly skilled mystery. I am come to tell your lordship that your orders have been obeyed.

WARWICK. I crave your pardon, Master Executioner; and I will see that you lose nothing by having no relics to sell. I have your word, have I, that nothing remains, not a bone, not a nail, not a hair?

THE EXECUTIONER. Her heart would not burn, my lord; but everything that was left is at the bottom of the river. You have heard the last of her.

WARWICK. [*With a wry smile, thinking of what* LADVENU *said.*] The last of her? Hm! I wonder!

EPILOGUE

A restless fitfully windy night in June 1456, full of summer lightning after many days of heat. KING CHARLES THE SEVENTH *of France, formerly Joan's Dauphin, now Charles the Victorious, aged 51, is in bed in one of his royal chateaux. The bed, raised on a dais of two steps, is towards the side of the room so as to avoid blocking a tall lancet window in the middle. Its canopy bears the royal arms in embroidery. Except for the canopy and the huge down pillows there is nothing to distinguish it from a broad settee with bed-clothes and a valance. Thus its occupant is in full view from the foot.*

CHARLES *is not asleep: he is reading in bed, or rather looking at the pictures in Fouquet's Boccaccio with his knees doubled up to make a reading-desk. Beside the bed on his left is a little table with a picture of the Virgin, lighted by candles of painted wax. The walls are hung from ceiling to floor with painted curtains which stir at times in the draughts. At first glance the prevailing yellow and red in these hanging pictures is somewhat flamelike when the folds breathe in the wind.*

The door is on CHARLES's *left, but in front of him close to the corner farthest from him. A large watchman's rattle, handsomely designed and gaily painted, is in the bed under his hand.*

CHARLES *turns a leaf. A distant clock strikes the half-hour softly.* CHARLES *shuts the book with a clap; throws it aside; snatches up the rattle; and whirls it energetically, making 'a deafening clatter.* LADVENU *enters, 25 years older, strange and stark in bearing, and still carrying the cross from Rouen.* CHARLES *evidently does not expect him; for he springs out of bed on the farther side from the door.*

CHARLES. Who are you? Where is my gentleman of the bedchamber? What do you want?

LADVENU. [*Solemnly.*] I bring you glad tidings of great joy. Rejoice, O king; for the taint is removed from your blood, and the stain from your crown. Justice, long delayed, is at last triumphant.

CHARLES. What are you talking about? Who are you?

LADVENU. I am Brother Martin.

CHARLES. And who, saving your reverence, may Brother Martin be?

LADVENU. I held this cross when The Maid perished in the fire. Twenty-five years have passed since then: nearly ten thousand days. And on every one of those days I have prayed to God to justify His daughter on earth as she is justified in heaven.

CHARLES. [*Reassured, sitting down on the foot of the bed.*] Oh, I remember now. I have heard of you. You have a bee in your bonnet about The Maid. Have you been at the inquiry?

LADVENU. I have given my testimony.

CHARLES. Is it over?

LADVENU. It is over.

CHARLES. Satisfactorily?

LADVENU. The ways of God are very strange.

CHARLES. How so?

LADVENU. At the trial which sent a saint to the stake as a heretic and a sorceress, the truth was told; the law was upheld; mercy was shewn beyond all custom; no wrong was done but the final and dreadful wrong of the lying sentence and the pitiless fire. At this inquiry from which I have just come, there was shameless perjury, courtly corruption, calumny of the dead who did their duty according to their lights, cowardly evasion of the issue, testimony made of idle tales that could not impose on a ploughboy. Yet out of this insult to justice, this defamation of the Church, this orgy of lying and foolishness, the truth is set in the noonday sun on the hilltop; the white robe of innocence is cleansed from the smirch of the burning faggots; the holy life is sanctified; the true heart that lived through the flame is consecrated; a great lie is silenced for ever; and a great wrong is set right before all men.

CHARLES. My friend: provided they can no longer say that I was crowned by a witch and a heretic, I shall not fuss about how the trick has been done. Joan would not have fussed about it if it came all right in the end: she was not that sort: I knew her. Is her rehabilitation complete? I made it pretty clear that there was to be no nonsense about it.

LADVENU. It is solemnly declared that her judges were full of corruption, cozenage, fraud, and malice. Four falsehoods.

CHARLES. Never mind the falsehoods: her judges are dead.

LADVENU. The sentence on her is broken, annulled, annihilated, set aside as non-existent, without value or effect.

CHARLES. Good. Nobody can challenge my consecration now, can they?

LADVENU. Not Charlemagne nor King David himself was more sacredly crowned.

CHARLES. [*Rising.*] Excellent. Think of what that means to me!

LADVENU. I think of what it means to her!

CHARLES. You cannot. None of us ever knew what anything meant to her. She was like nobody else; and she must take care of herself wherever she is; for *I* cannot take care of her; and neither can you, whatever you may think: you are not big enough. But I will tell you this about her. If you could bring her back to life, they would burn her again within six months, for all their present adoration of her. And you would hold up the cross, too, just the same. So [*crossing himself*] let her rest; and let you and I mind our own business, and not meddle with hers.

LADVENU. God forbid that I should have no share in her, nor she in me! [*He turns and strides out as he came, saying:*] Henceforth my path will not lie through palaces, nor my conversation be with kings.

CHARLES. [*Following him towards the door, and shouting after him:*] Much good may it do you, holy man! [*He returns to the middle of the chamber, where he halts, and says quizzically to himself:*] That was a funny chap. How did he get in? Where are my people? [*He goes impatiently to the bed, and swings the rattle. A rush of wind through the open door sets the walls swaying agitatedly. The candles go out. He calls in the darkness:*] Hallo! Someone come and shut the windows: everything is being blown all over the place. [*A flash of summer lightning shews up the lancet window. A figure is seen in silhouette against it.*] Who is there? Who is that? Help! Murder! [*Thunder. He jumps into bed, and hides under the clothes.*]

JOAN'S VOICE. Easy, Charlie, easy. What art making all that noise for? No one can hear thee. Thou'rt asleep. [*She is dimly seen in a pallid greenish light by the bedside.*]

CHARLES. [*Peeping out.*] Joan! Are you a ghost, Joan?

JOAN. Hardly even that, lad. Can a poor burnt-up lass have a ghost? I am but a dream that thou'rt dreaming. [*The light increases: they become plainly visible as he sits up.*] Thou looks older, lad.

CHARLES. I am older. Am I really asleep?

JOAN. Fallen asleep over thy silly book.

CHARLES. That's funny.

JOAN. Not so funny as that I am dead, is it?

CHARLES. Are you really dead?

JOAN. As dead as anybody ever is, laddie. I am out of the body.

CHARLES. Just fancy! Did it hurt much?

JOAN. Did what hurt much?

CHARLES. Being burnt.

JOAN. Oh, that! I cannot remember very well. I think it did at first; but then it all got mixed up; and I was not in my right mind until I was free of the body. But do not thou go handling fire and thinking it will not hurt thee. How hast been ever since?

CHARLES. Oh, not so bad. Do you know, I actually lead my army out and win battles? Down into the moat up to my waist in mud and blood. Up the ladders with the stones and hot pitch raining down. Like you.

JOAN. No! Did I make a man of thee after all, Charlie?

CHARLES. I am Charles the Victorious now. I had to be brave because you were. Agnes put a little pluck into me too.

JOAN. Agnes! Who was Agnes?

CHARLES. Agnes Sorel. A woman I fell in love with. I dream of her often. I never dreamed of you before.

JOAN. Is she dead, like me?

CHARLES. Yes. But she was not like you. She was very beautiful.

JOAN. [*Laughing heartily.*] Ha ha! I was no beauty: I was always a rough one: a regular soldier. I might almost as well have been a man. Pity I wasnt: I should not have bothered you all so much then. But my head was in the skies; and the glory of God was upon me; and, man or woman, I should have bothered you as long as your noses were in the mud. Now tell me what has happened since you wise men knew no better than to make a heap of cinders of me?

CHARLES. Your mother and brothers have sued the courts to have your case tried over again. And the courts have declared that your judges were full of corruption and cozenage, fraud and malice.

JOAN. Not they. They were as honest a lot of poor fools as ever burned their betters.

CHARLES. The sentence on you is broken, annihilated, annulled; null, non-existent, without value or effect.

JOAN. I was burned, all the same. Can they unburn me?

CHARLES. If they could, they would think twice before they did it. But they have decreed that a beautiful cross be placed where the stake stood, for your perpetual memory and for your salvation.

JOAN. It is the memory and the salvation that sanctify the cross, not the cross that sanctifies the memory and the salvation. [*She turns away, forgetting him.*] I shall outlast that cross. I shall be remembered when men will have forgotten where Rouen stood.

CHARLES. There you go with your self-conceit, the same as ever! I think you might say a word of thanks to me for having had justice done at last.

CAUCHON. [*Appearing at the window between them.*] Liar!

CHARLES. Thank you.

JOAN. Why, if it isnt Peter Cauchon! How are you, Peter? What luck have you had since you burned me?

CAUCHON. None. I arraign the justice of Man. It is not the justice of God.

JOAN. Still dreaming of justice. Peter? See what justice came to with me! But what has happened to thee? Art dead or alive?

CAUCHON. Dead. Dishonored. They pursued me beyond the grave. They excommunicated my dead body: they dug it up and flung it into the common sewer.

JOAN. Your dead body did not feel the spade and the sewer as my live body felt the fire.

CAUCHON. But this thing that they have done against me hurts justice; destroys faith; saps the foundation of the Church. The solid earth sways like the treacherous sea beneath the feet of men and spirits alike when the innocent are slain in the name of law, and their wrongs are undone by slandering the pure of heart.

JOAN. Well, well, Peter, I hope men will be the better for remembering me; and they would not remember me so well if you had not burned me.

CAUCHON. They will be the worse for remembering me: they will see in me evil triumphing over good, falsehood over truth, cruelty over mercy, hell over heaven. Their courage will rise as they think of you, only to faint as they think of me. Yet God is my witness I was just: I was merciful: I was faithful to my light: I could do no other than I did.

CHARLES. [*Scrambling out of the sheets and enthroning himself on the side of the bed.*] Yes: it is always you good men that do the big mischiefs. Look at me! I am not Charles the Good, nor Charles the Wise, nor Charles the Bold. Joan's worshippers may even call me Charles the Coward because I did not pull her out of the fire. But I have done less harm than any of you. You people with your heads in the sky spend all your time trying to turn the world upside down; but I take the world as it is, and say that top-side-up is right-side-up; and I keep my nose pretty close to the ground. And I ask you, what king of France has done better, or been a better fellow in his little way?

JOAN. Art really king of France, Charlie? Be the English gone?

DUNOIS. [*Coming through the tapestry on* JOAN's *left, the candles relighting themselves at the same moment, and illuminating his armor and surcoat cheerfully.*] I have kept my word: the English are gone.

JOAN. Praised be God! now is fair France a province in heaven. Tell me all about the fighting, Jack. Was it thou that led them? Wert thou God's captain to thy death?

DUNOIS. I am not dead. My body is very comfortably asleep in my bed at Chateaudun; but my spirit is called here by yours.

JOAN. And you fought them my way, Jack: eh? Not the old way, chaffering for ransoms; but The Maid's way: staking life against death, with the heart high and humble and void of malice, and nothing counting under God but France free and French. Was it my way, Jack?

DUNOIS. Faith, it was any way that would win. But the way that won was always your way. I give you best, lassie. I wrote a fine letter to set you right at the new trial. Perhaps I should never have let the priests burn you; but I was busy fighting; and it was the Church's business, not mine. There was no use in both of us being burned, was there?

CAUCHON. Ay! put the blame on the priests. But I, who am beyond praise and blame, tell you that the world is saved neither by its priests nor its soldiers, but by God and His Saints. The Church Militant sent this woman to the fire; but even as she burned, the flames whitened into the radiance of the Church Triumphant.

The clock strikes the third quarter. A rough male voice is heard trolling an improvised tune.

Rum tum trumpledum,
  Bacon fat and rumpledum,
Old Saint mumpledum,
Pull his tail and stumpledum
  Oh my Ma—ry Ann!

A *ruffianly English* SOLDIER *comes through the curtains and marches between* DUNOIS *and* JOAN.

DUNOIS. What villainous troubadour taught you that doggrel?

THE SOLDIER. No troubadour. We made it up ourselves as we marched.

We were not gentlefolks and troubadours. Music straight out of the heart of the people, as you might say. Rum tum trumpledum, Bacon fat and rumpledum, Old Saint mumpledum, Pull his tail and stumpledum: that dont mean anything, you know; but it keeps you marching. Your servant, ladies and gentlemen. Who asked for a saint?

JOAN. Be you a saint?

THE SOLDIER. Yes, lady, straight from hell.

DUNOIS. A saint, and from hell!

THE SOLDIER. Yes, noble captain: I have a day off. Every year, you know. Thats my allowance for my one good action.

CAUCHON. Wretch! In all the years of your life did you do only one good action?

THE SOLDIER. I never thought about it: it came natural like. But they scored it up for me.

CHARLES. What was it?

THE SOLDIER. Why, the silliest thing you ever heard of. I—

JOAN. [*Interrupting him by strolling across to the bed, where she sits beside* CHARLES.] He tied two sticks together, and gave them to a poor lass that was going to be burned.

THE SOLDIER. Right. Who told you that?

JOAN. Never mind. Would you know her if you saw her again?

THE SOLDIER. Not I. There are so many girls! and they all expect you to remember them as if there was only one in the world. This one must have been a prime sort; for I have a day off every year for her; and so, until twelve o'clock punctually, I am a saint, at your service, noble lords and lovely ladies.

CHARLES. And after twelve?

THE SOLDIER. After twelve, back to the only place fit for the likes of me.

JOAN. [*Rising.*] Back there! You! that gave the lass the cross!

THE SOLDIER. [*Excusing his unsoldierly conduct.*] Well, she asked for it; and they were going to burn her. She had as good a right to a cross as they had; and they had dozens of them. It was her funeral, not theirs. Where was the harm in it?

JOAN. Man: I am not reproaching you. But I cannot bear to think of you in torment.

THE SOLDIER. [*Cheerfully.*] No great torment, lady. You see I was used to worse.

CHARLES. What! worse than hell?

THE SOLDIER. Fifteen years' service in the French wars. Hell was a treat after that.

JOAN *throws up her arms, and takes refuge from despair of humanity before the picture of the Virgin.*

THE SOLDIER. [*Continuing.*]—Suits me somehow. The day off was dull at first, like a wet Sunday. I dont mind it so much now. They tell me I can have as many as I like as soon as I want them.

CHARLES. What is hell like?

THE SOLDIER. You wont find it so bad, sir. Jolly. Like as if you were always drunk without the trouble and expense of drinking. Tip top company too: emperors and popes and kings and all sorts. They chip me about giving that young judy the cross; but I dont care: I stand up to them proper, and tell them that if she hadnt a better right to it than they, she'd be where they are. That dumbfounds them, that does. All they can do is gnash their teeth, hell fashion; and I just laugh, and go off singing the old chanty: Rum tum trumple—Hullo! Who's that knocking at the door?

They listen. A long gentle knocking is heard.

CHARLES. Come in.

The door opens; and an old priest, white-haired, bent, with a silly but benevolent smile, comes in and trots over to JOAN.

THE NEWCOMER. Excuse me, gentle lords and ladies. Do not let me disturb you. Only a poor old harmless English rector. Formerly chaplain to the cardinal: to my lord of Winchester. John de Stogumber, at your service. [*He looks at them inquiringly.*] Did you say anything? I am a little deaf, unfortunately. Also a little—well, not always in my right mind, perhaps; but still, it is a small village with a few simple people. I suffice: I suffice: they love me there; and I am able to do a little good. I am well connected, you see; and they indulge me.

JOAN. Poor old John! What brought thee to this state?

DE STOGUMBER. I tell my folks they must be very careful. I say to them, 'If you only saw what you think about you would think quite differently about it. It would give you a great shock. Oh, a great shock.' And they all say 'Yes, parson: we all know you are a kind man, and would not harm a fly.' That is a great comfort to me. For I am not cruel by nature, you know.

THE SOLDIER. Who said you were?

DE STOGUMBER. Well, you see, I did a very cruel thing once because I did not know what cruelty was like. I had not seen it, you know. That is the great thing: you must see it. And then you are redeemed and saved.

CAUCHON. Were not the sufferings of our Lord Christ enough for you?

DE STOGUMBER. No. Oh no: not at all. I had seen them in pictures, and read of them in books, and been greatly moved by them, as I thought. But it was no use: it was not our Lord that redeemed me, but a young woman whom I saw actually burned to death. It was dreadful: oh, most dreadful. But it saved me. I have been a different man ever since, though a little astray in my wits sometimes.

CAUCHON. Must then a Christ perish in torment in every age to save those that have no imagination?

JOAN. Well, if I saved all those he would have been cruel to if he had not been cruel to me, I was not burnt for nothing, was I?

DE STOGUMBER. Oh no; it was not you. My sight is bad: I cannot distinguish your features: but you are not she: oh no: she was burned to a cinder: dead and gone, dead and gone.

THE EXECUTIONER. [*Stepping from behind the bed curtains on* CHARLES's *right, the bed being between them.*] She is more alive than you, old man. Her heart would not burn; and it would not drown. I was a master at my craft: better than the master of Paris, better than the master of Toulouse; but I could not kill The Maid. She is up and alive everywhere.

THE EARL OF WARWICK. [*Sallying from the bed curtains on the other side, and coming to* JOAN's *left hand.*] Madam: my congratulations on your rehabilitation. I feel that I owe you an apology.

JOAN. Oh, please dont mention it.

WARWICK. [*Pleasantly.*] The burning was purely political. There was no personal feeling against you, I assure you.

JOAN. I bear no malice, my lord.

WARWICK. Just so. Very kind of you to meet me in that way: a touch of true breeding. But I must insist on apologizing very amply. The truth is, these political necessities sometimes turn out to be political mistakes; and this one was a veritable howler; for your spirit conquered us, madam, in spite of our faggots. History will remember me for your sake, though the incidents of the connection were perhaps a little unfortunate.

JOAN. Ay, perhaps just a little, you funny man.

WARWICK. Still, when they make you a saint, you will owe your halo to me, just as this lucky monarch owes his crown to you.

JOAN. [*Turning from him.*] I shall owe nothing to any man: I owe everything to the spirit of God that was within me. But fancy me a saint! What would St Catherine and St Margaret say if the farm girl was cocked up beside them!

A *clerical-looking* GENTLEMAN *in black frockcoat and trousers, and tall hat, in the fashion of the year* 1920, *suddenly appears before them in the corner on their right. They all stare at him. Then they burst into uncontrollable laughter.*

THE GENTLEMAN. Why this mirth, gentlemen?

WARWICK. I congratulate you on having invented a most extraordinarily comic dress.

THE GENTLEMAN. I do not understand. You are all in fancy dress: I am properly dressed.

DUNOIS. All dress is fancy dress, is it not, except our natural skins?

THE GENTLEMAN. Pardon me: I am here on serious business, and cannot engage in frivolous discussions. [*He takes out a paper, and assumes a dry official manner.*] I am sent to announce to you that Joan of Arc, formerly known as The Maid, having been the subject of an inquiry instituted by the Bishop of Orleans—

JOAN. [*Interrupting.*] Ah! They remember me still in Orleans.

THE GENTLEMAN. [*Emphatically, to mark his indignation at the interruption.*]—by the Bishop of Orleans into the claim of the said Joan of Arc to be canonized as a saint—

JOAN. [*Again interrupting.*] But I never made any such claim.

THE GENTLEMAN. [*As before.*]—the Church has examined the claim exhaustively in the usual course, and, having admitted the said Joan successively to the ranks of Venerable and Blessed,—

JOAN. [*Chuckling.*] Me venerable!

THE GENTLEMAN.—has finally declared her to have been endowed with heroic virtues and favored with private revelations, and calls the said Venerable and Blessed Joan to the communion of the Church Triumphant as Saint Joan.

JOAN. [*Rapt.*] Saint Joan!

THE GENTLEMAN. On every thirtieth day of May, being the anniversary of the death of the said most blessed daughter of God, there shall in every Catholic church to the end of time be celebrated a special office in commemoration of her; and it shall be lawful to dedicate a special chapel to her, and to place her image on its altar in every such church. And it shall be lawful and laudable for the faithful to kneel and address their prayers through her to the Mercy Seat.

JOAN. Oh no. It is for the saint to kneel. [*She falls on her knees, still rapt.*]

THE GENTLEMAN. [*Putting up his paper, and retiring beside the EXCUTIONER.*] In Basilica Vaticana, the sixteenth day of May, nineteen hundred and twenty.

DUNOIS. [*Raising JOAN.*] Half an hour to burn you, dear Saint, and four centuries to find out the truth about you!

DE STOGUMBER. Sir: I was chaplain to the Cardinal of Winchester once. They always would call him the Cardinal of England. It would be a great comfort to me and to my master to see a fair statue to The Maid in Winchester Cathedral. Will they put one there, do you think?

THE GENTLEMAN. As the building is temporarily in the hands of the Anglican heresy, I cannot answer for that.

A *vision of the statue in Winchester Cathedral is seen through the window.*

DE STOGUMBER. Oh look! look! that is Winchester.

JOAN. Is that meant to be me? I was stiffer on my feet.

The vision fades.

THE GENTLEMAN. I have been requested by the temporal authorities of France to mention that the multiplication of public statues to The Maid threatens to become an obstruction to traffic. I do so as a matter of courtesy to the said authorities, but must point out on behalf of the Church that The Maid's horse is no greater obstruction to traffic than any other horse.

JOAN. Eh! I am glad they have not forgotten my horse.

A vision of the statue before Rheims Cathedral appears.

JOAN. Is that funny little thing me too?

CHARLES. That is Rheims Cathedral where you had me crowned. It must be you.

JOAN. Who has broken my sword? My sword was never broken. It is the sword of France.

DUNOIS. Never mind. Swords can be mended. Your soul is unbroken; and you are the soul of France.

The vision fades. The ARCHBISHOP *and the* INQUISITOR *are now seen on the right and left of* CAUCHON.

JOAN. My sword shall conquer yet: the sword that never struck a blow. Though men destroyed my body, yet in my soul I have seen God.

CAUCHON. [*Kneeling to her.*] The girls in the field praise thee; for thou hast raised their eyes; and they see that there is nothing between them and heaven.

DUNOIS. [*Kneeling to her.*] The dying soldiers praise thee, because thou art a shield of glory between them and the judgment.

THE ARCHBISHOP. [*Kneeling to her.*] The princes of the Church praise thee, because thou hast redeemed the faith their worldlinesses have dragged through the mire.

WARWICK. [*Kneeling to her.*] The cunning counsellors praise thee, because thou hast cut the knots in which they have tied their own souls.

DE STOGUMBER. [*Kneeling to her.*] The foolish old men on their deathbeds praise thee, because their sins against thee are turned into blessings.

THE INQUISITOR. [*Kneeling to her.*] The judges in the blindness and bondage of the law praise thee, because thou hast vindicated the vision and the freedom of the living soul.

THE SOLDIER. [*Kneeling to her.*] The wicked out of hell praise thee, because thou hast shewn them that the fire that is not quenched is a holy fire.

THE EXECUTIONER. [*Kneeling to her.*] The tormentors and executioners praise thee, because thou hast shewn that their hands are guiltless of the death of the soul.

CHARLES. [*Kneeling to her.*] The unpretending praise thee, because thou hast taken upon thyself the heroic burdens that are too heavy for them.

JOAN. Woe unto me when all men praise me! I bid you remember that I am a saint, and that saints can work miracles. And now tell me: shall I rise from the dead, and come back to you a living woman?

A sudden darkness blots out the walls of the room as they all spring to their feet in consternation. Only the figures and the bed remain visible.

JOAN. What! Must I burn again? Are none of you ready to receive me?

CAUCHON. The heretic is always better dead. And mortal eyes cannot distinguish the saint from the heretic. Spare them. [*He goes out as he came.*]

DUNOIS. Forgive us, Joan: we are not yet good enough for you. I shall go back to my bed. [*He also goes.*]

WARWICK. We sincerely regret our little mistake; but political necessities, though occasionally erroneous, are still imperative; so if you will be good enough to excuse me—[*He steals discreetly away.*]

THE ARCHBISHOP. Your return would not make me the man you once thought me. The utmost I can say is that though I dare not bless you, I hope I may one day enter into your blessedness. Meanwhile, however—[*He goes.*]

THE INQUISITOR. I who am of the dead, testified that day that you were innocent. But I do not see how The Inquisition could possibly be dispensed with under existing circumstances. Therefore—[*He goes.*]

DE STOGUMBER. Oh, do not come back: you must not come back. I must die in peace. Give us peace in our time, O Lord! [*He goes.*]

THE GENTLEMAN. The possibility of your resurrection was not contemplated in the recent proceedings for your canonization. I must return to Rome for fresh instructions. [*He bows formally, and withdraws.*]

THE EXECUTIONER. As a master in my profession I have to consider its interests. And, after all, my first duty is to my wife and children. I must have time to think over this. [*He goes.*]

CHARLES. Poor old Joan! They have all run away from you except this blackguard who has to go back to hell at twelve o'clock. And what can I do but follow Jack Dunois' example, and go back to bed too? [*He does so.*]

JOAN. [*Sadly.*] Goodnight, Charlie.

CHARLES. [*Mumbling in his pillows.*] Goo ni. [*He sleeps. The darkness envelops the bed.*]

JOAN. [*To the* SOLDIER.] And you, my one faithful? What comfort have you for Saint Joan?

THE SOLDIER. Well, what do they all amount to, these kings and captains and bishops and lawyers and such like? They just leave you in the ditch to bleed to death; and the next thing is, you meet them down there, for all the airs they give themselves. What I say is, you have as good a right to your notions as they have to theirs, and perhaps better. [*Settling himself for a lecture on the subject.*] You see, it's like this. If—[*The first stroke of midnight is heard softly from a distant bell.*] Excuse me: a pressing appointment—[*He goes on tiptoe.*]

The last remaining rays of light gather into a white radiance descending on JOAN. *The hour continues to strike.*

JOAN. O God that madest this beautiful earth, when will it be ready to receive Thy saints? How long, O Lord, how long?